INSIGHT GUIDE

COSTA RICA

APA PUBLICATIONS
Part of the Langenscheidt Publishing Group

L

INSIGHT GUIDE COSTA RICA

ABOUT THIS BOOK

Editorial

Project Editor
Paul Murphy
Managing Editor
Huw Clough
Editorial Director
Brian Bell

Distribution

UK & Ireland
GeoCenter International Ltd
The Viables Centre
Harrow Way
Basingstoke
Hants RG22 4BJ
Fax: (44) 1256-817988

United States
Langenscheidt Publishers, Inc.
46–35 54th Road
Maspeth, NY 11378
Fax: (718) 784-0640

Worldwide
APA Publications GmbH & Co.
Verlag KG (Singapore branch)
38 Joo Koon Road
Singapore 628990
Tel: (65) 865-1600
Fax: (65) 861-6438

Printing

Insight Print Services (Pte) Ltd
38 Joo Koon Road
Singapore 628990
Tel: (65) 865-1600
Fax: (65) 861-6438

© 2000 APA Publications GmbH & Co.
Verlag KG (Singapore branch)
All Rights Reserved
First Edition 1992
Third Edition 1999 (Updated 2000)

CONTACTING THE EDITORS
Although every effort is made to
provide accurate information in
this publication, we live in a
fast-changing world and would
appreciate it if readers would
call our attention to any errors or
outdated information that may
occur by writing to us at:
Insight Guides, P.O. Box 7910,
London SE1 1WE, England.
Fax: (44 20) 7403-0290.
e-mail:
insight@apaguide.demon.co.uk

This guidebook combines the interests and enthusiasms of two of the world's best known information providers: Insight Guides, whose titles have set the standard for visual travel guides since 1970, and Discovery Channel, the world's premier source of nonfiction television programming.

The editors of Insight Guides provide both practical advice and general understanding about a destination's history, culture, institutions and people. Discovery Channel and its Web site, www.discovery.com, help millions of viewers explore their world from the comfort of their own home and also encourage them to explore it firsthand.

How to use this book
The book has been carefully structured both to convey an understanding of Costa Rica and its culture and to guide readers through its many sights and natural attractions:

The **Features** section, with a yellow color bar, covers the country's **history** and **culture** in lively authoritative essays written by specialists.

The **Places** section, with a blue bar, provides full details of all the sights and areas worth

EXPLORE YOUR WORLD

The contributors

This new edition, which builds on the earlier edition edited by **Harvey** and **Dona Haber**, was edited by **Paul Murphy**, assisted by managing editor **Huw Clough**. Harvey and Dona contributed most of the book's historical pieces, with the new feature on the recent Nicaraguan influx by *Tico Times* journalist **Carol Weir**. Carol also did much valuable updating work on many other parts of the book.

Marine biologist and long-time Central America expert **Henry Genthe** wrote the Sports article and several of the Places chapters. **Cindy Hilbrink** wrote on rural aspects of Costa Rica. **David Burnie**, a biologist and natural history writer, wrote features on the flora and fauna.

Other writers whose expert text has been adapted and updated from earlier editions include **Moisés Leon**, **John McPhaul**, **Juan Bernal Ponce**, **Tony Avirgan**, **Martha Honey**, **Marjorie Ross-Cerdas**, **Mary Sheldon**, and **Alexander Skutch**.

Glyn Genin, an Insight regular, provided many of the photographs, as did Henry Genthe (*see above*). In San José, **John Skiffingham** also delved deep into his vast picture library,

Michael and **Patricia Fogden** are among the world's top wildlife photographers and **André Bärtschi** is a natural history specialist who works in the rainforests. Valuable contributions were also made by **Chip** and **Jill Isenhart** and **Buddy Mays**.

John Leach indexed and proofread the book.

seeing. The chief places of interest are coordinated by number with specially drawn maps.

The **Travel Tips** listings section, with an orange bar at the back of the book, offers a convenient point of reference for information on travel, accommodation, restaurants and other practical aspects of the country. Information may be located quickly by using the index printed on the back cover flap, which also serves as a handy bookmark.

Map Legend

──‥──	International Boundary
────	Province Boundary
⊖	Border Crossing
─‥─	National Park/Reserve
────	Ferry Route
✈ ✈	Airport: International/Regional
🚌	Bus Station
Ⓟ	Parking
❶	Tourist Information
✉	Post Office
🏛 † ⛪	Church/Ruins
☾	Mosque
✡	Synagogue
🏰	Castle/Ruins
∴	Archaeological Site
∩	Cave
⚑	Statue/Monument
★	Place of Interest

The main places of interest in the Places section are coordinated by number with a full-colour map (e.g. ❶), and a symbol at the top of every right-hand page tells you where to find the map.

CONTENTS

A map of Costa Rica can be found on the inside front cover, and a map of National Parks and Reserves can be found on the inside back cover.

Keeping
cool in the
shade

Travel Tips

Insight on ...

Places

Information panels

THE HAPPY MEDIUM

Amid the turmoil that often characterizes Central America

Costa Rica is a land at peace with itself and nature

Nestled betwen Nicaragua and Panama on the Central American isthmus, Costa Rica is a small, democratic and peaceful country, with a level of social development that always surprises first-time visitors and belies its definition as a Third-World nation. Lacking the clichéd images and iconographic characteristics of other Latin American countries, such as Mexico, Peru or Brazil, it has nonetheless become famous for its natural environment and for its efforts in helping bring lasting peace to a troubled region.

Since Don Pepe Figueres abolished Costa Rica's armed forces in 1949 the government has been able to devote a large percentage of its resources to education, health and conservation. And currently a quarter of the country is protected in national parks, biological reserves, wildlife refuges and private reserves. With more than 850 species of birds, 250 mammals and some 5 per cent of the world's total biodiversity, Costa Rica is a paradise for anyone who delights in the unspoiled natural world.

A land of dense jungles, active volcanoes and pristine white sand beaches, this is a tiny country (the size of the US state of West Virginia), but it is full of geophysical contrasts which make it seem much bigger. A third of the country's population (total 3½ million) live in the temperate Central Valley that houses the modern capital of San José. But as any *Tico*, (Costa Rican), will tell you, the "real" Costa Rica will only be found in the *campo*, or rural areas.

It was an official at the World Bank who termed Costa Rica as the Land of the Happy Medium. And while its economy is far from perfect the country is also known as the Switzerland of Central America, on account of its high living standard and temperate climate. It is often more European than Latino and predominantly middle-class. With a per capita income of around $2,400, Costa Rica's people can rely on the state to provide quality health care, public schools and other affordable services such as electricity and clean water, while its neighbors lavish equal amounts on national defense and putting down military coups.

Since 1994 tourism has been the country's leading industry, before coffee and bananas. More than 800,000 visitors now arrive each year, the vast majority of them coming from North America and Europe. A sophisticated tourism industry is in place, with accommodations ranging from luxury lodges to homey bed-and-breakfasts. Eco- and adventure tourism are the buzzwords that encompass activities as diverse as birdwatching and whitewater rafting. Costa Rica has come a long way from the Banana Republic it once was, but without losing its essential charm. ❑

PRECEDING PAGES: the Gaudy Tree Frog; cloud forest of Cerro de la Muerte; the spreading Cenicero tree dots the grassy plains of Guanacaste; black sand beach in Limón province.

LEFT: poison dart frogs, formerly used by indigenous people for tipping arrows.

COAST TO COAST

Costa Rica may be small in area but it is big in interest, with two oceans, rushing rivers, fiery volcanoes and chilly peaks touching nearly 4,000 meters

Costa Rica lies at the heart of the Central American isthmus and these days few people mistake it for an island in the Caribbean. Traveling around the countryside gives you the sense of being in a large country; geophysically there are so many things going on. There is the feeling that it would take months to really explore it all. Yet, in reality, it is quite small. From northwest to southwest it measures 460 km (285 miles) and at its narrowest point it is only 120 km (74 miles).

Neighbors

Costa Rica is bounded on the north by Nicaragua, and to the south by Panamá; two countries often in the international news, for the wrong reasons, and profoundly different from this usually benevolent and peaceful land. To the east is the tranquil Caribbean Sea and to the west is the tumultuous Pacific Ocean. Costa Rica is as complex and perhaps more diverse than any place of its size on earth; divided into several distinct regions, each of them looks like an entirely separate place.

A fertile land

Perhaps it is the hot coastal plains in the tropical zones, with their rolling wild grasses and plantations of palm and banana, or the thickly-forested valleys and coastlines, fringed with beaches of every description, that drew many of the early travelers here. Or perhaps it is the fertile central plateau in the temperate zone, at 975–1,980 meters (3,200–6,500 ft), with its rich, fecund cloud forests and magical tropical jungles, which has attracted an international community of conservationists, biologists, bird-watchers, environmentalists, naturalists and the ecologically attuned. Many a Northern European or *gringo* from the midwestern or northern United States or Canada has found Costa Rica to be an ideal new home, with its cool highlands of gently rolling, wooded pastureland,

LEFT: a prehistoric-looking mature green iguana.
RIGHT: shy but curious *Tica* welcome

reminiscent more of Switzerland than of a tropical country.

Running as veins of a precious ore through the body of the country is a network of waterways. They rise and fall through the mountains, flow to the sea and provide a seemingly endless source of fresh water and hydraulic power.

The soil of the Central Valley is exceptionally fertile, due primarily to the volcanic ash that has fallen through the centuries. This rich, drainable soil is ideal for producing Costa Rica's coffee, and traveling through the high country, you can view seemingly endless coffee *fincas,* with their deep green, jewel-like foliage, flowing up impossibly steep ridges, and across the floor of great alluvial valleys.

The coast

Never far away is the coastline. Indeed, there are many easily accessible points throughout this country from where you can simultaneously view both the Atlantic and the Pacific oceans. The Atlantic Coast measures only 220 km (135 miles) in length, while the Pacific Coast of Costa Rica, with its deep gulfs and indentations, is several times that length. On the Pacific there is the Nicoya peninsula to the north, and the Osa peninsula to the south. Each of these large peninsulas harbors numerous small islands. And, remote and mysterious, many miles off of the Pacific Coast, is the exceptionally beautiful, still pristine Cocos Island.

Peaks of delight

Although most of Costa Rica's volcanoes are extinct, some are still active. Poás Volcano, at

2,700 meters (8,900 ft), is located near to the town of Alajuela, and has what may be the world's largest crater, measuring more than a mile in diameter; and Irazú Volcano, at 3,440 meters (11,320 ft), not far from the city of Cartago, is occasionaly active, and can be viewed at relatively close range.

At 1,630 meters (5,350 ft) in height, Arenal is the most consistently active of Costa Rica's volcanoes. The rumbling, explosive spectacle of Arenal Volcano is the single most impressive pyrotechnic display in the whole country.

ABOVE: birders on Tortuguero's tree-lined canals.
RIGHT: Volcán Arenal letting off steam.

The highland mountains traverse Costa Rica, from the northwest to the southeast, in three ranges, rising to more than 3,800 meters (12,500 ft). These are the magnificent Guanacaste, Central and Talamanca ranges. Chirripó Grande, at 3,800 meters (12,500 ft), and Terbi, also at 3,800 meters (12,500 ft), are the highest elevation points in the country.

Climate

Although geographically situated in what earlier travelers used to call the "torrid zone," the great majority of Costa Rica's population never really feel torrid at any time of year, living for the most part on the Central Plateau, at elevations between around 450 meters (1,500 ft) and 1,400 meters (4,500 ft), in "perennial springtime" temperatures of between 20-26°C (68-78°F), day and night.

However, near the coasts the temperatures are indeed tropical and there are distinct alternating wet and dry seasons, at different times of year, for both the Atlantic and Pacific. There are certain times here when even the local residents are overwhelmed by the too-sensuous hot and humid midday air and are driven into the shade.

The famous tropical downpours usually arrive with great predictability in the afternoons during the wet seasons along the coasts and are undeniably awesome. If you are caught out in one, you will never forget the experience. Over the years, millions of words have been written about these extraordinary dramas of lightning, thunder and torrential rains; and, if you have never experienced it, well, it just isn't Kansas. After an evening of being humbled by these nightly displays, you'll know you're not in Dublin, Munich, or Tokyo, either.

Away from the tropical coasts, the climate is greatly determined by the altitude above sea level. At each level, temperatures are constant throughout a 24-hour cycle, regardless of the season, or time of year, from the heat of the coastal plains to the chilliness of the great volcanos and slopes of the mountain ranges.

From the edge of the almost tideless Caribbean Sea and the pounding Pacific coast; up and across the slopes of the volcanic *cordilleras*; and finally up to the highest peak of cold and brittle Chirripó, the visitor's experience of the Republic of Costa Rica is gloriously invigorating. ❑

Decisive Dates

PRE-COLOMBIAN ERA

40,000–4000 BC: First signs of human habitation of Central America: hunter-gatherers migrating southwards settled in small chiefdoms, developing diverse languages and cultures.

4000–1000 BC: Establishment of earliest settlements based on crop cultivation (including maize, yucca, and cotton).

1000 BC–AD 1500: Growth and expansion of organized, sedentary farming communities, who formed

A WARRIOR OF NICOYA.

trade and communication links with each other and as far afield as the Chibcha people of South America. By the time of the arrival of the Spaniards, five major cultural groups of natives predominated: the Caribs, the Borucas, the Nahua, the Corobicis, who were the oldest native group, and the most advanced group of all: the Chorotegas, who inhabited the Nicoya Peninsula.

1502: On his fourth voyage of discovery, Christopher Columbus drops anchor for two weeks off the island of Uvita (near Puerto Limón), where he encounters the Cariari tribe.

1519–60: The Spanish explore both coastlines of Costa Rica.

1561: An expedition from the Pacific coast finally manages to reach the the Valle Central. Juan Cavallón

founds the first town, Castillo de Garcimuñoz, which is relocated several times until becoming established as present-day Cartago.

1562: Juan Vazquez de Coronado explores the Valle Central and employs peaceful means to try to convert the *indígenas* (indigenous people).

1572: Beginning of Colonial Era, characterised by an almost continuous absence of labor. Costa Rica remains a poor colony for the next 250 years, largely ignored by Spain because of its lack of mineral resources.

1660–70: Atlantic coast cacao plantations bring the colony its first revenue, but are constantly raided by pirates.

1723: The tiny fledgling capital of Cartago is wiped out by erupting Irazu Volcano.

1787: Costa Rica is the only colony in the Audiencia Guatemala allowed to cultivate tobacco.

1821: On 15 September Guatemala announces its independence from Spain. The news reaches Cartago four weeks later.

1823: Civil war breaks out between the conservative imperialists in Cartago and Heredía, who want to join the Mexican Empire, and the republicans (*liberalistas*) who are in the majority in San José and Alajuela. The republicans finally secure Costa Rica's acceptance into the short-lived United Provinces of Central America, led by Guatemala. San José replaces Cartago as the national capital.

1824: Juan Mora Fernandez becomes Costa Rica's first head of state (until 1833). The inhabitants of the "Partido de Nicoya" (a region governed until then by Nicaragua, and roughly corresponding to today's Guanacaste) vote to join Costa Rica.

1825: The first constitution of the free state of Costa Rica is promulgated, and the cession of Guanacaste is made official by Congress.

1832: First coffee exports to Europe, via Chile.

1835: Braulio Carrillo becomes president, and uses dictatorial methods to introduce liberal reforms. Heredia, Cartago, and Alajuela all oppose these, form a "league" and declare war on San José, eventually winning the capital.

1838: After the collapse of the United Provinces of Central America, the president, Jose Maria Castro, announces the free and independent republic of Costa Rica.

1849: Juan Rafael Mora becomes president and is re-elected in 1853 and 1859. During his presidency coffee exports experience a sharp upswing.

1858: During the war against freebooter William Walker, who wants to turn Central America into a colony of the southern American states and introduce slavery, a decisive battle is fought near Santa Rosa. Walker is finally defeated by Costa Rica's troops in Rivas (Nicaragua).

1870: Tomas Guardia Gutierrez takes over power after a military coup, introduces a new liberal constitution, and remains in office until 1882.

1871: Railroad construction begins; the Atlantic Railway, from Cartago to Limón, is finally completed in 1890.

1880: First banana exports.

1882: The death penalty is abolished.

1886: Introduction of compulsory public education.

1890: First free and honest democratic elections in Central America bring José Joaquin Rodriguez to presidency.

1914-18: Costa Rica loses export markets because of World War I. Economic recession.

1917: Federico A. Tinoco takes power in a coup supported by the coffee barons. A popular uprising ends his dictatorship two years later.

1932: Costa Rica is affected by the world economic recession.

1934: A strike among banana workers in response to adverse working conditions at United Fruit Company leads to a series of concessions (including the right to strike and minimum wage).

1939–45: World War II – coffee exports stagnate. Costa Rica declares war on Germany, Japan, and Italy. German and Italian residents are dispossessed and deported.

1940–44: President Rafael Calderon successfully implements a series of social reforms.

1945: The Social Democratic Party (PSD) is founded, later to become the Partido Liberacion Nacional (PLN), under (Don Pepe) Jose Figueres.

1948: Calderon Guardia declares election results to be annulled and reassumes the presidency. Civil war ensues. The victorious *junta* led by Figueres takes over government.

1949: Under the terms of the new constitution the army is disbanded and replaced by a Civil Guard. Figueres hands over power to elected president Otilio Ulate, but governs the country again from 1953 to 1958 and 1970 to 1974. *

1979: The Sandinistas in Nicaragua topple the Somoza dictatorship. During the ensuing civil war, Costa Rica becomes a fallback area for Contra groups

and anti-Sandinistas. As a result of the war, hundreds of thousands of Nicaraguans seek refuge in Costa Rica.

1980: Slump in coffeee and banana markets causes onset of severe economic recession.

1983: President Luis Alberto Monge declares a state of "unarmed neutrality," leading to tensions with the United States.

1986: Oscar Arias Sanchez is elected president and prepares to restore peace to the region. For his efforts in instigating the Central American Peace Plan, "Esquipulas II", he is awarded Nobel Peace Prize in 1987.

1990: Social Christian Unity Party (PUSC) wins the elections. Rafel Angel Calderon Fournier, the son of Calderon Guardia, becomes the country's president.

Costa Rica sends a national team to the Soccer World Cup for the first time, and reaches the quarter finals.

1991: An earthquake strikes Limón province, killing over 60 people and causing extensive structural damage which still remains today.

1994: Jose M Figueres becomes Costa Rica's youngest-ever president, at the age of 39. However, his term is dogged by problems and scandals, including the bankruptcy and closure of Banco Anglo-Costarricense, the nation's oldest bank.

1996: Hurricane César strikes, killing dozens of Costa Ricans and causing over $100 million of damage.

1998: The Social Christian Unity Party (PUSC) wins general elections and Miguel Angel Rodriguez is sworn in as president. ❑

PRECEDING PAGES: Pre-Colombian ceramics from the National Museum, San José
LEFT: a Nicoyan warrior, set for battle.
RIGHT: a portrait of idyllic early Indian life by the chronologer Figueroa.

BEFORE COLUMBUS

The indians' early culture was largely agrarian. But, influenced by their
Mesoamerican neighbors, they learned to fashion goods from stone, jade and gold

On September 8, 1502, Christopher Columbus arrived on the Atlantic Coast of Costa Rica and took refuge in the calm waters just off the coast, between tiny Uvita Island and what is now the Port of Limón.

The native Indians greeted the Spaniards with interest and brought out goods to trade with them. They swam out to the ship carrying cotton cloth, shirts, tumbago pendants (an alloy made of copper and gold) and weapons such as clubs, bows and arrows.

Golden dreams

Dreaming of gold, Columbus had charted the coastal area from Honduras to Panamá and named it Veragua. However, he was so impressed by the golden mirrors that the Indians of Costa Rica wore about their necks, and by their many stories of gold and gold mines along the coast to the south, that he named the area the Rich Coast of Veragua.

Rich though it seemed to Columbus at the time, the newly discovered area was not to be a great, rich jewel in Spain's crown. In fact, the "Rich Coast" turned out to be one of the poorest of Spain's American colonies. Impassable mountains, impenetrable forests, raging rivers, unbearable heat, floods, disease, swamps, shortages of food, internal rivalries, lack of natural resources and a way to generate wealth all oppressed the settlers to the point where they were often reduced to living like the savages they had come to conquer: wearing goat hair garments or clothing made of bark, using cacao (chocolate beans) for currency, eking out a bare subsistence in the fields, using native methods to cultivate native crops.

This bleak reality, in contrast to the Spaniards' great dreams, remained to be discovered by those who followed. Columbus himself naively returned to Spain with dreams of returning to this rich land and requested of the king that he be named the Duke of Veragua.

LEFT: a ceremonial polychrome vessel.
ABOVE: gold ornament and battlewear.

To this day his descendents still use the title.

Yet if Columbus left the Rich Coast with overblown dreams of gold, riches and happily submissive Indians ready to labor for the Crown and his own personal dreams of wealth and fame, then what was life in the newly discovered land really like?

Natural riches

It was a rich land, though not in the mineral wealth to which Columbus aspired. Instead it was, and still is, rich in animal and plant life, rich in forests, mountains, rivers, swamps and grasslands. In the Atlantic watershed area, where much of the land is flat, navigable rivers and the tributaries were swelled in some areas by more than 400 cm (160 in) of rain a year. In the heavy tropical vegetation grew wild rubber trees, orchids and ferns. Fish, alligators and an occasional shark lived in the rivers. Water fowl, turkeys, iguanas, red monkeys, howler monkeys, boars, peccaries (wild pigs) and jaguars inhabited the forests.

To the north, in the Nicoya region, were tropical dry forests, also abundant in plant and animal life: on the broad, seasonally dry plains grew the beautiful wide, green Guanacaste tree; the *javillo* with its poisonous sap and thorny trunk; the *cenicero* with its flesh-colored flowers; the *guapinol*, and many varieties of cacti and spiny shrubs. White-faced monkeys, howler monkeys, red squirrels with grey tails, tapirs, coatis, deer, jaguars, mountain lions, coyotes and other animals lived in the forests, while in the trees, red and yellow macaws, and other parrots fluttered. Avocadoes, papayas, guavas and countless other fruits grew wild.

plants; supplementing their diets with wild fruits and game from the forests, fish and shrimp from the rivers, and crustaceans and small oysters from the ocean.

At the time of Columbus's arrival, the people of the Guanacaste/Nicoya region lived in well-developed settlements, some with populations as large as 20,000. These settlements, supported by the cultivation of corn, were built around central plazas, marketplaces and religious centers.

In the Atlantic Watershed/Central Highlands area, in the mountains near the present-day city of Turrialba, was a city with wide, cobblestone-

And the grasslands and swamps of the southern Pacific region, often called the Diquis region, were also lush with life, as were the often misty green hills and valleys of the Central Highlands, where broadleaf evergreen forests, palms and white oaks grew on the luxuriant hillsides and harbored innumerable species of birds, animals and plants.

Native settlers

Groups of indians with diverse languages and cultures lived throughout these areas in small chiefdoms. They were agricultural people, cultivating crops of *yuca*, corn, *pejibaye* (the bright orange fruit of palm) and numerous other

WHAT'S IN A NAME?

The Spanish colonists gave the indians the names by which we know them today (often the name of the chief at the time): the Chorotega, Bribri, Cacebar, Coctu, Corobicí, to name a few. We do not know the names the indians called themselves, and since some groups were completely wiped out before the Spanish came, we do not have names for them, or know what languages they spoke. Because of this, archaeologists usually refer to indian groups by the areas in which they lived: Guanacaste/Nicoya region, the Atlantic Watershed/Central Highlands region and the Diquis, or Southern Pacific region.

paved walkways, freshwater springs bubbling out of stone-lined pools, and a stone aqueduct system carrying fresh water to some of the stone mounds on which houses were built. This ancient city, called Guayabo, flourished and disappeared (approximately 1000 BC to AD 1400) before the arrival of the Spaniards. Other groups within the Atlantic Watershed/ Central Highlands region were less settled. They cultivated root crops and hunted what small game was available, and then moved on to new lands when the soil or supply of game became depleted.

In the Diquis region, the people also hunted,

the Americas. Linguistic and cultural influences, not to mention a wealth of artifacts and materials, were being exchanged not only within the country but from as far north as Mexico and as far south as Ecuador. The native Costa Ricans were enthusiastic traders and prized jade pieces, ceramic ware, gold and stone carvings from throughout Mesoamerica and South America.

The Nicoya area, with its quiet Pacific bays and safe anchorages, had long been a pre-Columbian commercial port. Merchant marines from ancient Ecuador, making ports of call all along the Pacific Coast of Mexico, Central and

cultivated root crops and lived in well-fortified villages which were strategically laid out to protect villagers from enemy attack.

Crossroads of the Americas

Influenced by some of the other great indigenous cultures of the Americas, the native people of Costa Rica had become skilled in the arts of ceramics, gold and metalwork, fine weaving, and stone carving. Costa Rica, it seems, was a kind of mercantile and cultural crossroads of

LEFT: a *mano*, or *metate* prehistoric corn grinder.
ABOVE: *conquistador* statue, San José.
ABOVE RIGHT: stone figure found at Guayabo.

South America, frequently stopped at sites in Nicoya, bringing the crafts and arts of Mexico, Central and South America to the people of the Nicoya region. Perhaps it was they who introduced Olmec influences to the area – or perhaps the Olmecs (and others) came themselves. Regardless, the influence of the Olmecs is strongly seen in the Pacific Northwest: in an impressive range of pottery styles; in utilitarian articles such as grinding stones; and in the practice of certain customs, such as the filing of a person's teeth into points.

Over the years, the pottery of Nicoya developed into a vigorous hybrid style that for centuries would be traded around Central America and southern Mexico. A collection of such work is available at the National Museum. Lively, bold, colorful work: large globular jars and vessels; figures of men and women, some with oversized genitals and physical deformities; animals of all kinds; mysterious effigies of man-birds; haunting funerary masks and some quieter pieces, almost luminously beautiful.

Mystery of the spheres

The Diquis region is the site of one of the great pre-Columbian riddles. Granite spheres (actually made of granite, andesite and sedimentary stone), some as small as oranges, some weigh-ing up to 14 metric tons (16 tons), measuring up to 2 meters (7 ft) in diameter and perfectly spherical to within a centimeter or two, have been found in their thousands, along river beds and arranged in cemetery sites. They are unique – none has been discovered anywhere else in the world. How were they made? How were they shaped to be so perfectly spherical? How were they transported over 30 km (20 miles) from the source of the stone to the cere-monial sites where they were arranged? And what do they mean? There are no answers: the giant spheres yield none of their secrets. They stand mute in their new locations, at the

THE RIDDLE OF JADE

In addition to the enigma of the country's lithic spheres (*see above*), there is another pre-Columbian riddle that perplexes historians and archaeologists. One of the great mysteries of Costa Rica is the source of jade for the many pieces found throughout the country. No quarries have ever been found in Costa Rica. Guatemala is believed to be the principal source, although some pieces may have come from Mexico.

Many of the objects appear to have been treasured for years, passed down as heirlooms – others appear to have arrived in one form and to have been re-sculpted to the tastes of their new owners. One interesting theory holds that some of the jade was brought to Costa Rica by pre-Columbian looters of Mayan burial sites, thus explaining the presence of Mayan hieroglyphs on the jade – which apparently had no value nor significance to the Costa Ricans.

The Jade Museum in San José has the largest display of jade in the Americas. The pieces are of great variety; notable oddities include a tooth with jade inset and jade breast supports, thought to have been worn by high-ranking women.

National Museum and in the gardens of expensive homes throughout the Central Valley. You can also see them, undisturbed in their original habitat, in a place on Isla Caño, near Corcovado National Park.

Gold and cotton

The Diquis region, along the South Pacific and extending into the Central Highlands, abounded with gold, which the indians washed out of rivers, obtained from shallow digs in the savannahs, from under groves of trees on hilltops, or in the plains. They became experts in the art of gold working and employed a variety of different techniques, including the "lost wax" method, to craft all manner of items: gold headbands, gold arm and leg bands, gold collars, patens, bracelets, beads, bells. Golden ornaments sewn on clothes. Gold tweezers for plucking away unwanted facial hair. Gold awls, fish-hooks and needles. Gold sheathing for teeth. Gold to use on decorative masks.

The people of the Diquis region also wove fine, white cotton cloth, which was prized throughout the country. It was often sewn into shirts, perhaps using golden needles, and was worn by both men and women as decoration or for ceremonial occasions. It was also used to wrap the bodies of the dead.

Wars, rituals and religion

Taken in isolation archaeological evidence on village life, diet, and the arts and commerce of the early Costa Rican people might suggest that life was plentiful, complete and quite idyllic. In fact it was anything but – war was almost continuous.

In the Guanacaste/Nicoya region, wars were fought between rival groups to obtain captives for human sacrifice (and consumption), and throughout Costa Rica there were wars to capture women and youths for slaves (who were sacrificed, sometimes brutally, on the deaths of their masters), to obtain the heads of enemies, which were carried as trophies, and to obtain access to new land. Sometimes, as in the Diquis region, men and women warred together.

Artifacts and skeletons found in unearthed graves suggest that the dead were honored; that funerals and burials of high-ranking people

LEFT: an elated Nicoya figure.
RIGHT: stone female carving, found at Guayabo.

were important and sometimes elaborate affairs. People of rank were buried with riches – and their slaves were killed in order to serve their masters once again in the other world.

Of their spiritual beliefs little is actually known, although much has been speculated. Phallic images and figures in pottery and stone, emphasizing male and female genitalia, suggest a religion focused on fertility and the practice of fertility rites, which probably included the music of pottery drums, bone and clay flutes, trumpets, ocarinas, clay and gourd rattles. Large vessels for the fermentation of corn, *yuca* or *pejibaye* suggest ritual inebriation. Drug para-

phernalia suggests the ritual use of coca. And there were medicine men, shamans, with vast knowledge of the flora of the forests, who cured illness, forecast the future and dealt with supernatural matters.

The proud pre-Columbian lineages disintegrated with the arrival of the Europeans, who captured their leaders, disrupted their communities, enslaved their people and destroyed their ceremonial and religious articles. The people's spirited artistry gave way to a lackluster mediocrity and dynamic spiritual beliefs were replaced by a half-hearted hybrid religion. Little by little, Costa Rica's rich pre-Columbian traditions were extinguished. ❏

CONQUEST

The conquest of Costa Rica followed the sad pattern of much of Central America,

bringing disease, death and slavery in the largely fruitless quest for gold

When Columbus set sail from Spain in 1492 on his first voyage to the New World, he was planning to find a group of islands near Japan, which he conceived to be about 2,400 nautical miles to the west of Spain. There he would build a great city and trade gold, gems and spices from the Indies today composed of Haiti and the Dominican Republic. One of his ships, the *Santa Maria*, had wrecked on a reef and, after a local indian chief helped him salvage the cargo, Columbus decided to build a fort there and leave 40 men to search for gold, while he returned to Spain with several captive indians. Columbus's return

with the cities of Europe. He would be a rich governor, lord of it all. And it so happened that his aims of discovering new lands over which he could rule, coincided with the interests of the Spanish Crown. The wars to oust the Moors from Spain had depleted the royal treasury. The promise of the wealth of the Indies was attractive indeed.

The voyages of Columbus

The first of his four voyages took Columbus to the Bahamas, which he insisted was an island in the Indies near Japan or China. However, also on this trip he established the first Spanish settlement in the New World, at Hispaniola, to Spain was triumphant. He was given a grand reception, was named Admiral of the Ocean Sea and was ordered to organize a second voyage to further explore Hispaniola.

The second expedition, outfitted with 17 ships and 1,000 male colonists, reached Hispaniola only to discover that the 40 settlers who had been left there had been killed after mistreating the indians. Undeterred, Columbus sailed on from that site to the north coast of Hispaniola, where he attempted the establishment of another settlement. Leaving his brother, Diego, in charge, he went off to explore the area, again in search of gold. But things did not go well in his absence. Settlers fought among themselves and with the indians. Frustrated gold hunters returned to Spain angry, they grumbled about the disappointingly small amounts of gold and the cruelties of Columbus, who, according to historic accounts, was indeed an arrogant commander. Things were beginning to go badly for Columbus, and the talk was undermining his reputation.

Nevertheless, a third voyage was planned and approved, and while Columbus was exploring the Atlantic coast of South America and claiming it for Spain, Hispaniola was seething with discontent. "Not enough gold!" was the cry, and "We can't eat this Indian food!" Columbus

The discovery of Costa Rica

It was on this voyage, sailing up and down the Atlantic Coast looking for a passage to what would later be called the Pacific, that Columbus discovered in Central America the Rich Coast of Veragua. He spent 18 days in what was later to be called Costa Rica, near the present-day port of Limón, in a place he called Cariari. There he made repairs to his damaged ships, the *Capitania*, *Gallega*, *Viscaína* and *Santiago de Palos*, while the near tideless ocean lapped on beautiful white and black sand beaches and coconut trees swayed in the gentle breezes. The respite was sorely needed: a violent storm off

tried to placate the rebels, as would his successors throughout Central America, by permitting them to enslave the indians. But even that failed to satisfy many. Large numbers of men returned to Spain demanding back pay and Columbus's head. The man sent to Hispaniola to quell the disturbances put Columbus in chains and sent him back to Spain. Columbus, however, through the intercession of Isabella and Ferdinand, managed to secure his release and set out on his fourth voyage.

LEFT: ritual drinking vessel.
ABOVE: Nicoyan phallic male figure.
ABOVE RIGHT: gold breastplate, Diquis region.

the coast of Honduras had caused considerable damage to his ships, and his men, one-third of whom were between the ages of 13 and 18, were sick and exhausted. Columbus himself, at 51 years of age, was almost prostrate with the pains of arthritis.

The return voyage, however, was difficult. His ships had been attacked by worms and foul weather, and were leaking badly. He made it only as far as Jamaica, and spent a year there, marooned, unable to get help from the governor of Hispaniola, who was worried that Columbus might usurp his position. There were food shortages and an attempted mutiny, but eventually Columbus and 100 of the original 135 men did return to Spain in 1504, shortly after the death of Queen Isabella.

Columbus spent his final years in failing health, attempting to secure the governorship, trade and other benefits which had been promised as part of his bargain with the queen. But the Catholic Monarchs refused even to see him, and the struggle to attain title, territory and wealth fell to his sons and their sons (Columbus' grandson was finally entitled Duke of Veragua in 1546) and to the *conquistadores* who followed him to the Americas and were his spiritual and material heirs. They too were to find hardships.

The *conquistadores*

It is tempting to characterize the Conquest of South America as a brutal cartoon: greedy, ruthless *conquistadores* bungling explorations, slitting each others' throats for gold, territory or gubernatorial titles, murdering, stealing from and enslaving the peoples of the land.

No small wonder then that it took 60 years from the time of Columbus's arrival at Limón until the first settlement in Costa Rica was established. The troublesome terrain, the unfriendly oceans, the extreme weather and the indians, who were not easily subdued, all played a large part in the delay – but it must be

GOLD FEVER

And, so the story goes, the indians of Costa Rica, wearing golden mirrors and necklaces, greeted the Spaniards, guided them around the area, and spoke of great mines of gold, pointing south.

"I have seen more signs of gold in the first two days than I saw in Hispaniola during four years," Columbus wrote to the Spanish king and queen.

He had struck it rich. He would be wealthy. He would be titled. His descendents would carry the noble names he won for them. He would return to Spain, reap the benefits of his discoveries and become a rich and titled man … or so he thought.

said that the continuous, jealous feuding among the *conquistadores* themselves was also a significant factor in the failure of the numerous colonization attempts.

Gold was consistently the big theme. When the *conquistadores* asked the indians about the location of the gold mines, the indians simply pointed south, ever south, to the fabled mines of Veragua. It gave the Spaniards the fever. But if the indians really knew where the mines were, they never revealed it, and to this day the great, legendary mines remain undiscovered.

The *conquistadores*, spurning the placer gold to be found in rivers, had to content themselves with taking the indians' gold, which they did –

until there was no more, and then they had to determine how to survive, let alone get rich.

More expeditions

In 1506, two years after Columbus returned to Spain, King Ferdinand sent the Governor Diego de Nicuesa and a group of settlers to establish a colony at Veragua. It was the first of a number of ill-fated attempts to establish settlements. Nicuesa's ship ran aground in Panamá and he and his group set about walking up the coast to their destination. Food shortages and tropical diseases were acute. The terrain was devastating. Indians along the way burned their own

young stowaway who was escaping his debts on Hispaniola, led an expedition across the isthmus and discovered the Pacific Ocean. It wasn't long before rudimentary shipyards appeared on the Pacific coast to accommodate would-be explorers who had sailed into Atlantic ports and walked across the isthmus, ready to set sail on the Pacific and continue their explorations. The Pacific was unexplored, had better anchorages, and was thought to have more gold.

The adventures of Gil González

The second inland expedition to Costa Rica occurred in 1522. It was led by Captain Gil

crops rather than yield their food. By the time the settlers finally arrived, their numbers had been halved.

Also around this time, expeditions from Spain were landing throughout the Atlantic coast of Central America. They were capturing indian slaves and sending them to work in the mines of Hispaniola, stealing the indians' gold and furiously searching for a passage across the continent to the other ocean.

Finally, in 1513, Vasco Nuñez de Balboa, a

LEFT: Columbus and *conquistadores*.
ABOVE: the *Pinta* founders in a storm.
ABOVE RIGHT: the Virgin of the Navigators.

González, and it too ended without establishing a settlement. Faulty ships hastily constructed on the Pacific Coast of Panamá took water and forced González and his men to abandon the sea and move forward on foot.

The expeditions of González, which included a walk of 224 leagues (well over 800 km) from the south Pacific coast of Costa Rica to the north, and into Nicaragua, have a mythic quality to them – at least as they are recorded for the king by the party's accountant. At the age of 65, and suffering from arthritis which was aggravated by the unceasing rain, González sometimes had to be carried on a litter, but he insisted on completing the arduous trip.

Once Gonzalez rested for 15 days in the home of the Terraba chief near Borruca. According to his accounts, he baptized some 32,000 indians here, collecting golden items of vast value.

Another encounter was with Chief Diríagen, who appeared one day with 500 indians, each carrying one or two turkeys, 17 women covered head to foot in gold disks, 10 men with standards, five trumpeters and other attendants, bringing 200 golden hatchets. The party stopped in front of the house where González was staying, the trumpeters played their trumpets and then chiefs, women and lords entered.

was aroused by the enormous amounts of gold González had collected and by González's refusal to give up his claim on Nicaragua. The affair ended with González fleeing Panamá with his treasure.

Pestilence and slavery

The indians of Nicoya and Nicaragua were not so fortunate as González, who got away with his life and his treasure. The expedition had brought smallpox, influenza and plague to the area, and tens of thousands of indians died of the diseases. Survivors of the epidemics faced another danger: impressment into slavery. Indi-

When González asked their business, Diríagen replied that they had come to see the men with beards who rode upon strange beasts. Probably Diríagen had come to ascertain the number and strength of the Spaniards, because he declined to be baptized and three days after his visit, returned and attacked the Spaniards, perhaps in attempt to get his gold back. It was an attack that González and less than 20 men, at least according to the story, easily repelled.

González ran into trouble later on with the greedy Pedrarias, governor of Panamá, who was responsible for the deaths of many Spanish *conquistadores*, including Balboa, his son-in-law, whom he had beheaded. Pedrarias's ire

ans from the Nicoya region, who then lived in large population centers and were vulnerable to such attacks, were captured, branded with hot irons and shipped off to Panamá and Peru to be sold as slaves.

The second attempted Costa Rican settlement was at Villa Bruselas, near present-day Orotina, not far from the large port city of Puntarenas. It lasted only three years and succumbed to feuding among the settlers and indian attacks.

During this period, the *conquistadores* who arrived in Central America were free to exploit the indians in virtually whatever way they wished. The Spanish policy of *requerimiento*, which went into effect in 1510, permitted settlers to make war on (kill) indians who did not become baptized, a convenient justification for the killing of indians and the continued plundering of their gold.

Forced labor

Later, *encomienda*, a royal grant from the Crown, gave settlers in Central America the right to force indians to labor without compensation – or to demand goods as tribute. It was, in effect, slavery. The indians were re-located to live on the land where they worked, and were considered the property of the grant holder. Until the Crown had approved the system of *encomienda*, the *conquistadores* could not realize their aspirations of becoming landed aristocracy. Without indians to work the land, all of the rights and assumed privileges of title had no real value.

Encomienda was not as widely practiced in Costa Rica as it was in the other Central American colonies for a variety of reasons; the indian labor force in Costa Rica was smaller, the Costa Rican indians were not unified and living in large population centers as were, for example, the Mayans of Guatemala. Instead, they lived in smaller, autonomous groups spread throughout the country. Thus the Spaniards weren't able to simply move in and conquer large numbers in a single effort as they had in Mexico.

Moreover, the Costa Rican indians did not adapt well to slavery and fiercely resisted its imposition. Many fought and died avoiding enslavement, and many others fled to the mountains, where they could not be followed. And, finally, the practice of *encomienda* was abolished well before large numbers of settlers arrived in Costa Rica.

Church intervention

The Church proved to have an uneasy time with the *encomienda* system, however, and after campaigning by many churchmen, including Friar Bartolmé de las Casas, a former *conqusitador*, *encomienda* was abolished in 1542, when it was repealed by the New Laws.

This set off violent protests among the settlers, who believed that they could not survive without slave labor. In Nicaragua, feelings ran so high that an armed uprising of colonists

murdered the bishop who had supported *encomienda*'s repeal. Settlers petitioned the king to revoke the New Laws, stating that they had invested their lives and possessions into settling the new land and the Crown had derived much benefit from their sacrifices, but, to his credit, the king refused.

Repartimiento

Still, the Crown had to support the colonists in their need for labor. *Encomienda* was replaced by a system called *repartimiento* which required all indian men between the ages of 16 and 60 to labor one week of each month for private indi-

viduals, religious institutions, municipalities and government offices. On paper, the system was supposed to provide indians with compensation for their labor and leave them free to work their own fields the other three weeks of the month, but, in practice, abuses were entered in to and the system functioned differently. Indians were required to devote considerably more than a week's labor to the Spaniards as they had to walk very long distances, sometimes for days on end, from their villages to their work places. And they were charged for the food and any other goods they consumed – thus using up the miserably small amount of pay they were to have received for their labors.

LEFT: converting the indians with the Cross.
ABOVE: Catholic missionaries among the indians.

The first inland settlement

Years passed, but little changed. The search continued for the great gold mines of Veragua to which the indians had referred, but the mines were never found. Spanish *conquistadores* plundered the coastlines, taking what booty they could find, capturing Indians and enslaving them, fighting all the while among themselves for claims to the new lands. English pirates appeared on the scene, competing for gold and slaves. Spain's

DUKE OF VERAGUA

In 1546, Luis, the grandson of Christopher Columbus, was finally entitled Duke of Veragua. He set out with an expedition of 130 men to claim his legacy, but he was attacked by indians, lost most of his men and retreated in failure.

as the indians scarcely ever attempted to escape and return to their homes.

Cavallón also brought along horses, cows, goats, pigs, chickens and ducks to improve the community's chances of success. It was a well-planned and well-financed expedition – and so, finally, 60 years after Columbus had arrived in Veragua, the first inland settlement in Costa Rica was established. It was christened Garcimuñoz, after Cavallón's place of birth.

Central American colonies were developing and administrative centers grew up in Panamá, Nicaragua and Guatemala. In 1539, officials in Panamá used the name Costa Rica for the first time to distinguish the territory between Panamá and Nicaragua, but still there were no settlements.

In 1559, Phillip II of Spain insisted that Costa Rica be populated, this time well inland, and in 1561, Juan de Cavallón arrived with a group of 90 Spaniards recruited from Guatemala and Nicaragua, along with a team of black slaves and "auxillary" Indians from Nicaragua. Bringing Indians from one area to another was a common practice among the *conquistadores*,

Juan Vásquez de Coronado

Hailed by some historians as the true conqueror of Costa Rica, Coronado moved the Garcimunõz settlement to the Cartago Valley to a place called El Guarco, and it was there, for the first time, that a permanent community took root. Coronado's tactics with the indians of Costa Rica were different from those of his predecessors. While he fully intended to settle their lands, and take what gold he could, he was friendly towards them, treated them with respect and requested, rather than demanded, labor and tribute.

Coronado was pressured by his soldiers and the settlers, who weren't particularly interested in peace, to be more aggressive with the indians. The settlers wanted food, gold and labor, or at least the promise of wealth and an easier life. During this time, they were continuously threatening to desert Costa Rica, claiming life was too difficult. Coronado's peaceful strategies were effective, however, and allowed the colony to flourish and grow.

Pacification and punishment

Among Coronado's successes was the surrender (pacification, it was called) of a local chief, Quitao, who called a meeting of all the chiefs in the area and announced that he was sick and tired of running around and hiding in the jungles and was ready to submit to the Spaniards. He told the other chiefs they were free to decide for themselves what they would do. The chiefs asked Quitao to decide for them and he replied that he would, but they must be advised that they would have to serve the king and his representative and those who did not go along would be severely punished. Then, as a token of his submission, he sent 150 indians to serve the Spanish, an act that was "cause for great admiration among the Spaniards."

Coronado's explorations through Costa Rica are recorded with his keen, almost affectionate observations of the indians. In the Diquis region, visiting the Coctu, he wrote of the well-organized and well-developed villages, unlike anything he had previously seen. He noted that the people had much gold, which they acquired from tribes on the Atlantic Coast and scooped from the rivers, and much cotton clothing. He described them as a very good-looking people, bellicose, skillful in their manners, and very honest, "a thing rarely seen in indians."

It was among the Coctu that Coronado met the "most good-looking indian" he had ever seen, Chief Corrohore, who asked his assistance in recovering his sister, Dulcehe, who had been kidnapped by a neighboring chief. Coronado's efforts on behalf of Corrohore were successful and Dulcehe was returned.

It was not always peaceful, however. Coronado, known for making peace among some of the warring tribes of Costa Rica, also joined them in their wars against one another. As well, there were indian uprisings in the colony. On

returning after an exploration Coronado, found that all the indians of the area, including Quitao, were at war with the Spanish. (The Spanish had been taking indian corn.) Indians in Orosi had killed eight Spaniards and their horses, and his old friends, the chiefs Aserri, Currirabá, Yurustí, Quircó and Purirsí, had been made prisoners. In an attempt to calm the situation, Coronado went to speak to the indians. Unfortunately, he lost his temper and ordered two of them to be dismembered.

The lack of gold and food, and the indian revolts imposed continuous hardships on the settlers. Supplies and new settlers were brought

in from Nicaragua, but the life was almost unendurable for the Spaniards. In 1569, settlers demanded indian slaves, threatening to abandon the colony if their demands weren't met, and Perafán de Ribera, Coronado's successor, an old man of 74 years and in frail health, went against the laws of Spain and permitted the settlers to make slaves of the indians.

The late 1560s marked the end of the Conquest of Costa Rica. By then the indigenous people of the new colony had been killed, had died of diseases, had submitted to the Spaniards or had fled to the forests of Talamanca. The land was now available to the settlers from Spain to come and make a new life. ❏

LEFT: the return of Dulcehe by Coronado.
RIGHT: Don Juan de Cavallón.

COLONIALISM AND INDEPENDENCE

After being a forgotten downbeat colony which received its independence by mail,
Costa Rica discovered coffee and a fledgling democracy

The Costa Rican colony grew slowly. In 1573, there was a total of 50 families in Cartago, and a fledgling community that would later become San José. Spanish immigrants arrived from Extremadura, in the west of Spain, from Andalucia, in the south, with its strong Moorish influences, and from Castile, the heart of old Spain. The Spanish had also founded Espiritú Santo de Esparza and Nicoya on the Pacific Coast, and, although the population of Costa Rica was slowly growing, life was anything but easy.

Riches to rags

During the Conquest, *conquistadores* had loaded their ships and lined their pockets with gold and had sent their obligatory percentages off to the royal treasury, which had swelled with their contributions. But by the end of the 16th century, the gold was gone, there was little Spanish currency available and it appeared as though there was no way to generate wealth. Cacao beans were used as money and barter became common. Even the few goods the colonists "bought" from Spain were traded for wheat flour, pigs, lard, chickens, tobacco and the liquor, which they produced on their farms. Most families lived on isolated farms in the Central Valle. They used primitive methods of agriculture; social and even church life was non-existent, and they lived in a state of grim impoverishment.

The forgotten colony

By now Spain was paying scant attention to its far-flung colony and even the colonial governor in Guatemala made little effort. It was, after all, a three-month trip from Guatemala by horse, and truly, there was little reason to travel to Costa Rica.

However, this was a rare land, in which even the governor and his aristocratic friends are said to have lowered their heads to the sun and dirt-

---

LEFT: the infamous English pirate Henry Morgan.
RIGHT: Miskito bandits, scourge of the colonists.

ied their hands in the soil of their own fields. The work was hard, but the hilly, green land, irrigated by rivers, was fertile and beautiful, and the climate was gentle. Colonists grew wheat, vegetables, sugar, and raised livestock and poultry. Slowly but surely the seeds of business began to grow.

GENERAL PETER SLAM.

The birth of commerce

The first export of the Costa Rican colony was mules. They were walked along the Mule Road to Panamá, where they were sold to hardy souls who needed the beasts to bear the goods they were carrying from the Atlantic to Pacific Coasts. Later came cacao production on the Atlantic Coast, and then tobacco, in the Central Plateau. In an attempt to give Costa Rica a product to export and a dependable income that could be taxed, the Crown set up tobacco processing plants and granted to Costa Rica sole rights within the colonies to grow tobacco. But Costa Rican tobacco was not of good quality, and there was not a large market for it.

On the Atlantic Coast, piracy and slave-trading were the business of the day. The Atlantic waters were continually plundered by English pirates, including the likes of Drake, Mansfield, Morgan and Owens, and by French, Dutch and Portuguese buccaneers, all attempting to control the territory so they could cross the isthmus, from the Atlantic to the Pacific, and thus avoid the Spaniards in Panamá.

The Miskitos

In 1641 a slave ship wrecked off the coast of Nicaragua/Honduras. The black slaves on board the ship escaped onto the Atlantic Coast. They later by the pirate Owens and the Miskitos, who were under orders to do so by the British-controlled Jamaican governor. (The British and the Spanish were then at war.)

Protection money

By 1779 things had become so bad that the Miskitos requested tribute of the Costa Rican government – and the government actually began to leave them "presents." The Miskitos would visit Matina and waiting for them would be a Napoleonic coat of bright fabric and shiny buttons, a three-cornered hat, or other equally attractive gifts.

Saqueo y incendio de la Ciudad de Esparza por los piratas ingleses.

were well-liked by the indians, who intermarried with them, and, over the years, they developed an identity and language of their own. They were called the Miskitos. British pirates allied with the Miskitos, and together they wreaked havoc on the Atlantic Coast of Costa Rica and on the cacao cultivation which was well under way there. For the Miskitos, the undefended plantations offered little resistance. They simply sailed in for their biannual raids, took the cacao, captured the black slaves and set off again.

In 1742, after many years of such devastation, the government built Fort San Fernando in Matina, only to have it destroyed five years

Many years later, in 1841, President Braulio Carrillo refused to continue paying tribute – or making gifts – to the Miskitos and threatened to bring the resources of the country to war against them. Probably because cacao production had dwindled greatly by then, the Miskitos stopped raiding Matina. Traces of their influence remain in the Atlantic coast area, however, and many of the place names there come from the Miskito language: Talamanca (Talamalka), Sixoala, Cahuita.

Indian resettlement

Owing to its mountainous terrain and inaccessibility, the Talamanca region of Costa Rica had escaped the Conquest. Groups of indians, some of them refugees who had fled oppressive conditions elsewhere in the country, lived there, undisturbed by the invading Spaniards. However, as more colonists arrived in Costa Rica and began to clear land, build roads and farm, the small size of the available indian labor force became a serious problem. The solution was to begin raids on Talamanca. After numerous, unsuccessful raids and attempts to conquer Talamanca, with counter attacks and cruel revenges on both sides, hundreds of indians were "re-located" to the Central Valley by the Indian Resettlement Policies of 1747.

class distinctions and onerous trade restrictions, largely passed them by.

Independence – by mail!

Costa Ricans like to relate that they received their independence from Spain by mail. In fact, a courier aboard a mule arrived in the Central Valley of Costa Rica with the news on October 13, 1821, nearly a month after colonial officials in Guatemala City had declared independence for Costa Rica from the Spanish Empire.

The news sparked ambivalence, confusion and conflict over what independence meant for the backwater region of Costa Rica. Being the

In the central valley, communities were being established and were growing. In 1706, the village of Cubujugui, which later became Heredia, was founded; in 1737, Villa Nueva de la Boca del Monte, now San José, was born; and in 1782, Villa Hermosa, now Alajuela, began.

Costa Ricans, with their attention on subsistence and survival, remained largely unaffected by the currents of thought and the conflicts that led to Central America's struggle for independence from Spain. The discord that was brewing elsewhere in Central America, fueled by

LEFT: English pirates sack a village near the Pacific.
ABOVE: a public beheading in Talamanca.

province furthest removed from the colonial capital, Costa Rica came under the least - influence of the Spanish Crown, the Catholic Church, the colonial bureaucracy and the monopolistic Guatemalan traders who dominated colonial life in the rest of Central America.

Tucked away in the recesses of the country's central highlands, leaders of the four small communities of San José, Cartago, Heredia and Alajuela began a debate over what to do next.

Which way now?

Taking their cues from the 1812 Spanish Constitution – written with the distinguished participation of liberal Costa Rican Florencio de Castillo – local leaders drafted their first constitution, the *Pacto de Concordia,* on December 1, 1821. However, a split quickly developed over whether or not to follow the lead of other Central American countries in joining the Mexican Iturbide Empire, or to opt for total independence.

Leaders of the towns of San José and Alajuela, inspired by the revolutionary ideas that were then sweeping the world, argued for independence, while those of Cartago and Heredia leaned toward the Empire. There were even those who argued passionately that Costa

Rica should become a part of Colombia, at the time ruled by Simón Bolívar.

The disagreements reflected the basic disparity in the respective characters of the cities. Cartago, the old capital, and Heredia, had been founded to create Catholic congregations out of the early settlers, who were religiously reticent. And so these towns evolved into centers of conservative thought and were more closely linked to the old colonial bureaucracy.

By contrast San José was founded by settlers who were banished from Cartago for defying the strict colonial trading laws on smuggling, and Alajuela, too, developed into an on-the-

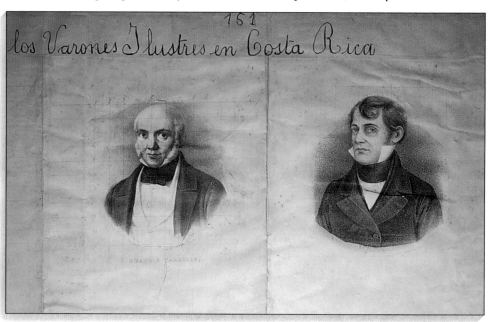

los Varones Ilustres en Costa Rica

THE OLD CAPITAL

The old capital of Cartago was founded in 1561 by Juan de Cavallón as Castillo de Garcimuñoz. The site and name were abandoned when Coronado moved all the inhabitants to El Guarco in the Cartago Valley. Then Perafán de Ribera moved it again, to Mata Redonda, near present-day Sabana. Later, the peripatetic city returned to the Cartago Valley, to its present location.

In 1723, Irazú Volcano erupted, covering Cartago in layers of ash. At that time, Costa Rica's capital comprised just 70 houses, a parish church and two shrines. It had no shops, no druggist, nor even a resident doctor.

fringe agricultural center where smuggling of tobacco flourished. Both towns developed more freewheeling, commercially-based liberal attitudes than those of their more stodgy neighbors.

The issue of whether or not Costa Rica would join the Mexican Empire was settled on April 5, 1823, when two armies from the rival cities met in battle on the Continental Divide between San José and Cartago in a skirmish which left 20 men dead. The victorious independence forces, led by a former merchant seaman named Gregorio José Ramírez, took the town of Cartago, assuring independence from the Mexican Empire. As it turned out, they need not have bothered. It was discovered that Augustine I of

Mexico had fallen several days before the battle, and with him went the Mexican Empire.

Farmers and teachers

Ramírez set a precedent by relinquishing power in order to return to his farm; an example that would be followed by other victorious Costa Rican conquerors. He later returned to put down an army coup, establishing civilian dominance over the military at a very early stage in the country's development.

Statehood was conferred upon a rather ambivalent Costa Rica by the Federal Republic of Central America, a noble effort at creating a

nández, a teacher at one of Costa Rica's two elementary schools, who distinguished himself by conducting the affairs of state with prudence and humility.

The first printing presses arrived in Costa Rica under Mora Fernández and by the time his successor, another elementary school teacher named José Rafael Gallegas, was elected, (against his will) in 1833, several newspapers were in print. One of them, *La Tertulia*, published humiliating attacks on Gallegas, who, not much interested in the office to begin with, resigned as Head of State. One of *La Tertulia*'s major complaints was the social disintegration

"United States of Central America" out of the five provinces, with a capital in Guatemala City. But it was an effort doomed to failure because of the tenacity with which the elite class clung to the local colonial social order in other parts of Central America.

As Costa Rica, largely a nation of family farmers, lacked both an elite class and a well-defined social order, it offered neither great resistance to, nor enthusiasm for, the Confederation. As a sovereign federal state, the country elected its first Head of State, Juan Mora Fer-

which had befallen the community as a result of the first modest signs of prosperity brought on by the planting of coffee, near San José. That limited prosperity brought with it prostitution, gambling and the theft of property at levels which had been unknown during the more austere colonial era. A strong, no-nonsense authoritarian hand was called for, and a San José lawyer, named Braulio Carrillo, was the right man in the right place at the right time.

Braulio Carrillo

Carrillo imposed vagrancy laws, removed Costa Rica from the faltering Central American Federal Republic and enacted a number of liberal

LEFT: 19th-century heads of state.
ABOVE: early 20th-century Nicoya Indians.

reforms such as a civil and penal code. He also outlawed the church's right to tithe and earned the enmity of the other Central Valley townships by imposing a tax on rural land, using the revenues to build roads and ports. Braulio Carrillo also paid off Costa Rica's share of a debt to British bankers which had been incurred by the founders of the Central American Federation, a debt that other Central American countries would have hanging over them until well into the 20th century. The payback of the"English debt" eventually paid

ROTATING CAPITALS

To minimize the rivalries between the four main population centers of the day the honor of being capital was rotated among them every four years.

as an important new marketplace for Costa Rican coffee.

The domination that coffee gave to the citizens of San José and Carrillo's vigorous action in ordering that the country's institutions be formed around the new source of wealth, caused resentment from the other townships. In 1837, Cartago, Alajuela and Heredia challenged Carrillo and San José in the *Guerra de la Liga*. Emerging victorious from the battle, Carrillo moved the capital permanently to San José.

dividends in the form of good credit with which to invest in the country's new found source of wealth: coffee.

Coffee power

Carrillo had, with unabashed autocracy, already ordered public administration around the demands of the coffee economy when an English seaman, on his way back to England with a cargo of pelts stopped in Costa Rica in search of ballast for his ship. He loaded some 500,000 pounds of coffee into his hold and the Costa Rica–Liverpool connection was, inadvertently, established. Thus were the British Isles and, ultimately, the European continent, opened up

When his term was up in 1837, Braulio Carrillo left office, only to return in a military coup the following year, after his successor tried to roll back some of his reforms. Continuing to force the country down the road to a coffee-fueled progress, he proclaimed himself president-in-perpetuity.

General Morazán

By 1842, the new social order created by Carrillo rose up to overwhelm him. Members of the budding coffee oligarchy called on General Francisco Morazán, the hero of the Central American Federal Republic, who was ousted during a civil war in Guatemala three years earlier, to free them from what they conceived to be Carrillo's despotism. Morazán was welcomed as a liberator when he arrived in Costa Rica, in April of 1842, with an army of 500 mostly Salvadoran volunteers. The head of Carrillo's army, Vicente Villaseñor, met Morazán as the general and his men neared Alajuela on their march from the Pacific port of Caldera and offered to join forces with him. The *Pacto de Jocote* sealed, Carrillo fell and was forced into exile in El Salvador.

A special assembly named Morazán Provisional Head of the State of Costa Rica. The General received a hero's welcome in Heredia and Alajuela, but received a somewhat restrained and cooler reception in San José.

Morazán wore out his welcome when he attempted to use Costa Rica as a base to revive his moribund Confederation. The General sent missives to the other Central American countries calling for a National Constituent Assembly to revive his dream of a unified Central American nation, threatening to impose compliance by force of arms. When Morazán tried to conscript Costa Ricans to enforce his ultimatum, the people of San José revolted. After three days of fierce fighting, Morazán was captured and, on September 15, 1842, he was executed in San José's Central Park.

Less than three years later, Braulio Carrillo, too, was to meet a violent end, assassinated in El Salvador. Today, Costa Ricans have mixed feelings about Braulio Carrillo. He is remembered as both a despot and as a strong, sometimes benevolent leader who, perhaps, was the right man at the right time to force Costa Rica to break with its colonial past, placing the country firmly, if hesitatingly, on the path to nationhood.

William Walker

In 1855, a Tennessee adventurer named William Walker took control of Nicaragua. One of his aims was to institutionalize slavery there and in neighboring countries which he would then sell on to the United States. Certain US industrialists liked the plan and gave support to Walker. The following year, with an army of 300 fellow filibusters, he invaded Costa Rica, advancing as far as the site of the present Santa

Rosa National Park, where they entrenched themselves in the fotified Santa Rosa *casona*. However, the Costa Rican president, Juan Rafael Mora, a member of the coffee oligarchy, had been monitoring the threat and mustered a force of *campesinos* to repel Walker. The Costa Ricans were numerically superior, though many were poorly armed with little more than farming implements and rusty rifles. On May 20, 1856, they engaged Walker and in a 14-minute-long battle and forced him to retreat back towards the Nicaraguan border. The Costa Rican army followed and, at Rivas in Nicaragua, trapped Walker in a wooden fort.

A young drummer boy named Juan Santamaria volunteered to torch the fort, but while doing so was shot and died. With the fort in flames, Walker's men were routed and his Costa Rican adventure was over. Three years later, he met his end in front of a firing squad in Honduras. The name of Juan Santamaria lives on in Costa Rican folklore as a youthful hero and symbol of national freedom.

President Mora was not such a hero. Despite his victory, his domestic policies meant he was not a popular choice as leader. He rigged the elections of 1859, however, to win another term in office. He was deposed, attempted a coup d'état, and was executed. ❑

LEFT: a 19th-century mud-and-wattle home.
RIGHT: statue of Juan Santamaria, Alajuela.

THE 20TH CENTURY

Economic difficulties and the rising tide of reform came to a head in civil war, but today Costa Rica, a nation without an army, is Central America's peace broker

In 1889, with the drafting of the country's liberal constitution and the institution of a reliable quadrennial electoral process, Costa Rica entered an era of bucolic prosperity and political stability. The affairs of state were left in the hands of so-called "Olympian" political plutocrats who administered public affairs with a laissez-faire assurance.

The coffee coup

It was not all plain sailing, however, as the downward trickle of profits in the coffee economy failed to reach growing numbers of people, especially in the neglected urban centers. Faced with the closing of European coffee markets during World War I, Costa Rica's first reformist president, Alfredo Gonzáles Flores, instituted a tax on coffee. This incurred the wrath of the coffee establishment which backed the president's own army chief, Federico Tinoco, in a successful coup on January 27, 1917. Tinoco assumed the presidency and named his brother, Joaquín, to head the army.

The warrior priest

Popular reaction to the repressive Tinoco dictatorship brought Jorge Volio Jiménez onto the country's political stage with a dramatic flourish. The pious scion of a Cartago coffee family that gave Costa Rica several presidents, Volio began studying for the priesthood at Belgium's Leuven University in 1903. Heavily influenced by Belgian social Christian thinking, Volio returned to Costa Rica in 1910 to become pastor of the parish of Carmen de Heredia. No simple parish priest, in 1912, Volio denounced the silence of the Costa Rican government over the intervention of US Marines in Nicaragua and backed up his words by leading a group of Nicaraguan revolutionaries into battle. He was seriously wounded in the battle of Paz Centro, which took place in southern Nicaragua.

For his military adventure Volio was suspended from the Church, but was later reinstated and assigned to the Santa Ana parish. But his passion for social justice led him to more clashes with the conservative local hierarchy, and, in 1915, he left the priesthood to devote himself full-time to working for social change.

As the dictatorship became even more repressive, Volio and a handful of other Costa Ricans left the country and formed an armed resistance that plotted against the Tinocos, first from Panamá and then from Nicaragua. The revolutionary forces were defeated by government troops led by army chief Joaquín Tinoco in battles near the Nicaraguan border in early 1919. But the Tinoco dictatorship was brought down not by this armed resistance nor by a military one, but rather by school teachers and students who rioted after soldiers marched on them, during a demonstration, in July of 1919. On August 9, 1919, Federico Tinoco resigned the presidency. The next day, Joaquín Tinoco

---

PRECEDING PAGES: volunteer militiamen.
LEFT: young soldiers in a border dispute with Panamá.
RIGHT: animal trophies were once the fashion.

was gunned down as he walked in the street. The gunman was never identified.

Viva Volio!

His military defeat notwithstanding, Volio received a hero's welcome on his arrival in San José and the ready cry "Viva Volio!" expressed the hope for change in the country's stodgy political status quo. The title of "General" was subsequently conferred on Volio by the Costa Rican Congress. But much to Volio's consternation, the fall of Tinoco meant a return to business as usual in liberal Costa Rica. He formed the Reformist Party in 1923, which set an

Volio took matters into his own hands and commanded a force across the border to intervene. Concerned as to what an increasingly belligerent Volio might do with his force upon return, Jiménez ordered the General to be intercepted when he arrived in Liberia.

After a gunfight that left two government soldiers and Volio himself wounded, the General was apprehended. He was then brought back to San José where he was examined by the doctors. They diagnosed Volio as suffering from "nervous hypersensitivity." Rather than imprisoning the patriot, Jiménez, in consultation with Volio's family, allowed the General to be taken

agenda for agrarian reform, decent housing, job security and social protections, and ran for president on the Reformist ticket in that year against Ricardo Jiménez and Alberto Echandi.

He came in a close third in a vote that gave none of the candidates the required majority. A crisis was averted when Volio agreed to join forces with Jiménez, accepting the vice-presidency and a seat in Congress. But Volio did not see his pact with Jiménez as one of compromise. Instead, he used his seat in Congress to bewilder his fellow congressmen with forceful attacks on the country's upper classes.

When the government once again showed indifference to strife in neighboring Nicaragua,

to Belgium for psychiatric care and Volio's promising political career came to an ignominious end.

The growth of reform

Volio's own brand of reformism collapsed with his party, but the reformist movement was important in giving voice to the aspirations of broad sectors of society on the margins of the agro-export economy, and in inspiring young intellectuals to action.

One of those intellectuals was Manuel Mora, who, in his own words, "used to follow Volio around like a puppy dog." Disillusioned with Volio's political flirtation with Jiménez, Mora split with the Reformist Party to eventually form the Communist Party in 1931.

The Communists immediately made their presence felt in the lowland banana zones. In a strike in the banana zones in 1934, immortalized in the novel *Mamita Yunai* by labor organizer Carlos Luis Fallas, the Communists won wage guarantees and the right to unionize, but only after a torrid and sometimes violent battle with both government troops and the United Fruit Company.

Meanwhile, plummeting coffee prices during the Great Depression had created additional hardship for a great many Costa Ricans.

Calderón Guardia

The rising tide of reform finally found its champion when, as the economic crisis reached its breaking point, Costa Ricans elected Dr. Rafael Angel Calderón Guardia to the presidency in 1939. Inheritor of his father's humanitarian legacy and backed by the coffee establishment, Calderón Guardia seemed the perfect choice, as he won the election with more than 80 percent of the total vote.

Calderón Guardia, also steeped in social Christian doctrine at medical school in Bel-

ABOVE: mural in Costa Rica's Museum of Art: *Cultivating the Wild New Country.*

gium, carried out reforms beyond the hopes of even the most fervent reformers and the fears of the most entrenched liberal, creating a social security system, a labor code, and other social guarantees.

But after Costa Rica declared war on Germany and Japan following the attack on Pearl Harbor – a day before even the United States – Calderón Guardia added insult to injury for the coffee barons by using his wartime emergency powers to confiscate the lands of German families, some of whom had been in Costa Rica for generations and who had business dealings with and were intermarried within the oligarchy.

Having alienated himself from the traditional source of political power, Calderón Guardia made common cause with Manual Mora and his Communist Party, and the Catholic Church led by the socially-minded Archbishop Victor Sanabria. Together they defied the coffee barons and the economic liberals who had dominated Costa Rica since the end of the 19th century to expand the role of the state in providing for people's needs. The nascent bureaucracies would invariably be headed by a member of the Communist Party. Manuel Mora eventually would be named to head the country's army.

When the worldwide anti-Nazi alliances – which made this peculiar Church-State-Party pact feasible – vanished, so too did the popular support for Calderón's leadership. According to Mora, as the government clung to power during the 1948 Civil War to, in his words, "defend the social guarantees won by the people," he was paid a visit by an old friend who offered his support. It was the elderly and ailing General Jorge Volio Jiménez.

History has shown that the winners of that Civil War, led by José (Don Pepe) Figueres, had no intention of rolling back the social guarantees, but rather further institutionalized the legacy of nearly 30 years of reformist struggle. It was a legacy summed up by the immortal cry: "Viva Volio!"

The grandfather of Costa Rica

José Figueres is best known abroad for abolishing the army; but Costa Ricans remember him for the way in which he lived his life, and for the heritage of democracy that he created and solidified.

Don Pepe was born of Catalán parents, and for many that somehow explained his ego, his opinionated, self-righteous, impossibly princi-pled, obstinate, courageous, unyielding, unpre-dictable self. He was self-educated, and as a young man he virtually lived in the Boston Public Library, where he read as if ravenous for the purity of ideas, and became infected with the new and exciting spirit of North American liberalism. He returned to Costa Rica from Boston and New York City, in the 1920s, with a romantic vision and deeply-held belief in the nobility of the human spirit, and in a hope for social justice for the people of his country.

There he learned that it was as he had hoped and believed it would be: that placing social

services above his own personal profit offered a far greater reward.

Until 1942, Don Pepe had no real political experience. Then, on July 2, the *San Pablo*, a United Fruit Company vessel, was sunk by a German submarine in the Port of Limón. The Costa Ricans aboard were killed, and people everywhere were outraged and screaming for something to be done. The president, Rafael Angel Calderón, responded to the submarine attack and to the excitable flames of hatred that were rising up in the demands of the people by imprisoning the German and Italian citizens of the Atlantic region. Two days later, on July 4, a celebration planned to honor the US Day of In-dependence turned into a riot. A gathering of 20,000 people in San José's Central Park turned violent, as the window of a medical doctor who had studied in Germany was smashed. Rioting and looting followed, and the government not only did nothing to control the mob, but, some said, they actually encouraged it.

The aftermath of the riots was one of fear and suspicion. Businessmen who had been looted were afraid to speak out and seek redress; instead, cowed by fear of further reprisals, they placed paid ads in the newspa-pers asserting their loyalty to Costa Rica. Don Pepe Figueres blamed Calderón, whose gov-ernment, he said, was responsible for public order and safety.

He decided to express "what everyone felt but was afraid to say," and purchased radio air time on "America Latina." In strident mocking tones he accused, the administration of an inability to govern. His acid denouncement of the government was interrupted mid-sentence as the director-general of the police arrived and hauled him away. The result was, perhaps all too predictably, the making of a martyr and national hero out of the imprisoned Don Pepe Figueres.

The seeds of revolution

Figueres spent the next two years in exile in Mexico. There he began to plan his revenge. Force, he was convinced, was the only way to overthrow the government of Rafael Angel Calderón. Always an avid reader, Figueres con-tinued his personal studies, made contacts, mutual help relationships and agreements with exiles, intellectuals and revolutionaries from other countries, and began stockpiling arms.

LA LUCHA SIN FIN

Don Pepe started a farm high in the mountains, south of San José, and called it *La Lucha Sin Fin* (The Endless Struggle). It was a success and he used the profits to provide schools, libraries, stores, movie houses, soccer fields and medical clinics for the local people. At *La Lucha*, Don Pepe worked at liberating the *campesino* from the ignorance and poverty that was his natural inheritance, and labored at turning some of the Utopian theory of which he had read into a workable reality. The day-to-day life on the farm provided lessons which in many ways he was later to apply to all Costa Rica.

In 1944, after a particularly violent and discreditable presidential election in Costa Rica, with shootings, ballot boxes being stuffed and stolen, and the voting process being degraded to a point well below any previous level, Teodoro Picado, Calderón's political successor, was elected president. Issues of a fraudulent election, the faltering economy, the Communist presence and widespread official corruption were just too much for Figueres, and he returned to Costa Rica in May of 1944. His apolitical days were over; it was a time for action. Determined to do something about Calderón, he jumped into opposition politics, but felt that the electoral process had been so badly corrupted that he would not run as the opposition candidate. He once again insisted that only a violent revolution would bring about the changes that he felt were inevitable and desperately necessary.

In the fateful 1948 presidential elections, Otilio Ulate, publisher of the *Diario de Costa Rica*, a San José newspaper, ran against Calderón. Ulate won by a substantial margin, but the *calderonistas* maintained control of congress. There were charges and countercharges of fraud. And, in the midst of all the violent confrontations, a large number of ballots were set ablaze.

The Electoral Tribunal, which had been entrusted to oversee fair elections, and to which the nation was looking for an electoral verdict, failed to issue one, perhaps in the hope that the candidates themselves would reach a compromise agreement.

With no action forthcoming from the Electoral Tribunal and no compromise possible between the candidates, the *calderonista*-controlled Congress, in an unprecedented act, annulled the presidential election. Ulate was arrested by Picado's police colonel, and his closest advisor, Dr. Carlos Luis Valverde, was shot and died the following day. In San José, businesses were closed and storefronts were boarded up. It felt as though a bomb were ready to go off.

Meanwhile, Figueres was in the mountains near his ranch, *La Lucha Sin Fin*, planning for the coming war.

LEFT: Don Pepe, the country's grandfather (left), and Oscar Arias, the Nobel Laureate (right).
RIGHT: a pensive Don Pepe.

Civil war

The War of National Liberation began on March 11, 1948. It consisted of a well-planned, albeit rather fortunate offensive, carried out by men with no formal military backgrounds, who were trained by *guerrilleros* from the Dominican Republic and Honduras, and armed with guns flown in from Guatemala.

Forty-four days later, 2,000 men, one in every 300 Costa Ricans, had been killed during the violent, sad war of liberation. Figueres' forces were victorious, despite the efforts of the Nicaraguan dictator Anastasio Somoza, and his invasion of the north of Costa Rica.

President Picado, who had never really believed an armed insurrection would occur, and who really had no heart for conflict, saw that a swiftly negotiated peace was essential. Picado announced his surrender.

The Second Republic

Don Pepe Figueres, as the acknowledged winner of the battle, and as the head of the victorious junta, entered San José five days after the cease-fire and led a triumphant parade. His National Liberation Army, festooned with flowers, marched up Avenida Central to the International Airport at La Sabana. Figueres addressed the people, outlining his goals and fundamental concepts, which he referred to as "the greatest good for the greatest number." More precisely, he described the four main objectives of what he called his Second Republic: the re-establishment of civic ethics, elimination of the spoils system in public administration, social progress without communism, and a greater sense of solidarity with other nations.

One of Figueres' first acts was to place a 10 percent tax on wealth, a law that was resented, badly administered and, in most cases, evaded by the affluent. He expanded the social security system, enacted full voting rights for all women, created a minimum wage, low-cost

the Constitutional Congress, did reflect many of the goals of the Second Republic. It included political and individual freedoms, and added new social guarantees. It established the principle of public regulation of private property and enterprise, and empowered the state to take actions assuring the widest distribution of wealth possible.

But arguably its finest social guarantee was to extend citizenship to everyone born in Costa Rica, an issue of great importance to the Afro-Caribbean people of the Atlantic region, who until that time had been treated as second-class persons.

national health care services for all, legislation on child support, and the nationalization of every bank in the country. The firing of large numbers of bureaucrats and schoolteachers, in an attempt to reorganize government agencies, exacerbated his declining popularity. And then the assets of individuals connected with the Calderón-Picado governments were frozen. Don Pepe's extreme and, to some, arbitrary politics, alienated many. Even the press became hostile to him.

Acceptance of his new vision was extremely difficult in what was then an atmosphere of mistrust and disharmony. Nevertheless, the Constitution of 1949, when it was finally accepted by

THE PRAGMATIC REVOLUTIONARY

The *junta* of Don Pepe was not universally popular and he suffered criticism from all quarters. He was accused of being a Communist by the right and a Nazi by the left. Indeed, his revolution had received funding from very conservative Costa Ricans; he had accepted military aid from the United States; he had also received armaments from a group called the Caribbean Legion, who had supplied him on the understanding that this revolution was to be the first of a series that would re-create the Central American region and oust many of the dictatorial regimes that had risen to power with the aid of the United States.

The end of the military

The new constitution also abolished the military. This was perhaps Figueres' most celebrated and memorable achievement, and one that he would point to over and over again. As he liked to explain, if a member of the family is ill, you should call the doctor, but that doesn't mean that the doctor has to continue to live with you for the rest of your life.

In a public ceremony, he delivered the keys of the Bella Vista military fortress to the Minister of Public Education, and told him to convert the old fort into a national museum. Don Pepe knew how to exploit the moment. With photographers standing by, he took a sledge-hammer and a symbolic smash at the wall of the fortress. Figueres supporters consider that dramatic act as a final blow to militarism. His enemies regard the aboliton of the military as a clever move, as, lacking the full backing of the military, he decided to get rid of it.

Calm before storm

The 1960s and 1970s were essentially peaceful and prosperous decades for Costa Rica, with the development of a welfare state and rights bills protecting indigenous peoples just two of the highlights of a progressive regime. In 1979, however, the anti-government Sandinista forces in neighboring Nicaragua toppled the Somoza dictatorship and, during the war, Costa Rica became a fallback area for Contra groups and anti-Sandinistas, largely on the insistence of the United States, to whom Costa Rica was financially indebted.

Equally bad news, if not worse, was the collapse of both the banana and coffee markets at the beginning of the 1980s. Throughout the decade debt continued to mount and by 1989 Costa Rica was in the red to the tune of a massive $5 billion.

The silver lining on the cloud hanging over the nation was provided by its president, Oscar Arias, who was acting as a peace mediator in the escalating regional conflicts. By now El Salvador, Honduras and Guatamala were also embroiled in various types of war or dispute and Costa Rica, for all its economic problems, was at least an oasis of peace. In 1987, Arias

was awarded the Nobel Peace Prize for his efforts to bring peace to Central America. He also managed to agree millions of dollars of aid for his country from the United States without compromising Costa Rica's neutral position.

A family affair

Despite the success of Oscar Arias abroad, he was voted out in 1990 in favour of Rafael Calderón Fournier, the son of post-war president Dr Rafael Calderón Guardia. Following a lackluster term, he was succeeded *by José Maria Figueres, son of Don Pepe, who was, of course, Calderón Guardia senior's arch *rival.

An unpleasant legacy of the Calderón era was the El Banco Anglo Costariccense affair. In 1994, just after the president left office, the nation's oldest government-owned bank went bust to the tune of more than $100 million. The legal battles and trials, charges and counter charges continue to this day.

Sadly, the young Figueres was unable to repeat his father's success, or even improve much on the previous miserable administration, *and proved to be one of Costa Rica's most unpopular presidents. In 1998 the Social Christian Unity Party (PUSC) won the election under Miguel Angel Rodriguez, who has pledged to liberalize certain key economic sectors. ❏

LEFT: national flag-waving politicos.
RIGHT: former president Oscar Arias, winner of the Nobel Peace Prize, with his family.

COSTA RICA
(THE HEART OF THE AMERICAS)

WHERE THE WORLD'S CHOICEST COFFEE GROWS.

SAN JOSE – THE WAY IT WAS

Thanks to coffee, San José enjoyed a golden age in the early 1900s. It became the toast of Central America, a bourgeois paradise, but, sadly, it was not to last

In 1737, the authorities ordered the construction of a thatch-covered hermitage on the flatlands of the Boca del Monte. It was to be the centerpoint of a new village to bring together the residents of the area, whose small homes were scattered over the valley. From this humble beginning began the city of San José.

For its first 39 years, it was still just a village, with mud covered streets and miserable little houses. Then an official ordered the construction of a tobacco factory, and it was from here that the country's tobacco industry monopoly was administered. It proved to be an activity that brought a certain degree of prosperity.

The coffee boom

Tobacco was a short-lived success, as was cacao but then came experimentation with a new crop: coffee. It grew with such ease and it bore fruit with such abundance that this once-small Central American colony very quickly left behind the squalor that it had known.

England was interested in not only buying this coffee, but also in loaning funds, on account, against the next harvest. The surrounding areas filled quickly with orderly rows of coffee plantations and the people, with their new wealth, sought the life of San José, thus transforming it into a prosperous coffee-growing center.

By the town square there was at first only the Church of Mercy and the Town Council building. But other conveniences, created to service the foreigners who were beginning to arrive, were soon set up.

At the end of the 18th century, the Education Building was erected, as was a cathedral, at the front of which stood a beautiful central park, where the indians and farmers held their weekly fairs. Money was minted at the Currency House, and, in order to support the militia, the Military Quarters were erected.

Social and cultural life

In 1821, Costa Rica gained its independence from the Spanish Empire and became a republic. The small village-town of San José soon grew into a city, a capital city, and its newly installed authorities struggled to improve the streets, build bridges and open roads to the ports. Guards, armed with rusty muskets, patrolled the brick-layered streets, illuminated at night by kerosene lamps.

In the dance parlors of the bourgeoisie, the quadrille was in vogue. An actor would recite poetry and a young lady would play Chopin ballads amidst conversations concerning the price of coffee in London.

Social and economic life was rigidly defined. The indian population was severely depleted, the black community was excluded from the central valley and provided manual labor, while the descendants of the Spanish lived in the central part of town where they built their large adobe houses with corridors opening onto enclosed vegetable gardens.

Cultural life centered around the Mora Theater, where fourth-rate companies would perform along with jugglers and an occasional virtuoso musician. The ladies would sit and listen, dressed in their regal dresses, while the gentlemen stood around, robed in their Spanish capes, and smoked and engaged in small-talk concerning politics.

Foreign visitors would stay in a rooming house and from there would visit the town; some considered the possibility of entering the coffee export business and others idly took notes for their travel diaries.

The European influence

Earnings from the export of coffee engendered an illustrious bourgeoisie. The members of this grander plantations were created in an effort to stay ahead of those whom they felt were their competitors.

Costa Rican architects visited the Universal Exposition of Paris and, along with other new and imported ideas, brought back metal buildings for schools. They imported finely-wrought metal plates for walls, steel columns, crests for the buildings and Italian mosaics. The homes of the coffee growers soon began to look like the mansions of the wealthy in New Orleans and Jamaica. French adobe walls, wide, inclined roofs, ornate verandas with white balustrades and woodwork cut in the style of gingerbread.

class traveled to France to have their children educated in Europe. When home in San José, the children missed the theaters, the boulevards, the cafés and the fine architecture of Europe. They were insistent on improving the appearance of their native capital city. As coffee production engendered greater prosperity, the leading planter families increased their investments, which led to rivalries among them. Ever

PRECEDING PAGES: an early attempt to lure tourists.
LEFT: downtown San José was conceived as a handsome place of fine buildings and grand statues.
ABOVE: First Avenue, San José, during the early years of the 20th century.

EARLY IMPRESSIONS

A German scientist, visiting during the mid-19th century, wrote: "There is not a building that calls attention for its beauty. The government buildings, the garrison and its gallery, the university and the theater are insignificant structures. The cathedral has an air of negligence and economy. There aren't even any chairs. The president of the republic has to sit with his followers on a wooden bench. By contrast a French journalist noted: "The presidential palace is an enchanting square building with an internal half-Spanish, half-Arab patio. A circular stair led to the congressional room where a ball was staged for me."

Jalousies and shades protected the windows made of colored glass through which the brilliant tropical sun shone.

The city's golden age

Towards the end of the 19th century, Monsieur Amon Faiseleau Duplantier, who received the concession to establish the streetcar system, divided his farm on the sunny slopes of the Torres River and there began the business of real estate sales. He was successful and the best of San José society fought for the urban lots. Soon the coffee plantations were replaced with tree-shaded streets and stately residences with large

the shape of a horseshoe was financed from the national budget and by a tax paid by the rich coffee growers.

By the early 1900s, the village had given way to a glowing city, which, even if it did not attain the elegant, urbane layout to which it aspired, developed a comfortable lifestyle permitted by its growing prosperity.

If the early European critics of Costa Rica had looked in the crystal ball and foreseen the amenities of San José at the turn of the 20th-century, they would surely have remained. In front of the theater was the elegant Hotel Francais. Nearby, the Petite Trianon was a coffee

gardens. Meanwhile, Minor Keith, who was occupied with developing The United Fruit Company and the railroad system to the Atlantic Coast, finished the Atlantic Railroad station in San José. At the same time, Mother Superior Barthelemy Rich was opening her prestigious girls' high school, *Colegio de Sión*, where the daughters of the bourgeoisie received their education.

On October 19, 1897, the president and a select audience entered the wide doors of the National Theater to inaugurate the building. That opening night featured a magnificent presentation of the opera *Faust*. The sumptuous building with its four levels and a floor plan in

house favored by high society, artists and diplomats; a little beyond, the windows of the Golden Eagle were filled with French wine and liquors and Spanish preserves and fine oils. *Talabarteria Inglesa* and *La Tiendita* satisfied the most demanding tastes in matters of decoration and leatherwork.

The Ford agency exhibited its 1912 model, which was priced at $975. It competed with a number of other import agencies, as well as real estate businesses, which offered farms, lots, beaches and Victorian residences. The streetcar ran to the limits of the city carrying great numbers of merchants, their employees and office workers.

The other side of the tracks

Not all members of San José society enjoyed a rose-colored life. The city had expanded too quickly, into vast, obscure and sad suburbs. World War I and the coffee crisis brought to wide sectors of the working population unemployment and salaries that were below poverty level. The Society of *Casas Baratas* began the construction of workers' housing units of the type known as *puerta ventana*, where several families would cram in narrow and poorly ventilated rooms.

To the south, where many blacks had once lived, and near the railroad station to the

End of an era

Under the pick and sledgehammer disappeared the magnificent National Palace, the Garrison, the National Library, the Union Club and many lovely residences. The city extended its arms beyond the suburbs, the inner city lost its sense of identity and was invaded by mediocre commercial constructions. Fast highways opened up and North American influence began to replace elegant European ideals.

San José spilled over and outward in a random fashion. Cars permitted the wealthy classes to move their residences from what had now become the depressed inner city to the

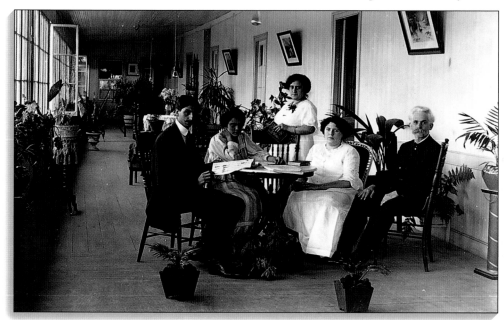

Pacific, there soon appeared barracks, warehouses and factories, where soap and candles were made. An industrial zone with beer factories, ice-making factories, printing presses, mechanics' shops and lumber mills slowly began to surround and envelop the elegant urban center.

With the advent of cement structures, the arrival of the new rich, and the industrialization of the city, there also came the desire to modernize, to create new statements and to destroy the past.

LEFT: San José, around 1928.
ABOVE: the leisured classes at home.

desirable suburbs of Escalente, Los Yoses, Curridabat, Paseo Colon, Sabana and Rohrmoser. By the 1960s, several neighborhood centers evolved, resembling the style of suburban North America.

Certainly San José would no longer win a prize as the most beautiful Central American city. But it still possesses a certain charm. You won't find the monumental scale of Guatemala City nor the cosmopolitan quality of Panamá City; yet there is a vital quality to the hustle and sheer movement of the place, and tangible remains of the coffee-growing bourgeoisie and their Neo-classical architecture and whimsical Caribbean-colonial style. ❑

THE PEOPLE OF COSTA RICA

Costa Ricans, or Ticos, come in all shapes, sizes and colors.

"We are all Ticos,"is the proud claim, though some Ticos fare better than others

Costa Ricans are both narcissistic and chauvinistic. And because of this they have acquired the curious and skilful art of being poor and not showing it. By any international standards, Costa Ricans are predominantly poor, but they do a very good job of not letting anyone take note of their poverty. There aren't the screamingly visible cardboard shanty towns that dominate the cityscape of other developing countries. People seen on the streets of the towns and cities are, more often than not, well-dressed. The homeless, the street people, are not omnipresent and evident as they are in Latin and Asian countries, and, indeed, in all of the large cities of North America.

Grace under pressure

Costa Ricans have a graceful sense of the universal corruption that surrounds them. They shake their heads, lamentably acknowledging it. They know that problems abound, both within and without. Almost endless problems beyond resolution. But there is not the nagging, complaining of the hopelessness. They actually believe that things can and will get better.

Travelers to Costa Rica find it difficult to identify the feeling, the sense, that Costa Ricans are somehow different from people in other Central and South American countries, yet they notice it in subtle ways.

Costa Ricans may not be perfect, though they are essentially a democratic, benevolent and peaceful race. However, the cities are greatly affecting their character. In the villages and small towns of Costa Rica there is a connectedness, a familial unity.

Perhaps that is why San José can feel unreal at times, as though it is out of place and time, because it is a basic contradiction to the terms of Costa Rica. San José is a city, yet Costa Ricans are much happier living and working in the terms of a village or a small town.

The US influence

To fly to Costa Rica, leaving behind the numbing babble of Los Angeles or the big cities of western Europe, and to head for a small town there, is to leap backwards to an earlier time. But it is not an earlier time in North American or even European lives, it is somewhere else,

A PROUD PEOPLE

"The blood that flows in the veins of the people of this Republic is too generous. The Costa Ricans are a people of such excellent mettle; ardently patriotic, they are very proud of their independence, their autonomy, and of a prosperity due almost wholly to industry. The country is one of flourishing villages. There it is that the population of Costa Rica dwells, since it is there that are found the hardy toilers who wrest from the earth the products which form the wealth of the land. An air of ease combined with antique simplicity characterizes these villages."

A.S. Calvert, *A Year of Costa Rica,* 1901

PRECEDING PAGES: Carnival time; ox-cart painter.
LEFT: *campesino* cultivating onions.
RIGHT: *gringa* and friendly frog.

somewhere more idealized and more precious. Like treasured remembrances of things past, you want to protect it, to shield it from the gross intrusion of foreign influence. You want to shut off the television set that is beaming satellite-relayed shows and commercials from the cities of the United States. Because the United States is by far the richest neighbor in the hemisphere, and therefore the most powerful broadcaster of image and ideology, Costa Rica knows a great deal more about the United States than the United States knows about Costa Rica. Ticos know the names of sports figures, actors and actresses, musicians and politicians from the

Yet somehow you feel that Costa Rica will endure, that there is somehow strength in the fragility, and that people all over the world will do whatever they can to ensure the survival and intelligent growth of this vulnerable country and its people.

A country apart

A Latin American writer recently observed: "The problem is that the Costa Rican looks too much to the North. He should be looking to the South." But even if they did, Ticos would insist that they are different from most Latinos because of what they call their "whiteness,"

USA, and they know the strange collection of fact and fallacy that one derives from watching American television shows and going to movies made in Hollywood.

A fragile world

Costa Rica is fragile, surrounded by Nicaragua and Panamá, with questionable advice and political succor from the US Agency for International Development, with Japanese investors buying whatever appears profitable, with political and economic refugees coming in from other parts of Central America, with drug dealers finding the shores and ports of the country defenceless against their traffic.

THE TICO SPIRIT

Costa Ricans call themselves Ticos in a reference to their common use of the diminutive ending: "*Un momentico, por favor.*" There is a sweetness to the way in which they speak Spanish.

Ticos are politically temperate, shy and unaggressive, yet, today more than ever, they are actively democratic. Once it was only the game; more of a pretense, a love of the rules and trappings of democracy. "Hey, look at me, I voted!" Today, it is stronger, more involved, more functional, more passionate. Demonstrations, protests, strikes, rallies and caucuses are common. Yet the people remain mostly prudent, respectful and discreet.

their European heritage. Just go to Guatemala, Panamá or El Salvador, and observe the differences. And yet these other countries are only short distances away, only miles apart. The Costa Rican is as different from these other Latin people as, say, the Swiss is to the Italian, or as the German is to the Dane. And the Costa Rican revels in the difference and is unabashedly proud of it.

Costa Rica welcomes foreign investors. There are duty-free zones, tax-free incentives to foreigners setting up industry, other incentives to those creating tourist facilities. Several institutions exist, created by the government to

manner and accent. The indians of Costa Rica belong to six linguistic groups, though they increasingly use Spanish, and debate as to whether it is more important to retain their indigenous cultural identity or to assimilate more into the main Costa Rican culture.

The Chinese-Costa Ricans are called *Chinos*. In some of the smaller towns they are ubiquitous and seem to own many of the bars, restaurants and retail stores. Yet all these different races are *Costarricense*, and much of the time they swagger with superiority over their Central American neighbors. They like being Ticos, and they believe in this rare place.

encourage people to come and view the marvels of the country, and to invest there.

A complex racial makeup

Racially and ethnically, Costa Rica is not a simple place. The blacks of the Atlantic Coast are the country's largest and most visible minority. They speak English and talk with pride of their blackness and their Jamaican heritage. The gregarious people of Guanacaste have dark skin, resemble their Nicaraguan neighbors in

LEFT: *pipas*, drinking coconuts for sale at a roadside stand in Limón province.
ABOVE: Puntarenas schoolboys.

The Atlantic railway

The construction of the railway to the Atlantic Coast, during the latter part of the 19th century, brought new waves of immigrants: among the builders, managers and technicians of the Northern Railway Company were English, Irish and North Americans. The largest group, however, were the workers, West Indian blacks, who built the tracks, the endless numbers of bridges, the docks and the wide, rectangular streets of the Port City of Limón.

Blacks remained along the isolated Atlantic Coast, and they continue living there today, enriching those coastal communities with a distinct Afro-Caribbean flavor.

Chinese laborers from southern China joined the blacks on the railroad project in 1873, essentially as slaves, or what were euphemistically referred to as "indentured workers," but they escaped this labor as soon as they figured out how to do so to work as domestic servants, cooks, small shopkeepers and grocers in developing rural areas and port cities.

The management of the railroad company had serious difficulties with the Chinese. In an attempt to try an alternative working force, they imported several hundred Italian rural laborers. But the disagreeable working conditions soon led the Italians to leave the railroad project, as

with numerous dissidents, all fleeing the Pinochet dictatorship of Chile.

Since the 1960s, Costa Rican laws favoring North American and European retirees, have led to the establishment of a large number of comparatively wealthy *gringos* in the Central Valley area. And the arrival in Costa Rica of many ecologically-concerned North Americans and Europeans has stimulated major changes in the country's environmental awareness.

Black settlers

As early as 1825, Afro-Caribbeans came to Costa Rica to fish, hunt turtles and market

had the Chinese before them. Many of them remained in Costa Rica, and in 1959 they were joined by other Italian farmers who settled in a government-sponsored colony, San Vito, in the Southern Pacific region of Costa Rica.

During the past couple of decades, onerous political conditions and deteriorating economic circumstances in their home countries have brought significant numbers of South Americans to Costa Rica: middle-class, educated Chileans, Argentinians and Uruguayans. These groups have greatly enhanced Costa Rica's cultural sensibilities over the past 20 years. As an example the exceptional *Teatro El Angel* was virtually transplanted to San José, along

ORIGIN OF THE SPECIES

Tradition holds that most Costa Ricans descended from hard-working rural Spanish farmers; that they came from good, simple, unpretentious, egalitarian stock. Yet among colonial immigrants to Costa Rica from the Iberian peninsula there were Spanish Jews and Arabs, Catalans and Basques, and a great many people from the Middle East.

Then in the 19th century, lured by the promise of coffee prosperity, German and English settlers set up import-export trades, while Lebanese, Turks and Polish Jews became powerful local merchants. Clearly these were no simple agrarian folk.

coconuts. These immigrants were part of a migration from the West Indies to the Central American Atlantic Coast. From Panamá to Honduras, they came looking for work to support themselves and their families. Many were transient. One man might harvest cacao in Limón, then find employment on the barges in Nicaragua and next labor on the construction of the Panamá Canal. They went where there was work.

In 1872, under contract from Minor C. Keith, who was later to become the founder of the

BLOOD ON THE TRACKS

After 4,000 West Indians died during the laying of the first 32 km (20 miles) of the Atlantic Railroad, businessman Minor C. Keith simply imported another 10,000 laborers.

fields of the Atlantic United Fruit Company is well-documented. And when United Fruit left the Atlantic region and moved to the Pacific Coast, the unemployed blacks were left behind. Many emigrated out and away from Costa Rica, for much the same reason that had motivated their parents to immigrate to the country in the first place: they were again seeking work. Those who stayed behind lived for the most part at subsistence level, often just producing what they could from the small plots of land that they had

United Fruit Company, blacks from the West Indies came to work on the construction of the Atlantic railroad. They proved more successful than previous laborers imported by Keith, in their ability to tolerate the working conditions, which included exposure to yellow fever, malaria and poisonous snakes, as well as very severe physical labor and oppressive management. But they were certainly not invulnerable and they too died in their thousands.

The maltreatment of workers in the banana

settled on. They retained their English language and their Protestant religion, remaining proudly separate from the Hispanic Costa Ricans.

Others came to the Atlantic Coast on their own, looking for any kind of work available and to escape the poverty of their native islands. Some ultimately were given land along the railroad right-of-way and others rose from the ranks of laborers to become managers in the banana business. Most originally planned to earn whatever money they could and then to return to their islands; yet many remained in Costa Rica, where for many years they were subject to racist immigration and residency laws that restricted their movement.

LEFT: the ubiquitous Costa Rican *pulpería* (neighborhood store) and its proud owner.
ABOVE: *Josefinas* making merry at the beach.

Assimilation

When the new Constitution of 1949 declared that anyone born in Costa Rica had automatic citizenship, doors finally opened for blacks. They began to send their children to public schools, to enter politics. When, in the 1950s, the value of cacao soared on the international market, many of the squatter-farmers were able to achieve a certain prosperity. And, in an ironic reversal of historical patterns, they hired Hispanics to work their fields.

Many of the subsequent generation of blacks were well-educated and, preferring the professions to farming, left the Limón area. Indeed,

Chinese immigrants

The first Chinese to set foot in Costa Rica were 77 indentured servants, in 1855. Almost 20 years later, despite the existence of a law against the permanent settlement in Costa Rica of African and Asian races, contractors for the Atlantic railroad imported "one thousand healthy, robust Chinese of good customs and addicted to work." These two groups were to become the founding fathers of the Chinese colony of Costa Rica.

Those contracted by the railroad quickly left that work, and, as their fortunes improved, set up small eateries, grocery and liquor stores.

many left Costa Rica entirely to find jobs in Panamá, the United States or elsewhere. Those middle-class, educated blacks who have remained in Costa Rica have many times married Hispanics, but their assimilation into Costa Rican society is not a complete one, due mostly to a curious two-sided racism that exists. The blacks usually consider themselves more civilized and superior to the Hispanic Costa Ricans, and the Hispanic Costa Ricans usually insist that blacks are racially inferior.

Today, fewer than 5 percent of the Costa Rican population as a whole, and fewer than 25 percent of the population of the Atlantic Coast of Costa Rica, are black.

A steady trickle of Chinese immigrant laborers followed, the newcomers getting assistance from those who were already established. Through work contracts and credit assistance from other Chinese, they set up commercial ventures along the railway system, the port cities and in growing rural communities throughout the country. Their small-scale businesses required little capital investment, only a minimal acquaintance with the language, and allowed all members of the growing family network to become involved in tending the business. Chinese family traditions upheld the authority of elders and reinforced an already strong generational hierarchy and well-defined division of labor, plus a strong work ethic. Because of this their businesses flourished.

Chinese colonies headed by businessmen associations similar to those established in California and elsewhere, evolved into strong business groups in the cities and towns of Costa Rica. By the turn of the century a number of Chinese immigrants had become wealthy businessmen, who then sponsored the immigration of other family members and acquaintances. Recent events have also served to reinforce this influx from the East. The prospect of the British colony of Hong Kong being transfered to Chinese hands caused a steady flow of Asian

retaining marriages established in China, with childhood brides. Money which they sent to China was often used to finance family enterprises back home and contribute to the development of their home communities.

The successful Costa Rican-Chinese traveled to China to oversee his holdings, raise a family and invest towards retirement in the home of his ancestors. During his absence from Costa Rica, his business was managed by close younger kin. To the Costa Ricans it seemed as though these older Chinese did not die, but simply disappeared, leaving in their place younger replacements.

immigrants from Hong Kong, as long ago as the 1970s. In a survey in the 1980s, it was reported that there were over 100 Asian-owned and-run restaurants in San José and the surrounding districts. Today, there are probably many more.

Mixed marriages

Among the first generations to settle in Costa Rica, many male immigrants began living with local Costa Rican women, white women, while

However, since the Communist takeover in 1949, return to their Chinese homeland has become less attractive, and most Costa Rican Chinese have forsaken hope of a permanent return to China.

Those Chinese born of Costa Rican mothers and raised in Costa Rica consider themselves full members of Costa Rican society, identifying heartily with its ways and traditions, while, at the same time, expressing a strong sense of devotion to their immigrant forefathers. Although many among them have married Hispanics, much against the overwhelming and loud opposition of their parents and the foreboding ostracism of the Chinese community,

LEFT: shimmering beauty queens at the Hotel Cariari. **ABOVE:** shining sisters of devotion at a town fair in Guanacaste province.

they have, nevertheless, retained venerable family traditions that express Chinese values of ancestral wisdom and family solidarity. Many young Costa Rican-Chinese have now joined the ranks of the professionally educated; yet, although they are doctors, lawyers, engineers, business administrators and university professors, they continue to contribute to and oversee the family businesses that allowed their ancestors to achieve economic success in Costa Rica.

> ### LIMÓN CARNIVAL
>
> Chinese participation in the social life of the towns they settled is nowhere more in evidence than at the Limón Carnival, when the traditional Chinese dragon snakes its way alongside flamboyantly-costumed Caribbean dancers.

monial groups, grew corn and were culturally similar to groups of Southern Mexico. These peoples were devastated during the Conquest by disease and by slave traders who carried them into Panamá and Peru. Their descendents are today mostly integrated into contemporary Costa Rican life.

Other indian groups, today spread over much of Costa Rica, spoke dialects originating in Colombia, and were divided into clans: the Guaymi, the Terrabas, the Borucas and, in the

Indigenous people

Archaeologists have recently estimated that some 60,000 native people were in Costa Rica when Columbus arrived. Today, however, less than 15,000 native people remain in the entire country.

The history of the indians of Costa Rica is much like that of the other indigenous peoples of the American continent. The Europeans brought diseases to which the native populations had no immunity. Entire tribes were obliterated before they had even seen a white man.

The Chorotegas, cousins of the Nicaro, inhabited Guanacaste and the Nicoya Peninsula in pre-Columbian times. They lived in patri-

Talamanca mountains, the Bribri and Cabecares. These people lived in matrilineal societies in clearings in the jungles. With the coming of the Europeans, many of them fled their villages and moved further into the almost inaccessible jungle regions of the southern mountains and thus were not easily found and subdued. Much of their culture has been preserved by their descendents who still speak their original language and live in the remote regions of the Talamanca Mountains. Despite the influence of Christian missionaries, they have not forsaken their animistic religious traditions. The Bribri call their deity "Sibu" and use shamans, with their vast knowledge of the rainforest's medicinal herbs, to cure illnesses.

Further south, along the Panamá border, the Guaymi indians live in their traditional areas, which span political boundaries.

Modern temptations

Yet no matter how remote their jungle reserves, the indians are not isolated from contemporary culture. Battery-powered televisions bring pressure to consume soft drinks and junk food, as well as images of the First World to these people who are living without electricity and running water.

INVASION OF THE ANTS

Even today, the native tribes refer disparagingly to the white man as "*hormiga*" (ant), a creature which wipes out everything in its path.

which, perhaps unfortunately for the indians, contain a significant proportion of the country's mineral wealth.

Many indians complain bitterly of the encroachment of the contemporary society which threatens their language, their cultural identity and their way of life. Caught in time between two worlds, slowly relinquishing the old, but not yet embracing the new, they are vulnerable. In the 500 years since the Conquest, little has changed for the aboriginal Costa Rican people. The stranger

The cultural imperialism of the airwaves is persistently penetrating the sanctuary of those who for 500 years have resisted the *conquistadores*. And, among the young, the temptations of this world are great and the desire to assimilate strong.

Today, the indigenous peoples live on reserves authorized for them in 1971. By law, non-indians cannot own land inside these areas, but the law has been difficult to enforce and non-indians have moved into these territories,

still dominates things and the choice between isolation and assimilation is still painful.

The *gringo*

They are unmistakable in San José, standing out amidst the dense, crazy streets and violently crowded sidewalks, their blonde heads rising above everyone else's. They are as enormous crane-like birds, searching for something. These *gringos*, so highly visible, easily catch the eye. They have been coming here for a long time. In 1888, 1,500 "good, humble, thrifty Italians of a superior race," were brought here to work the Atlantic railway, and later settled on the country's southern peninsula.

LEFT: heady blossoms off to market; melon seller at the 10th Avenue open-air market in San José.
ABOVE: *boyero* ("cowboy") with his Brahman oxen.

Early in the 19th century, attracted by the promise of wealth from coffee, the French, Germans and English came to Costa Rica. Many married Costa Rican women, and most became thoroughly assimilated into the aggregate of Tico culture.

Latter-day settlers

In the 1950s, Quakers from the United States came seeking a place of peace in Costa Rica and found it in the cloud forest of Monteverde, where they formed a community dedicated to a life of harmony with the land and fellow man.

From the United States and as far afield as

Europe have come large numbers of retirees (recently estimated at over 35,000) seeking peace and a restful existence in the sun. The *pensionado* is a non-national living in Costa Rica with a guaranteed monthly income. Most often these people are retired North Americans who have come to Costa Rica for the warm climate and for the higher standard of living their dollar affords them.

Today, too, there are large numbers of young and environmentally-concerned people who come to carry out ecological work in Costa Rica. For them the country is a laboratory, a place in the world where the viability of living in harmony with the environment can be demonstrated to the world at large.

Most recently, Costa Rica has also become a safe haven for those fleeing the problems elsewhere in Central America. This has caused undeniable difficulties, though in general the country has absorbed them with its typical mix of grace and tolerance.

The effect of tourism

The most dramatic influx of people today is the result of the country's flourishing tourism industry. However, while Costa Ricans are proud to show off their beautiful land, this brings fresh problems of a new kind. The *campesino* is stripped of his land for a biological reserve, dairy farmers are unable to afford fresh pasture because property speculators have driven prices sky high. But while profits flow abroad to large hotel groups, promised local benefits often amount to little more than the meagre wages of waiters, hotel maids, gardeners and pool attendants. ❏

HEALTH AND EDUCATION

The standards of health and education in Costa Rica are anything but Third World. In 1920, infant mortality was nearly 26 percent. Today it is less than 2 percent. A century ago the annual mortality rate was 41 per thousand. By 1944 it had dropped to 18 and today it is less than four.

According to World Health Organisation figures, the average Costa Rican man lives to be over 75 years old, better than the longevity rates for the average US citizen and several European nations. *

This is not sheer luck, or just the quality of the air they breathe; without the burden of supporting any armed forces, Costa Rica is able to invest around 10 percent of its GNP on health care and the quality is so high that it is said even Beverley Hills residents come here for plastic surgery.

Costa Rica is also an exceptionally literate nation, which claims 93 percent literacy across the population aged 10 and over. Again, this is a figure that surpasses the US and many European nations.

The country has always been progressive in electing teachers to high political posts and, in 1869, it was the first country in the world to make education both mandatory and free of charge.

Ticos and Nicas

osta Rica's poor stepsister, Nicaragua, reminds Ticos of what their country's fortune could have been, given slightly different geographic and political conditions.

An estimated 250,000 to 500,000 Nicaraguans – fleeing nearly 50 percent unemployment and harsh living conditions in their home country – work in Costa Rica, many of them illegally. Most form part of the country's growing informal sector, with low wages, under-the-table payments and no access to the country's socialized health service. Many work as maids, gardeners, or construction workers, or sell snacks or trinkets in the streets. The sugar cane and coffee industries depend on Nicaraguan workers for their harvests. Perhaps it is not surprising that they are prepared to work for such low wages when you consider that the average per capita income in their own country is just $1,000 per year. Only Haiti in the western hemisphere has lower income levels.

Not all Nicaraguan refugees are poor, however. Middle-class and upper-class supporters of the Somoza regime came in the 1980s, seeking refuge from Nicaragua's civil war. Many have opened successful businesses.

When former president José María Figueres signed an accord in mid-1997, allowing all Nicaraguans in the country a five-month window to apply for work permits, thus obtaining health and other benefits, lines of applicants at the Nicaraguan embassy stretched around the block.

Always a troubling issue in Central America, immigration became more polemic when the US adopted a harsh immigration law in early 1997. Though the law was later toned down and mass deportations avoided, thousands of Nicaraguans chose Costa Rica instead of the US as their destination in the search for a better life.

Immigration officials of the southern Nicaraguan port of San Carlos estimate some 5,000 people enter Costa Rica illegally each month. The two countries share a 320-km (200-mile) border.

Shanty towns full of Nicaraguan immigrants ring the capital. and many squat on, rent or own farms in the Northern Zone. Ticos are often prejudiced against their northern neighbors, who are stereotyped as "dirty", and often unfairly blamed for crimes including murder and theft. In 1996 and 1997, two separate

high-profile kidnappings – one of a Swiss tour guide and German tourist, the other of two Dutch administrators of a teak farm – were carried out by Nicaraguans, thus increasing suspicion and a feeling of animosity towards the wider community.

Thick-accented and darker-skinned than most Costa Ricans, who like to forget that the province of Guanacaste was once part of Nicaragua, "Nicas" are generally quieter and more serious than Ticos. They are also hard workers and many people prefer to hire Nicaraguans as domestic help. Nicaraguans also bring with them a love of poetry and music, and a tradition of camaraderie and willingness to help each other.

Nicaragua was hit very badly in 1998 by drought

as a result of the weather phenomenon known as El Niño. Some 40 percent of the country's entire crop, including staples such as beans, rice and corn, was lost and this further increased pressures on Nicas to leave their country.

In March 1998, 29 Nicaraguans tragically drowned when their heavily-laden boat, *El Cairo*, overturned on the choppy waters of Lake Nicaragua. Most of the victims were on their way to Costa Rica to seek employment. It is thought that the boat may have been carrying up to 70 people, almost twice its official capacity. It was a pointed reminder of the desperation that drives so many Nicaraguans to leave their homeland and loved ones, and risk everything to come to a land where they are not wanted.   ❑

LEFT: cellist of the National Symphony Orchestra, San José. **ABOVE:** a less fortunate Nicaraguan immigrant.

NATIONAL PARKS

With so much of its land under protected status, Costa Rica is the flagbearer for the forces of conservation. But, while many battles have been won, the war goes on

An astonishing 27 percent of Costa Rica is designated as national park, biological reserve, wildlife refuge or some other category of protected area, both private and public. Increasingly, individuals and groups are purchasing tracts of Costa Rican wilderness in order to preserve it. And so more than a quarter of the country has been set aside in some capacity or other by human beings to protect it from the potential exploitation and ravages of other human beings. No other country in the world comes even close to such a statistic.

Heroes and villains

The story of the creation of Costa Rica's parks and protected areas is one of drama, ideals and sacrifice. One of the earliest in an international lineage of protectors was Nils Olaf Wessberg, who, with his wife, Karen, came to Costa Rica from Sweden in 1955 and bought a farm in Nicoya near Montezuma. Fervent naturalists, they built a home of palm leaves, determined to live in harmony with the land. Yet even in this removed corner of the world they did not escape what many call progress, and they watched, dismayed, as the destruction of virgin forest took place at Cabo Blanco, on the Nicoya peninsula. Nils became an activist, working ardently to raise money to purchase the property and thereby preserve it.

After three years and 1,000 pages of letters he raised the $30,000 he needed to buy the 1,200 hectares (3,000 acres) that constitutes the Cabo Blanco Strict Nature Reserve. Today, a plaque inside the park is a memorial to Nils, who, while trying to establish another park in the Osa Peninsula, was murdered by those who had vested interests in preventing his work.

Another individual, Mario Boza, a student of Costa Rican forestry, was able to put his conservation ideas to work in the creation of Santa Rosa, the country's first national park. In 1969,

the Forestry Law trumpeted the creation of the Santa Rosa National Monument and established the National Parks Department. But of course, with little funding and personnel to enforce it, the new law went unrecognized and the land continued to be used as it had been in the past, as grazing pasture for the cattle of nearby

NATURAL WONDERLAND

There are many astounding statistics concerning Costa Rica's natural abundance. In a space that occupies less than three ten-thousandths of the earth's surface are 5 percent of all of the plant and animal species on the planet. In total this numbers somewhere between 500,000 and a million, species of flora and fauna including: 50,000 species of insects (some the size of small mammals!); over 1,000 species of orchids; 800 ferns (more than in all North America and Mexico); 208 species of mammals; 850 species of birds; 200 species of reptiles (half of which are snakes) and thousands of species of moths and butterflies.

PRECEDING PAGES: dusk at Braulio Carrillo; heliconias on the jungle floor; iguanas at La Orotina.
LEFT: jaguars. **RIGHT:** the *bejuquillo* vine snake.

ranchers and as homesteads of squatters who cleared the land by slashing and burning it.

Unable to halt the destruction through bureaucratic channels, Boza went to the people through the press. "Santa Rosa in Flames; National Park Being Ruined" read the headlines. The public were outraged and park authorities were duly authorized to move out the squatters and protect the land from the encroachment of livestock and agriculture.

Rodrigo Carazo, president of Costa Rica from 1978 to 1982, described the national parks system as "splendid natural laboratories which we offer to the international scientific commu-

the country, the Central Valley – covers the land with concrete and asphalt, and it continues at a frenzied pace. Extensive soil erosion, an effect of the rapid deforestation of the country by the destructive use of land for cattle grazing, causes a phenomenal loss of topsoil.

Threats to the watershed as well as the nation's extensive hydroelectric system also result. Uncontrolled dumping of toxic wastes from banana, coffee and fertilizer industries have contaminated coastal and inland waters. Agricultural chemicals used in pesticides, once employed only on the traditional export crops of bananas and sugar, are now being used by

nity and also to children, young people and adults who should not be denied the joy of direct contact with nature in its pristine state. All of this represents the contribution of the Costa Rican people to peace among men and good will among nations."

The economy versus the ecology

As admirable as Costa Rica's conservation initiatives may be, the environmental efforts of this Third World country are counter to its economic development. Parks are, after all, expensive. Urban sprawl – resulting from the concentration of more than 60 percent of the country's population in the most fertile area of

vegetable and flower growers and result in, among other things, the virtual elimination of large species such as armadillos and crocodiles along the Tempisque River. The crazed rush to feed the demands for exotic plywood by the First World is resulting in the deforestation of the land surrounding the magnificent Tortuguero canals. And so it goes on.

In its attempts to imitate much of North America and the First World, the country experiences the inevitable conflict between consumption and conservation. Trying to balance these forces are whole armies of international naturalists. Environmentalists and ecologists from all over the world come to

Costa Rica to join the side of "the good guys". Today, Costa Rica has environmental experts in abundance, and dozens of international conservation organizations work on behalf of the country's ecological efforts.

Conservation by education

Believing that true conservation can only be accomplished by the will of the people, the national parks system has made a great effort to educate the Ticos most affected by the transfer of land into parks. The co-operation of these people is necessary for the parks' survival. For example, the custom of hunting species for

of the workings of the national parks; and through their work and contributions to the many foundations working in Costa Rica.

Sometimes eco-projects even cross Costa Rica's borders. Current projects already in operation include the extension of La Amistad National Park, which spans the border of Panamá, and will soon be expanded into a park system; and also the proposed Peace Park, a joint effort with Nicaragua along the San Juan River, which comprises the border between the two nations. These are just two examples of the potential for national parks to engender co-operative international relations.

whom the parks is a refuge must often be changed. Large animals, such as pumas and jaguars, require an extensive amount of free territory in order to survive. Convincing people not to kill them, despite the fact that the cats are a constant threat to livestock, is an enormous and often thankless task.

Eco-tourists and traditional travelers to Costa Rica support the national parks system by coming to visit them; by staying at the private reserves, by viewing and understanding some

LEFT: the arboreal fruit-eating kinkajou (martella).
ABOVE: sometimes you have to look very carefully to unravel the jungle's camouflage.

Future perfect?

Yet is this good news enough? The fact that Costa Rica is thought of as a safe, quiet democratic place is perhaps both the nation's great blessing and her problem. Ironically the world will not be sufficiently moved to donate aid and attention and media coverage continually to such a gentle democratic place.

It is not clear yet as to which side will prevail, the conservationists or the economic development-at-all-costs forces; it is not predictable whether Costa Rica will become a successful environmental model for the nations of the world or just another failed experiment in ecological idealism. ❏

A Tropical Forest Watcher's Guide

Don't be disappointed if, on your first few visits to the tropical rainforest you fail to see any of the hundreds of bird species and spectacular large cats, monkeys and sloths that are listed as living there. In fact, your first impression of the forest will probably be of a great green wall of vegetation, not the spectacular variety of colorful animals you had hoped to see. However, be assured a great diversity of organisms do

inhabit the tropical forest and their very survival, which may span millennia, depends not least on how successful they are in avoiding the attention of predators, which include humans.

Before setting off into the forest do your homework. Study specialist guidebooks that describe animals living in the area and familiarise yourself with the characteristics that are used to identify them, such as color, shape and behavior.

Determine the time of day or night when they are most active. A good pair of binoculars is essential. They can also be used backwards as a powerful magnifying glass. Take every opportunity to charter a boat for lake or river trips. They are always worth the investment.

Observe safety tips before proceeding. Remember that even though it may look like Disneyland, it isn't. Here snakes slither, insects bite and animals may (in very rare cases) become aggressive. Notify someone of your intentions: where you are going, when you plan to arrive, when to expect you back. Take water, insect repellent, flashlight, sunscreen, umbrella or rain poncho, and hat.

Look before you touch, step, sit or lean. Scan the trail for slippery rocks, mud, downed trees, ants and snakes. Then move ahead while you search the canopy for animals. Continually shift your gaze. Don't wander off into the woods following a bird without carefully looking where you step. Snakes are rare but potentially lethal. Consider carrying an anti-venom kit – and make sure you know how to administer it.

A general guideline: forest wildlife viewing is easiest and most productive along habitat "edges" next to rivers, beaches, open fields, roads and trail heads. Look for shapes, colors and behaviors that stand out and do not appear to "fit" the design of the forest vegetation.

In the dry season deciduous forests lose their leaves, opening the canopy for viewing; and water sources are frequented by thirsty animals.

Wildlife observation tips: seasoned forest watchers, like legendary animal trackers, are alert to certain small and easily overlooked clues that indicate the presence of animals or birds in the forest. Things rustling, or dropping from the forest canopy (especially on a windless day), and unexplained noises are often a sign that an animal is nearby. Seeds or leaves dropping from above are probably caused by parrots, monkeys or sloths in the canopy. Fruits, nuts, seed husks or leaf fragments in the trail mean a food tree is nearby and perhaps feeding animals or birds.

Large, dark shapes in tree crevices might be sleeping sloths, anteaters or monkeys. A hanging green tail may indicate an iguana. Logs on river banks could be crocodiles. Rotten tree sections are often home to amphibians, insects, fungi and mosses. Holes in trees might contain precious bird's nests.

When you've developed skills in seeing and identifying some of the plants and animals, think about what they eat and why they live where they do. Soon you will begin to understand the complexity that makes the forest so mesmerising. ❏

LEFT: a colorful small forest dweller.
RIGHT: birdwatchers at Monteverde.

Ecosystems of Costa Rica

For its size, this country contains a remarkable variety of natural ecosystems. A journey of a few miles is often enough to take you from one to another, each with its own quite different plants and animals. Much of this variety is due to the country's mountains, which create a range of "life zones" at different altitudes and rainfall patterns. Some species of plants and animals live in several zones, but many are confined to just one.

Dry tropical forest

In some parts of Costa Rica – particularly the lowlands of Guanacaste – little rain falls for four or five months of the year. Here, the natural vegetation is dry tropical forest, with most of the trees shedding their leaves soon after the dry season begins. The trees are rarely more than about 30 meters (100ft) high, and there is usually a tangled understorey of spiny and thorny shrubs.

Although the trees are leafless during the dry season, few of them are fully dormant, and many burst into flower soon after their leaves have been shed. Among the most conspicuous of these dry-season flowerers is the guayacan or Cortes tree, which puts on a particularly spectacular display of waxy yellow blooms. Dry tropical forest abounds with reptiles, including rattlesnakes and large lizards called ctenosaurs, which often feed on the fallen guayacan flowers and fruit.

Rainforest

Across most of the Costa Rican lowlands, the climate is wet and warm enough for trees to keep growing for much of the year. The result of this non-stop growth is generally called rainforest, although, strictly speaking, botanists restrict this term for the wettest forests of all. Unlike the trees in tropical dry forests, rainforest trees are evergreen, and their dense crowns form a continuous canopy that casts a deep and almost unbroken shade.

In lowland rainforest, the canopy trees generally reach up to 50 meters (165ft), and many have buttress roots. Scattered among them are emergents – giant trees that rise above the canopy, and which may reach 60 meters (200ft) or more. With increasing altitude, the canopy height starts to drop, while rainfall levels usually rise, typically reaching a maximum at about 1,000 meters (3,300ft). Above this height, rainfall begins to decline again, but on slopes facing the prevailing wind the forest is often enveloped by cloud. At mid- and higher altitudes, the trees are often laden with epiphytic plants, such as bromeliads, orchids and ferns.

Epiphytes use trees as living perches in their quest for light, and they generally do their hosts little harm. However, where high rainfall allows them to grow unchecked, their combined weight sometimes brings branches crashing to the ground.

Costa Rica's rainforests – both on low ground and at altitude – harbour an immense variety of life, but actually seeing wild animals is not as easy as it sounds. With the exception of monkeys and agoutis, most forest mammals are nocturnal. Some birds feed on or near the forest floor, and a number specialize in following columns of army ants, snapping up small animals that flee the ants' advancing front. However, the full richness of rainforest wildlife is in the canopy overhead, where a complex community of species lives with minimal contact with the ground.

Páramo

On Costa Rica's highest peaks, the forest gives way to a treeless landscape known as páramo. Cold and frequently swathed in cloud, páramo seems a world away from the warmth and lushness of lower altitudes. This ecosystem is dominated by tough, low-growing shrubs that can withstand strong winds. Páramo is also found in the Andes, and Costa Rica's scattered patches of it – for example, in the Talamanca - Mountains – are the northernmost in the Americas.

Freshwater wetlands

Costa Rica's topography means that its rivers are generally short and fast-flowing, quickly completing their journey from the interior to the sea. Sudden fluctuations in water level – brought on by tropical downpours – are a common event, and freshwater animals are experts at taking cover when flow levels abruptly increase. On lower ground, where the flow is more sluggish, river wildlife is more varied. Animals of particular note include caimans, which often bask on the banks, and one of the world's few bipedal lizards, the basilisk, which escapes danger by running across the water on its back legs.

Small forest streams usually flow beneath a continuous overhead canopy, but most rivers are broad enough to allow light to reach the forest floor. The result is a linear "light gap", and a profusion of plant growth of the kind rarely seen inside forests themselves. Some of the most eye-catching species are heliconias, or lobster-claws, which are pollinated by hummingbirds. They often spring up on mudbanks and sandbars, but rarely grow in deep shade.

Costa Rica's largest body of freshwater – Lake Arenal – has a distinctly highland feel, and while it teems with fish, its bird life is unexceptional. By contrast, the shallow lakes and marshes of Palo Verde National Park and Caño Negro are much more productive ecosystems. These seasonal wetlands attract a wide variety of wading birds, particularly when water levels are low, and prey is more easy to catch.

Mangrove swamps

Mangroves are the natural vegetation of muddy, low-lying coasts throughout the tropics. In Costa Rica, there are five species of mangrove, and they form extensive forests on both the Caribbean and Pacific shores. None of the five species is closely related to each other, but they have all evolved a collection of adaptations for surviving in seawater and saline silt, for which they are known to botanists as halophytes. These adaptations include mechanisms for getting rid of excess salt, and also elaborate roots that anchor them in the shifting mud.

Although they are often inaccessible, smelly and hot, Costa Rican mangrove swamps abound with life, with crabs being a particular specialty. These include not only hordes of fiddler crabs, which pick over the

mud for particles of food, but also fist-sized land crabs, and the mangrove tree crab, which feeds on mangrove leaves and leaps acrobatically from branch to branch. Even mangrove mud makes an important contribution to the marine food chain, for the nutrient-rich algae and other small organisms it produces.

Coasts and coral reefs

Apart from mangrove swamps, Costa Rica's coastline consists largely of extensive beaches – often of dark volcanic sand – low-lying rocks and a small number of offshore islands. Although the two coasts are never far apart, their marine life is quite different, and their physical differences also affect other animals. Brown

pelicans, for example, feed on both coasts, but they only breed on the Pacific, where the rocky islands give them the protection that they need. The spectacular frigatebird is also a much more common sight in the Pacific Ocean than in the waters of the Caribbean.

Costa Rica has a number of small coral reefs on its Pacific coast, but only one significant area on the Caribbean, at Cahuita. Reef-building corals need sunlight to grow, and they can only survive in clear water. This limits them to areas well away from the mouths of silt-laden rivers, but it also makes them vulnerable to any increase in silt run-off. Unfortunately, in recent years the Cahuita reef has been affected by deforestation, which has increased silt levels in the surrounding water. ❑

LEFT: the density of the rainforest, seen from above.
RIGHT: malachite butterfly in Braulio Carillo Park.

A PASSION FOR PLANTS

From the beautiful to the bizarre, Costa Rica's many species of flora offer a vibrant introduction to the kaleidoscopic plant wealth of the tropics

For many visitors to Costa Rica, first contact with the country's spectacular plant life comes at the hotel reception desk. As likely as not, the desk will be adorned by a vase of heliconias – strikingly angular red or orange flowers, also known as lobster claws, which grow in the country's forests.

Heliconias are typical of the outsize blooms that flourish in Costa Rica's warm and humid climate. As a rule of thumb, the biggest and most robust flowers – including heliconias – are pollinated by birds or bats, while more delicate flowers are pollinated by insects. This second category includes most of the country's orchids – another group of plants for which Costa Rica is justly famous.

INTRODUCED PLANTS

Costa Rica has a vast number of native plants, including about a thousand different species of trees. To add to this botanical richness many other species have been introduced from different parts of the tropics, either for food or for ornament. The food plants include bananas, which arrived in the Americas in the early 1500s, coffee, mangoes and sugar cane, and also the African oil palm, first planted on a large scale in the 1960s.

Many of the showiest garden and roadside plants are from distant parts of the world. Among the most eye-catching are jacarandas, South American trees that produce a mass of purplish-blue flowers.

▷ **GIANT LEAVES**
Elephant ears takes its name from its enormous leaves, over 1.2m (4ft) long. Originally from southern and southeast Asia, they are common on marshy ground by streams. Also known as giant taro, these plants have edible roots and stems.

◁ **LANDING PLATFORM**
Popular garden plants throughout Costa Rica, bird-of-paradise flowers are pollinated by birds. The flower has a built-in perch.

◁ NATIONAL FLOWER

Like most of the country's orchids, Cattleya skinneri – the national flower – normally lives high up on trees, and is very difficult to spot from the ground. A visit to an orchid garden is the easiest way to see it.

▷ PRIZED ORNAMENTALS

Named after a 19th-century German naturalist, kohlerias have hanging tubular flowers, and live in damp, shady places on the forest floor. The family that they belong to is widespread throughout the tropics, and includes many popular indoor plants, such as African violets and gloxinias.

◁ BLUE BLOOMS

The blue passionflower (Passiflora caerulea) is found throughout Costa Rica. Like other passionflowers, it produces juicy berries, and its seeds are spread by animals.

▷ SYMBOLIC FLOWERS

Legend has it that Spanish missionaries named the orange passionflower after Christ's crucifixion: the flower's three stigmas, for example, represent the three nails.

△ LOBSTER CLAWS

The flowers of heliconias, or lobster claws, are clasped by brilliantly-coloured flaps. In some species, the flowerhead stays upright, but in others it gradually topples over as it grows.

▽ NECTAR STATION

The nectar-rich flowers of ginger lilies have a magnetic effect on butterflies and on nectar-drinking birds. These shoulder-high relatives of edible ginger come from India and southeast Asia and are widely grown in Costa Rica as garden plants.

THE PLANTS THAT GROW ON PLANTS

Costa Rica's forests are home to an immense variety of epiphytes, or plants that grow on the shoulders of other plants, often far above the ground. Epiphytes manage this remarkable feat by collecting rainwater, and by scavenging nutrients from any organic debris that is washed or blown their way.

Of all the country's epiphytes, bromeliads are the most conspicuous. Tank bromeliads, like the one shown above, collect water by funneling it into a central reservoir formed by their leaves. These plants can be over 1 meter (3ft) across, and their tanks can hold several liters of water. Other epiphytes, including most orchids, have specialized roots that absorb water and nutrients before they have a chance to drain away.

In forests, a different collection of plants – including philodendrons and the Swiss cheese plant (Monstera deliciosa) – start life rooted in the ground, but soon head for the sunlit treetops. In the wild, the cheese plant and its relatives have a bizarre growth pattern. If the plant climbs up a tree that turns out to be too short, it simply drops back to the forest floor and searches for another one.

THE SPORTS SCENE

Activity holidays are booming in Costa Rica. Getting wet – whether
by spilling out of a raft or falling off a board – is usually part of the game

Ticos love sports and are always happy to have visiting foreigners join them for an important game of soccer or basketball. In the past decade a fitness craze has swept the country, joggers and cyclists are a common sight puffing up the hills of the Central Valley in the early morning. On weekends, the enormous La Sabana Park, on the west side of San José, is filled with thousands of athletes: soccer teams, basketball players, swimmers, volleyball players, roller-blade teams and base-ball enthusiasts. On the Central Valley plateau, private golf and tennis clubs with complete health spas cater for wealthy suburbanites.

It is for the country's burgeoning watersports, however, that visitors are coming in increas-ingly greater numbers to Costa Rica, to surf isolated beaches, to windsurf on magnificent Lake Arenal, and to enjoy some of the best whitewater rafting in the world.

Whitewater rafting

The brightly colored inflatable raft rushes down a chute of cascading whitewater, then plunges over and through waves that are nearly 2 meters (6 ft) high. Those in the raft gleefully dig their paddles into the frothing water, and then shriek with delight as they maneuver the raft between boulders the size of small cars. After a while, a calm spot on the river is reached, an eddy, and from there the raft passengers take pause and look up from the roaring river course, to inhale and appreciate the beauty of the Reventazón Gorge. The scenery includes the colossally broad panorama of the canyon, and rolling fields of coffee, sugar cane, wild grasses and radiant flowers blooming unexpectedly in the canopy of trees that lean over the river.

Whitewater rafting is relatively new to Costa Rica, and it is rapidly growing in popularity, for Costa Rica has more accessible whitewater

rivers and rapids than any other place in the world. It is, of course, the unique geography of the country that makes it one of the world's great destinations for rafters. To have the right kind of rapids it is necessary to have a river that descends in a fairly steep gradient. The four mountain chains that wind down the axis of Costa Rica provide the perfect basis for these conditions. The Talamanca range and the Cor-dillera Central have many steep, wide, peren-nial rivers which are regularly supplied with bounteous rainfall.

The variety of these rivers provides an enor-mous range of wilderness experiences. Some offer idyllic float trips through luscious land-scapes with abundant wildlife, while others contain explosive whitewater and raging rapids which challenge the most experienced rafter.

The Sarapiquí

The Sarapiquí River flows through the low-lands of Heredia, providing stunning scenery

---

PRECEDING PAGES: rafting on the Reventazón river.
LEFT: surf's up at Playa Dominical.
RIGHT: a windsurfer enjoys a breezy, late afternoon sail into the sunset at Lake Arenal.

and exceptional whitewater. About a two-hour drive from San José, the upper portion of the Sarapiquí contains moderate rapids that are suitable for novice paddlers. On the calm, lower section of the river, the jungle closes in and gives rafters the opportunity to relax for a while and view the monkeys, otters and abundant water fowl of the area.

The Reventazón

The head of the Reventazón River is a 90-minute drive from San José and offers some of Costa Rica's most challenging whitewater and spectacular scenery. Rafting companies run four sections of the river. The first, which is just below the hydro-electric power plant of Cachí, is steep and contains continuous rapids of moderate to high difficulty. The second section, from Tucurrique to Angostura, is suited to novice paddlers and provides splendid views of the surrounding volcanoes.

The final two sections of the Reventazón, from Angostura to Siquirres, have some of the most challenging whitewater in the world.

The Pacuare

Many consider Costa Rica's most famous whitewater river to be the Pacuare. Accessible

WHITEWATER RAFTING – THE MAJOR PLAYERS

Despite its perilous appearance, whitewater rafting, also known as river running, is a relatively safe sport. And it offers anyone in moderately good health an exhilarating way to observe the scenery and wildlife of the country. Several professional outfitters provide all of the necessities: life preservers, helmets and rafts, and their guides have been through training in the classroom and on the rivers. Most Costa Rican head guides have been trained at whitewater schools in the USA and many have worked with the world's best.

The first whitewater exploration of Costa Rican rivers was made by Costa Rica Expeditions on the Reventazón River in 1978 and the following year the same company were the pioneers of commercial whitewater rafting in Central America. Ríos Tropicales, founded in 1985, started rafting on the Sarapiquí and Sucio Rivers and local graduates of their kayaking school have represented Costa Rica at the World Championships of Whitewater Racing. Aventuras Naturales, is the third major company in this field. Others of varying expertise have also recently sprung up in San José, Turrialba and elsewhere. Many offer day-trip packages from San José, including transportation, breakfast and lunch, at very reasonable rates.

from the Central Valley via Turrialba, it passes through a deep gorge in dense jungle that contains rich flora and wildlife. Most groups spend two or more days descending this river from Tres Equis to Siquirres, and camping in riverside sites within view of thundering waterfalls and great flocks of birds.

On the Pacific side of Costa Rica, the river system offers the longest of the uninterrupted stretches of whitewater in Costa Rica. Most rafting parties take around four days to travel the 80 km (50 miles) from Chiles to Crujo, allowing time for exploring the waterfalls and for relaxing in camp.

Surfing

During the past few years, Costa Rica's unending beaches have been discovered by surfers from North America, Australia and Europe. They generally concur that the quality of Costa Rica's surf is in the top four – along with California, Hawaii and Australia. Moreover, they find that the surf here is plentiful and relatively uncrowded, the water temperature is a comfortable 27°C (80°F) throughout the year, and that there is still the rare experience of having a wave all to oneself, just offshore a pristine and empty beach.

A map of Costa Rica reveals what may not be

The Corobicí

This is the gentlest of Costa Rica's rafting rivers (designated Class 1 flat water), and is ideal for rafters who are also birdwatchers. In the adjacent Palo Verde National Park, over 300 species of birds have been observed and most can be seen from rafts on the Corobicí. Because the river's perennial flow is controlled by a dam on Lake Arenal, it becomes an oasis that attracts birds, monkeys and lizards during the dry season in Guanacaste.

LEFT: surfers appreciate the beautifully-shaped waves on the Pacific seaboard.
ABOVE: wave jumping on Lake Arenal.

too obvious from driving on the highway up or down the coasts: there are masses of beaches and, often, few access roads to many of them. In fact, there are some 200 km (120 miles) of Atlantic Coast and 1,000 km (630 miles) of Pacific shore, sculpted with sandy beaches, rocky headlands, offshore reefs and river mouths near coastal jungles.

There is also a great number of open beaches that are exposed to ocean swells coming from many directions. Much of the coastline is removed from civilization, and there may be no facilities, food or emergency services within many miles. A four-wheel drive vehicle is often essential, especially during the rainy season.

Popular surf spots

With hundreds of miles of coastline, there are many undiscovered, nameless surfing beaches. but among the favourites are the following.

Jacó, a Pacific beach town located southeast of the Gulf of Nicoya, is less than two hours by car or bus from San José. It is a long, silty beach trapped between two jungle-covered rocky points, with waves that are particularly good for body surfing or boogie boarding. The surf is easily accessible, just beyond the patios of many of the hotels and cabinas. For non-surfers, however, the beach is unattractive and the currents and riptides are strong.

Jacó is often used as a base for trips to other surfing areas nearby. Just under 3 km (2 miles) to the south is Playa Hermosa. It is possible to hitchhike, rent a bike or take a bus with a surf-board around the point south of Jacó to this beach. South from Jacó to Playa Panamá are many excellent undiscovered and unexploited surfing spots.

North of Jacó, near Puntarenas, the sandspit at the mouth of the Barranca River produces what is reputed to be one of the longest left-breaking waves in the world.

Far to the north, the beaches of Guanacaste Province have some of the best surf anywhere,

SWELLS AND BREAKS

Wave-making conditions are complex in Costa Rica. On the Pacific Coast, swells originating from storms in the north and central Pacific Ocean occur frequently from November through March. South swells from distant storms prevail for the remainder of the year. Pacific beaches are shaped by sediment which is carried to the sea by major rivers. The silt migrates up and down the coast on strong onshore currents. Sandbars produce beach breaks with long and fast right and left rides along much of the coast. Sandspits form at the river mouths, and create long, and often clean, point breaks. But because the sand bottom is unstable, bars and sandspits

change with the season. Tides and winds also strongly influence wave shape.

From December to April, large swells caused by winds and storms originating in the Caribbean arrive at Costa Rica's east-coast beaches. The steep, fast-moving waves break over shallow coral reefs, often in shapes and sizes that rival those of the north shore of Oahu, in Hawaii. Smaller west swells from tradewinds originating in the West Indies prevail from June through August. The only months when there is generally little or no surf on the east coast are September through November.

To check on conditions call Surf Report, tel: 220 206.

particularly during the dry season when steady offshore winds help to create the waves. The break near Roca de la Bruja (Witch's Rock) at Playa Naranjo, in the Santa Rosa National Park, is one of the best-known and most spectacular waves. Getting there requires a very long, bumpy journey in a four-wheel drive vehicle along nearly impassable roads, but the sight is certainly worth the discomfort.

The Nicoya Peninsula to the south of Guanacaste is scalloped with one beach after another, and many of them, such as Nosara, have rideable waves. Some of the best surfing in the country is found in remote Pavones on the southern Pacific coast.

Near Limón, some two and a half hours east of San José, are Playa Blanca and Playa Portete, both of which are good, popular surfing beaches. Approximately one hour south of Limón, Puerto Viejo, a tranquil Caribbean village, is the site of the sometimes awesome Salsa Brava, a surf break that now seems to have acquired an international reputation. From December through March, consistent, large north swells hit the coral reef in Puerto Viejo with tremendous force.

Windsurfing

In January 1991 a television sports network hosted and filmed Costa Rica's first windsurfing contest. The event served as an announcement to the world that the country warranted recognition as an outstanding destination for international windsurfers. During the competition, strong tradewinds whipped the picturesque Lake Arenal into a sea of white water and waves, creating ideal conditions for European and North American windsurfers.

The few pioneers who have sailed Arenal favorably compare this lake with the world's best windsurfing locations, such as the Columbia River Gorge in Oregon and Maui in the Hawaiian Islands (with the only caveat that the waves are sometimes rather choppy).

Almost every other day between January and April, consistent winds of around 20 knots whip the waves to a metre-high swell along the length of Arenal, creating excellent short board sailing conditions. For the rest of the season,

lighter winds predominate and are ideal for longboard sailing. Lake Arenal, is however, not a suitable place for beginners. Sideshore winds are consistent and blow across the full width of the lake. During high winds, steep swells provide the right conditions to practice acrobatic speed runs, jumps and loops. The water is a comfortable 18–21°C (64–70°F) year-round. The Hotel Tilawa and the River Rock Lodge are good places to hire equipment.

Another excellent windsurfing destination is the nearby Coter Lake. If you are looking for the "funnel effect" try Bahia Salinas, near La Cruz, in the far north west of the country.

Golf

Golf is growing in popularity in Costa Rica. The Hotel Cariari and Country Club, outside San José, is the country's championship course. Until now it has been Costa Rica's only 18-hole course. However, new 18-hole facilities have been developed at Bahia Culebra, on the Nicoya Peninsula, and at the Playa Conchal Hotel, in Guanacaste.

There are also a number of reasonably good nine-hole courses at Tango Mar, which overlooks the Gulf of Nicoya; Costa Rica Country Club in Escazú; the Los Reyes Country Club, La Guácima. and the El Castillo Country Club, above Heredia. ❑

LEFT: divers explore Isla del Caño's beautiful coral reef. **RIGHT:** bougainvillea frames the fairways at Cariari Country Club golf course.

BIG FINS AND FRESH FISH

Costa Rica is a paradise for both fresh and saltwater fishing. It's quiet too:

you'll run into other fishing folk only if you really want to

The king of game fish swims calmly towards Costa Rica's Caribbean Coast. At 70 kilos (150 pounds), he fears no predators, except sharks, as he cruises towards the mouth of the Colorado River.

Where the tarpon has been is a mystery to man. He could be coming from Florida, South America or West Africa. He might have been in local waters the entire time.

But now he is with an ocean school of 100 fish of the same size. Suddenly they spot a school of titi, a small sardine-like fish, and chase them to the surface. The tarpon cause an acre of the Caribbean to explode as they churn

RULES OF ENGAGEMENT

In tarpon fishing, the rules of angling must be suspended or reversed, otherwise there's no chance of success. The first trick that goes against all that you've ever learned is to retrieve the lure with the rod tip low – at water level or, better yet, in the water. That way, when it's time to set the hook, the rod tip can be brought up and backwards in a long arc. The maneuver must be repeated rapidly at least three times with a force that would tear the hook out of the mouth of almost any other fish.

Tarpon sometimes strike like a rocket, hurtling 5 meters (16 ft) straight up as they hit the plug. At other times it is hard to tell whether or not one of these giant

fish is even on your hook. If you react fast enough, and if you're lucky, the tarpon will be hooked before it makes its first jump. If you're not so lucky, you'll see your lure thrown into the air as the great silver fish seems to explode out of the water and reach for the clouds. A tarpon's jump is like no other in fishing. They reach incredibly high; twist right, twist left, flip over, fall back on the line and do everything possible to get free.

Usually the tarpon succeeds. Usually you lose. The success rate of experts is to land about one out of every 10 hooked. though try telling that to your friends when you go back after a day's tarpon fishing empty-handed!

the water and devour the titi. If you are lucky enough to witness this scene, it's simply a matter of casting into the chaos to get into contact with what many consider the most exciting aquatic quarry on earth.

Tarpon enter the river mouths all along the Caribbean coast of Costa Rica, from the Colorado River in the north, to the Sixaola River, which forms the border with Panamá. In most rivers, they swim a few hundred meters upstream in search of food and return to the sea.

Only in the Río Colorado do they keep going upriver, following the titi, in an incredible journey of more than 200 km (124 miles) to Lake Nicaragua, close to the Pacific Ocean.

Freshwater lakes

As the tarpon begin their long swim, they pass a series of thin fingers of water stretching northward almost to the border with Nicaragua. These freshwater "lakes" are full of a variety of exotic fish that make great sport on light tackle. One of the most fascinating is the alligator gar, known in Costa Rica as *gaspar*. Looking like a holdover from prehistoric times, this fish has a long, narrow snout as full of sharp teeth as an alligator's. Its coffee-colored body is covered with tough skin and large scales. Its tail is broad and powerful. The meat of the "gaspar" is firm and sweet, not unlike that of shrimps. But the eggs should never be eaten as they are highly toxic to humans.

The tarpon is not alone in his upriver swims. Snook also make the long journey following the titi. And following them all are bull sharks.

The sharks, like the tarpon, continue all the way to Lake Nicaragua. Their presence has led many people to believe that there are "freshwater sharks" in the lake. Actually, they are just visitors from the faraway Caribbean.

Snook are the mainstay of sport fishing in Costa Rica. Large snook are plentiful along all parts of the Caribbean and Pacific coasts, as well as in rivers throughout the country.

All along the Río San Juan, there are lesser rivers flowing into it from Costa Rica. The confluence of the San Juan with the Colorado, Sarapiquí, San Carlos, Infernito, Pocosol,

Medio Queso and Frío Rivers all offer some excellent angling for tarpon and snook. None is heavily fished and all require a bit of enterprise to reach. But those who make the effort are usually well rewarded.

The Río Frío

An exception to this rule of relative inaccessibility is the Río Frío which passes right through "downtown" Los Chiles, which is an approximate three-hour drive, on paved roads, from San José.

The Río Frío is full of tarpon, snook, white drum, gar and other exotic species. Some

ROLLING FOR AIR

Tarpon are one of the few fish that are capable of taking in air directly through the mouth rather than by filtering water through their gills. This ability is necessary because these big active fish need more oxygen than they can get from the waters that they sometimes inhabit.

This method of direct breathing accounts for the phenomenon known as "rolling", when they come to the surface and flop on their side while gulping air. This unusual adaptation also makes it possible for tarpon to swim freely between saltwater and freshwater and even in oxygen-depleted water.

LEFT: many visitors get to land a sailfish; a *guapote* caught in Lake Arenal.
RIGHT: a proud fisherman with his freshly caught *mahi-mahi* (dolphin fish), off the Nicoya coast.

people fish right from the municipal landing in Los Chiles. Others, who have boats, launch them there and venture north or south. For those who don't have a boat, it is possible to rent a *panga*, driven by a knowledgeable local person who also acts as a guide. These *pangas* can be found at the municipal landing.

Some tarpon, as they swim up the Río San Juan, apparently take diversions far into the side rivers. This is the case with the Río Frío. Thirty minutes by boat south of Los Chiles is the convergence of the Río Frío and the Río Sabogal. Here tarpon up to 45 kilos (100 pounds) seem to be present at all times.

Every morning and every evening the giant fish, too big to be in a narrow river, leap high into the air, re-entering the water with a thundering splash. It is a sight every fishing enthusiast would love to see. It can also be one of the most frustrating experiences imaginable, because there are days when these fish just won't take a lure. However, just the sight is well worth the trip – and there's always a good chance of hooking into one of them.

More river fish

The Río Frío, as well as most of the other rivers of Costa Rica, is full of a fish often overlooked by anglers. The *machacha,* a silvery speedster, is an unusual fish in that is primarily a vegetarian. They can often be found under the overhang of *chilemate* trees waiting for ripe fruit to fall into the water. Costa Ricans fish for them using pieces of banana or tomato, but *machacha* will also take small lures or flies running, changing directions, diving and leaping into the air. They can grow up to 9 kilos (20 pounds) and two to five pounders are common and offer great sport. Their flesh is bony but tasteful.

Up a few of the rivers that feed into the San Juan, particularly the Sarapiquí, can be found the *bobo*, a difficult but rewarding quarry. These fish, which weigh up to 14 kilos (30 pounds), feed on shallow, fast-moving water. They are relatives of the saltwater mullet and are pure vegetarians. But they can be taken on small spinners and they offer great sport as they fight hard through the rapids.

In these Atlantic slope rivers can be found other exotic species including the *mojarra*, a strong, sharp-toothed, brightly-colored pan fish resembling a perch on steroids.

Sea angling

For most people, fishing off the Pacific coast of Costa Rica means angling for sail fish, marlin and tuna. All along the Pacific coast there are sport fishing operations springing up and all are finding success.

Operators in the Gulf of Papagayo were the first, and the area was often shown to have the most productive sail fishing in the world. Sails here are not the scrawny Atlantic variety. They are hefty, healthy Pacific sail fish averaging over 45 kilos (100 pounds). Fought on 7-kilo (15-pound) line or less, they offer fantastic sport and a spectacular show full of graceful jumps. Laws require that all sails (except record catches) are released and this is generally respected by fishermen.

In recent years, marlin have been discovered throughout most of the Pacific coast. Dolphin, tuna and rainbow runner are plentiful offshore and the spectacular rooster fish and snook can be found close to land. Offshore reefs also offer great fishing for snapper, including the prized *cubbera.*

Often overlooked are the fishing possibilities from the Pacific beaches. Every beach on the Pacific coast offers the chance to take various types of jack and drum as well as trophy-sized snook from the surf. Mouths of rivers and streams often attract congregations of snook. Casting from rocks often locates snapper and rooster fish.

Roosters abound on Costa Rica's Pacific coast. The wide-bodied, powerful fish with the long, spiky dorsal fin that gives it its name, is particularly plentiful around the rocks in Puntarenas or the nearby Pacific port of Caldera. Once hooked, the rooster fish raises its comb and speeds away across the surface, offering a unique show and fight.

LICENSED TO FISH

You can buy a fishing license from specialist suppliers Deportes Keko, Calle 20 and Ave 4–6 in San José.

force of a rhino and if it gets there it will almost certainly cut the line on underbrush.

The *guapote* is a spectacular fish. A breeding male has large bulbous protrusions above the eyes that "light up", displaying many colors on its flank. *Guapote* in Lake Arenal, the main place where they are fished, weigh up to 9 kilos (20 pounds) or more, although a 7-kilo (15-pound) fish is about as much as most can handle. The *guapote pinto*, or painted guapote, can be found in rivers that flow into the San Juan. ❏

The *guapote*

The star of Costa Rica's few lakes is the *guapote*. Some people call this fish the "rainbow bass", although taxonomically it has nothing to do with bass. The main similarity to bass is in the way it is fished, casting or flipping plugs or spinner baits.

Once hooked, the resemblance is soon forgotten. The *guapote* is to a bass what a diesel is to an HO model train. It is not a light tackle fish. Once hooked, it heads for cover with the

LEFT: unfamiliar faces in the fish market.
ABOVE: fishing for trout and *machin* in the breathtaking mountains around San Isidro del General.

TROUT AND MACHIN

Trout have never done well in Costa Rica. Despite numerous attempts to stock them in high mountain streams, they have never really thrived. Trout fishing is possible in the breathtaking mountains between San José and San Isidro del General, such as the Rio Savegre in the San Gerardo de Dota valley area, and, even if the fish are somewhat small, the scenery alone makes a day spent here worthwhile.

If you cannot find trout then a good substitute is the *machin*, which is found in rivers where trout would be expected. It puts up a vigorous fight, very similar to that of a trout.

TICO COOKING

When you can try Painted Rooster and Married Man on the menu in Costa Rica's
sodas, why spend time at fast-food or international restaurants?

While it is possible to order everything from *sushi* to *huevos rancheros* (Mexican-style eggs) in Costa Rica, part of the joy of travelling is sampling local cuisine.

The Ticos' basic diet is simple, low fat and rich in proteins and carbohydrates. Fruits, fresh vegetables, beef and abundant salads are the

coriander, paprika and a small amount of hot chilli. "English sauce", the native version of Worcestershire sauce, is also used, albeit sparingly, by most cooks. Jalapeño chillies, from the mountain towns of Zarcero and Cervantes, are very good and not as hot as the Mexican varieties. In fact, most Costa Ricans do not like

trademarks of Costa Rican cooking. *Picadillos* are found in every Tico home: diced potatoes, *chayotes* (water squash or vegetable pears) or string beans are mixed with finely chopped meat, tomatoes, onions, fresh coriander, bell peppers and whatever the cook feels may add flavor to the pot. Leftover *picadillos*, fried with rice, are served for breakfast, usually with hot *tortillas*, and are called *amanecido*.

Costa Ricans season their food with a mixture of dry spices called *condimentos mixtos* (mixed seasoning), which are readily available at the markets. There are many different brands of liquid sauces as well. Most often these contain cornflour, salt, garlic, black pepper, onion,

very spicy food, although tabasco and chilli sauce is always on the table in inexpensive restaurants.

Gallo pinto and casado

The classic Costa Rican dish of *gallo pinto* (literally, painted rooster) is rice and black or red beans mixed with seasonings including onion, garlic and finely chopped bell pepper. While predominantly a breakfast dish in the city, rural Costa Ricans eat *gallo pinto* three times daily, accompanied by homemade corn tortillas. For breakfast they order it with scrambled or fried eggs and sour cream, or *natilla*.

For lunch, businesspeople, professionals,

students and farmers alike usually have a *casado* (meaning married man), a hearty combination including rice, beans, cabbage salad, fried plantains and chicken, fish or beef. An example of Tico macho humour, the name *casado* derives from the ordinary daily fare a man supposedly receives after he is married.

More Tico favourites

Another typical dish is *olla de carne* (meat pot), a hearty stew that includes a small amount of beef and many vegetables common to the region: often *nampi* and *camote* (both relatives of the sweet potato), *chayote* (water squash), carrots and potatoes. It is usually served with white rice – something Ticos feel no meal is complete without. This dish can be traced back to Cervantes' novel *Don Quixote*.

The *olla podrida* is the great-grandparent of the soup the people in Costa Rica love the most. What gives the distinct flavor to the Costa Rican version is the mixture of vegetables cooked in it: yucca, green plantain, sweet potato, *tannia*, *tacacos*, taro, pumpkin, carrot, *cho-cho*, onion, cabbage and whatever else is to hand.

Another interesting soup that is available at neighborhood restaurants throught the country, is *sopa negra,* made with black beans, onions, fresh coriander and hard-boiled eggs.

For lunch or dinner, *arroz con pollo* (rice with chicken) or *arroz con mariscos* (rice with seafood) are filling, inexpensive meals served in *sodas* and hotel restaurants.

Other local favorites include *lengua* (cow's tongue), and *mondongillo* (cow's stomach lining). While tongue is tender and often deliciously prepared, *mondongillo* has a strong taste and is not liked by most foreigners.

The ubiquitous accompaniment to most meals is plantains – a sweet relative of the banana. It must be cooked before eating and is usually cut into strips and fried in oil or lard (called *manteca*).

Bocas and bebidas

Most bars serve *bocas* ("mouthfuls") with drinks in the same tradition as Spanish *tapas*. Traditionally they were complimentary but these days are increasingly sold separately.

Favorite *bocas* include *ceviche* (raw fish marinated in lemon juice), *carne en salsa* (meat stewed in a tomato sauce), fried cassava, and fried chicken. Beer, rum and *guaro* (an aniseed drink) are favorite local tipples.

Special occasions

On weekends, Costa Ricans love to eat *chicharrones* – chittlins or deep-fried pig skin (including the layer of fat just below the skin). The concoction is served with tortillas and wedges of lemon, which are supposed to cut the grease.

At Christmas, everyone eats *tamales*, which

PRECEDING PAGES: an astonishing tropical fruit bounty.
LEFT: the bustling San José restaurant scene.
RIGHT: succulent *gambas* (shrimps).

COSTA RICAN NOUVELLE CUISINE

The concept of Costa Rican nouvelle cuisine may sound like a contradiction in terms, but increasing exportation of food has stirred new interest in the country's vegetables and fruits. New recipes and traditional ones alike have been imaginatively rewritten.

Pejibaye soup, a delicate orange creamy broth, features at banquets. The common, but never ordinary, mashed black beans (*frijoles*), well-seasoned with onions, sweet peppers and coriander, are now served at formal dinners as hors d'oeuvres. Posh restaurants offer native cooking nights, starring such delicacies as plantain soufflé and pork-filled cassava pastries.

are pieces of dough made from ground corn beaten with lard and certain spices, stuffed with different fillings, then wrapped in corn husks and steamed. The dish is of Aztec origin and is still eaten in Mexico and the whole of Central America. It is very rarely the same in any two countries. In Costa Rica, *tamales* are traditionally filled with tender bits of pork, rice, olives, carrots and olives.

Easter fare

Since colonial times, the Easter meal has been an important and traditional celebration. The Catholic Church's prohibition on eating red

meat during Lent explains why fish, pastries and sweets are made available for the Easter celebration. Since the 19th century*, bacalao con papas* (salted cod and potatoes) has been traditionally prepared for Easter. Huge quantities of salted cod are imported from Europe especially for this occasion.

Just before Easter week, particularly in and around Cartago, a type of fruit similar to the pumpkin, but oval and quite large, is sold in the streets. These are *chiverres*, and a preserve made with them, called *cabellito de angel* (angel's hair), is eaten during Easter throughout the Central Valley.

Costa Rican *ceviche* is an Easter speciality,

but is available all year round at any neighborhood *cevicheria*. It is prepared by marinating small cubes of white fresh fish in a sauce made with lime juice, olive oil, fresh coriander, onions and bell peppers, for at least 12 hours. Most Costa Rican cooks believe in keeping the lime juice to a minimum and using coriander freely to perfume the fish. It is similar to the Mexican dish of the same name, and both show the influence of the Aztecs.

Fresh *palmito* (heart of palm) is also traditionally eaten during Lent, but can be bought any time pickled in vinegar. *Palmito* and rice is an elegant, festive dish served with grated cheese on top.

Flor de itabo is the flower of a plant often used in the fences of the coffee farms. It is a very white bunch of lily-like flowers, which are also eaten for Easter, stewed in butter with eggs and tomato.

Regional cooking

Costa Rica may only be a small country, yet it enjoys several clearly differentiated regional cuisines.

The foods of Limón are exotically tropical and flavorsome. The area offers a wide diversity of dishes influenced by African and West Indian cooking. The names of the ingredients (*haki, yokotaw, bami, calaloo*) have the beat of Calypso and reggae, as do the names of the dishes themselves (*tie-a-leave, dokunu, johnny cake*). You will also find strong traces of Chinese cuisine, as there are many Chinese living in the area.

The trademark of the cooking of Limón is coconut. Coconut oil and milk are used generously in most recipes, including the traditional rice-and-beans. For this popular dish, rice is cooked in a pot filled with red beans, coconut milk and aromatic herbs. It is the regional - variation of the traditional *gallo pinto*, but in Limón it's served on Sundays and on festive occasions.

From their African background the *Limonenses* have kept the original names of many ingredients, the use of tubers, such as the yam, and green leaves in soups and stews. Their African heritage also shows in their use of herbal teas made with an infinite variety of plants. From their ancestors' hard lives in the sugar plantations of the West Indies, the *Limonenses* have inherited many products that were included in the daily rations of the slaves: breadfruit, salted cod, mangoes, *cassava*, plantains and a great variety of tropical fruits.

And from the demands and preferences of their British masters they have retained several recipes for cakes, pastries and breads.

In Guanacaste, pre-Columbian traditions in cooking are very much alive. A larger variety of corn dishes are cooked there than in the rest of the country, including delicious pastries. *Tamales*, *chorreadas*, *tanelas* and many other regional delicacies can still be found throughout Guanacaste. Some beach hotels there are starting to include them on their menus.

region during colonial times to work in the kitchens of the haciendas. They also left their mark on many exotic recipes still cooked in that province. *Ajiaco* and *bajo*, stews made with a mixture of meats and vegetables, maintain their African origins.

On the Pacific coast, Puntarenas presents recipes using ingredients from the sea, including *guiso de cambute* (conch stew) and dishes featuring different combinations of fresh shrimp, lobster and squid. *Patacones*, crisp green plantain sliced and topped with black mashed beans, are a necessary accompaniment to fresh *ceviche*. ❑

Since cattle farming is one of Guanacaste's main resources, milk products there are often very good. *Bagaces* (a hard, salted cheese, used shredded and added to other recipes) has been, since the 19th century, an important part of the salary of the *peones* on the haciendas. *Cuajadas* (fresh cheese balls) are usually served at breakfast, to be eaten with hot *tortillas guanacastecas*, which are larger than the ones eaten in the rest of the country.

African slave women were brought to the

LEFT: *empanadas* (meat or vegetable patties) are a typical country fair food.
ABOVE: *gallo pinto*, the national dish.

THE CHOROTEGA LEGACY

Long before the white man arrived the indigenous Chorotega tribe prepared a very thin unleavened cornmeal pancake called the *tortilla*. It is the main ingredient of Costa Rican *gallitos*, a type of hors d'oeuvre made by wrapping them around mashed black beans, spicy meat, a spoonful of vegetable stew, pork rinds, or whatever else takes the chef's fancy.

The Chorotegas also prepared tamales, rectangular pieces of dough, stuffed with deer or turkey meat and a sauce made from tomatoes, pumpkin seeds and sweet peppers. The sauce, called *pipian*, is still prepared today in a very similar way.

FRUITS OF COSTA RICA

*Whether piled high in the market, served up on a plate or whipped into a milkshake,
Costa Rica's rainbow of fruits are a delightful assault on all the senses*

F ernandez de Oviedo, a Spanish writer who came to Costa Rica in the 16th century, was probably the first European to chronicle the country's astounding variety of tropical fruits. Enthusiastic at every new discovery, he pronounced the pineapple the "best-looking, most wonderful lady in the vegetable world".

De Oviedo probably didn't get to taste all of Costa Rica's different fruit. There are simply too many, and they are available for every possible taste preference, throughout the year. Get up early in the morning in San José and visit the Mercado Borbón, or the produce market off 10th Avenue, or the dozens of fruit stalls near the Coca Cola bus station. Or go to the open-air produce and fruit markets on Saturday morning, held in almost every town on the Central Plateau, to see and taste the season's harvest. Along the highways and main roads will be vendors of all kinds of fruit and fruit drinks. In this chapter, we take a look at Costa Rica's A–Z of fruits – from *anona* to *zapote*.

Anona

A strange-looking heart-shaped fruit, also called "the bullock's heart", the *anona* changes from green to a dark reddish-brown as it ripens. The sweet pulp is milk white and contains several large black seeds. After cutting it in half, eat it with a spoon, using the skin as a bowl. The *anona* is related to the custard-apple (*anona chirimoya*) found in the northern part of the country. It has a delicate sweetness and a delightful fragrance like rose-water. Mark Twain described it as "deliciousness itself".

Breadfruit

Breadfruit, like bananas, is grown in the Atlantic region of Costa Rica. This fruit of Polynesian origin was introduced to the West Indies by Captain Bligh, and the Jamaicans planted it in Limón. The breadfruit is an attractive, ornamental tree with large leaves, and the fruit is an ingredient in many Caribbean dishes.

Caimitos and other stars

The *caimito* or Costa Rican star apple looks just like a star when cut, similar in taste to the mangosteen (an exotic fruit found in Malaysia and Thailand). This glossy fruit varies in shade from purple to light green. The sweet flesh is usually eaten fresh, but in Limón you can still find it made into a mixture called "matrimony", prepared by scooping out the pulp and adding it to a glass of sour orange juice.

Carambolas, which also look like beautiful stars when cut in thin slices crosswise, are used as garnishes for desserts and for making juice. This shiny, five-sided pinkish-yellow fruit is about 5–8 cm (2–3 in) long.

Cashew fruit

An exotic cousin of the mango, the cashew fruit is best known for the kidney-shaped nut attached to its lower end. The fleshy portion, or apple, varying in color from brilliant yellow to flame-scarlet, is eaten fresh here. Its superb color and penetrating, almost pungent aroma make this one of the most delectable of all tropical fruits. The flesh is yellow, soft, very juicy and zesty. It is also used to make a jam, a wine and a refreshing beverage similar to lemonade, which retains the special aroma and flavor of the unique fruit. In the late 1970s, the government decided to plant many acres with cashews, to be exported abroad. The venture was a failure, but the trees are still there, and there was a wonderful side effect: parakeets and parrots adore the fruit, and many species that were almost extinct are now increasing their numbers while dining on abundant cashew apples. Beware, if the seeds are not roasted before eating, they are poisonous.

beverages. Foreigners find the flavor somewhat suggestive of a combination of pineapple and mango, but Ticos consider that to be heresy.

Guava

A bestselling book about the acclaimed Colombian writer Gabriel García Marquez has the provocative title *The Guava's Perfume*. You will better understand how the title elicits the Latin American experience if you visit a home when guava jelly is being cooked. The entire house fills with the aroma of this wonderful fruit. But cooking is not obligatory; you can simply eat the guava raw.

Granadilla

The sweet *granadilla* is a favorite all over Central America. This fruit is oval and orange to orange-brown. Within the hard, crisp skin a bundle of seeds is surrounded by an almost liquid, translucent and wonderfully tasteful pulp. Use a spoon to eat it.

Guanabana

Related to the *anona*, the *guanabana* is unrivaled for its use in sherbets and refreshing

Another fruit, called in English "Costa Rican guava" (*cas*), is yellow in color, round, and has soft white flesh. It is acidic, but highly valued for jelly-making and for drinks. If you see it on a menu, under "*naturales*", try a freshly-squeezed *jugo de cas* (*cas* juice).

Loquat

The loquat (níspero) is a small, oval-shaped fruit with a large seed, pale-yellow to orange in color. It is also called the Japanese medlar. The flesh, firm and meaty in some varieties, melting in others, is juicy and of a sprightly acid flavor. Although commonly eaten fresh, it can also be used in cooking.

LEFT: cashew apples; the gray part is the edible nut.
ABOVE: paw-paw near Turrialba. Squeeze a dash of lemon or lime juice on the flesh to give it a zing.

Mango

Alajuela's Central Park, where young and old gather to enjoy the good weather and each other's company, is full of mango trees, with their tempting fragrance, and that is why the town, second in importance only to San José, is called Mango City. Alajuela's mangoes are sweet, firm and delicate. The ripe *mangos* are sweeter and spicier, but smaller and softer than the unripe *mangas*. The mango aroma is spicy and alluring. Few other fruits have a historical background as developed as the mango, and few others are so inextricably connected with religious beliefs. Buddha himself is said to have

sell brown paper bags full of *mombínes* from August through October, the color varying from dark green to bright red, depending on ripeness. *Mombín* is usually eaten fresh, as is its cousin, the yellow *mombín*. Some refer to the yellow variety as the hogplum because hogs are very fond of it and fatten on the fruit that falls to the ground from wild trees in the forest.

The coco-plum (*icaco*), on the other hand, is never eaten fresh, but its white flesh is made into a sweet preserve, called *miel de icaco*. Another cousin, the *ambarella* (*yuplón*), was brought to Jamaica by Captain Bligh of the *Bounty*. It came to Costa Rica in the hands of

been presented with a mango grove, so that he might find rest beneath its graceful shade.

Besides eating them as dessert fruits, Costa Ricans make mangoes into chutney – that spicy sauce well-known to those who enjoy East Indian food – as well as preserves, sauces and pies. For many people mangoes are the very essence of summer.

Mombín

The Spaniards said the *mombín* (or *jocote*) was a type of plum when they first saw it, but it really has nothing in common with the plum. This fruit is juicy and spicy, unlike any other. The *tronador* is the best variety. Street vendors

English-speaking Jamaican immigrants, to the Port of Limón. It is eaten uncooked, with a little salt, or made into a preserve.

Nanzi

You'll recognize a *nanzi (nance)* by its fragrance. This small, round yellow fruit has been popular among Costa Ricans since pre-Columbian times, but foreigners tend to find its smell too strong. It is used for preserves, wines and jellies. *Nances en guaro* (*nanzis* in liqueur) are very good. Bottled in a strong liqueur and left to ferment for nine months, they take on an amber-brown color. Nanzi sherbets are also very popular.

Paw-paw

Paw-paw (or papaya) grows almost everywhere in the country, and most tourists are particularly enamored of a drink called *papaya en leche*, a sort of papaya milkshake. Papaya is also excellent as a meat tenderizer.

Pejibaye

This was a treasured food of the aboriginal Indians. You will surely see it on the fruit stands, with its glossy orange skin and black stripes, resembling a large acorn. Cooked and peeled, its yellow pulp tastes very good when a little mayonnaise is added to it to soften its rather dry texture. It cannot be eaten fresh. *Pejibaye* soup is one of the most exceptional dishes of Costa Rican nouvelle cuisine.

Rambutan

The most exotic sight in a fruit market in Costa Rica has to be the rambutan (*mamon chino*). The bunches of red and orange fruits, sometimes called "hairy lychees", look like gooseberries covered in fleshy spines. To eat them, simply cut the leathery rind with a sharp knife and pull it back from the pulp.

Rose-apple

The fragrance of the guava is only rivaled by that of the rose-apple (*manzana rosa*), a beautiful round fruit, whitish green to apricot-yellow in color, perfumed with the scent of the rose. The flesh is crisp, juicy and sweet. As a preserve or crystallized, it is delicious. If you eat it fresh, don't overdo it. Rose-apples must be eaten in small quantities. A relative of the rose-apple, the *ohia* or mountain-apple (*manzana de agua*) is a beautiful oval fruit, white to crimson in color. Its flesh is apple-like: crisp, white and juicy. *Ohia* jam is exquisite.

Sapodilla

One of the best fruits of tropical America, from the province of Guanacaste, is the *sapodilla* or naseberry, here called *chicozapote* or *níspero*. It is a dessert fruit, rarely cooked or preserved in any way. The French botanist Descourtilz described it as having the "sweet perfumes of honey, jasmine and lily of the valley."

LEFT: a mountain of melons at Cartago.
ABOVE: the humble *pejibaye* has become an unlikely star of Costa Rican nouvelle cuisine.

Zapote

A relative of the *sapodilla*, the *mammee-sapota* or marmalade-plum (*zapote*), kept Cortés and his army alive on their famous march from Mexico City to Honduras. The bright salmon-red color of the pulp catches the eyes of tourists walking the Avenida Central in San José. Street vendors, knowing the sales appeal of the beautiful color, cut the marmalade-plums in halves.

Beware, however, if you are not used to the very sweet fruits of the tropics then the flavor of the *zapote* may be rather cloying. Very ripe zapotes are used to make the most wonderful ice creams and sherbets. ❑

REFRESCOS

Refreshing fruit drinks such as *fresco de maracuyá* (passion-fruit) accompany every Costa Rican meal. One of the favorite and most nourishing is made from *mora* or blackberries. The berries are blended, strained and added to sugar water or milk. One of the more thirst-quenching drinks is made from *cas*, a type of guava.

A *tamarindo refresco* is similar in color and taste to apple juice. It is made from the seed pod of the tamarind tree. Tamarind seeds and pulp wrapped into balls the size of oranges are available at every market. The seeds are put into hot water to wash off the sticky tamarind and then are mixed with sugar and water.

COFFEE

When white coffee blossom blankets the fields of the Central Valley, their sweet jasmine-like fragrance filling the air, the Ticos call it "Costa Rican Snow"

You might well surmise that coffee is indigenous to Costa Rica, but it's not. The Spanish, French and Portuguese brought coffee beans to the New World from Ethiopia and Arabia. In the early 1800s, when seeds were first planted in Costa Rica, coffee plants were merely ornamental, grown to decorate

patios and courtyards with their glossy green leaves, seasonal white flowers and red berries. Costa Ricans had to be persuaded, even coerced, into growing them so the country might have a national export crop. Every Tico family was required by law to have at least a couple of bushes in the yard. The government awarded free plants to the poor and grants of land to anyone who was willing to plant coffee on it.

The Central Valley is the ideal place for the production of coffee. Its altitude, above 1,200 meters (4,000 ft), its temperatures, which average between 15°C and 28°C (59°F and 82°F), and its soil conditions are all perfect for coffee cultivation. Coffee *fincas* quickly occupied

much of the land, except for that needed to graze oxen. As the only Costa Rican export, the country's financial resources supported it. By 1840, coffee had become big business, carried by oxcart through mountains to the Pacific port at Puntarenas, and from there by ship to Chile from where it was transported to Europe. By the mid-1800s Costa Rica's oligarchy of coffee barons had risen to positions of power and wealth, for the most part through processing and exporting the golden bean, rather than by actually growing it.

A mixed blessing

Costa Rica was fortunate in its early development of the coffee industry, but at times it has been a mixed blessing. The country borrowed three million dollars from England to finance the Atlantic Railroad so coffee could be exported from the Atlantic port of Limón. And when coffee hit bottom on the international market in 1900, the result was a severe shortage of basic foods in Costa Rica that year.

This dependency on an overseas market beyond their control has left the Costa Ricans vulnerable on many occasions. Throughout the 20th century, coffee prices *fluctuated wildly and the health of the nation's economy varied accordingly.

Traditionally, banana, citrus and poro trees were planted in the coffee fields to provide

COFFEE TO EUROPE

In 1843, an English sea captain, William Le Lacheur, returning to England from the United States, stopped in at Costa Rica's Pacific port of Puntarenas in need of ballast for his empty ship. As it happened, 1843 was an exceptional year for coffee production and the farmers had more of the beans than they could sell.

They did a deal with Le Lacheur and loaded up the holds of his ship with coffee, allowing him to use the heavy sacks as ballast. He made the trip to England, around the Cape, and two years later he returned to pay the coffee planters their profit. And thus began the Costa Rican-European coffee trade.

some shade for the coffee plants. Later, coffee hybrids were developed that did not need shade and treeless fields allowed more yield per acre. These varieties, however, were found to deplete the soil more rapidly and required fertilizer to enrich it, adding to the cost of production. Today, many coffee-growers have returned to the traditional shade-loving plants.

The coffee plant itself is grown in nurseries until it's a year old, at which time it is transplanted to the field. Two years later it bears harvestable berries and, with care, will continue to bear for the next 30 to 40 years.

As coffee grows best in a mountainous climate, during school vacation and Christmas holidays, and it is traditional for entire families in rural areas to pick coffee together, some of the money earned going for Christmas presents and new outfits.

Costa Rican coffee has been traditionally mixed with other coffees to upgrade blends destined for worldwide export to give them a liveliness and body. But today, consumers demand the unadulterated stuff: 100 percent pure Costa Rican coffee. And the coffees from the highland regions around Poás, Barva de Heredia, Tres Rios and Tarrazú are rated by many aficionados among the best in the world.   ❑

mate, many of the hillsides in the Central Valley are covered with rows of the bright green bushes, reflecting the sun with their shiny, luxuriant leaves. Some of the fields seem almost vertical and it is difficult to see how pickers keep from tumbling down the slopes as they collect the berries. The answer lies in the ingenious solution of planting the trees directly behind one another so that the trunk of the downhill tree serves as a foothold for the pickers. Coffee is harvested from November to Jan-

LEFT: fast hands; Costa Rica has the greatest coffee productivity per acre in the world.
ABOVE: coffee pickers *circa* 1920.

CAFE BRITT

The best way to get a taste of the Costa Rica coffee experience is to take Cafe Britt's exceptional Coffee Tour. Located almost 1 km (½ mile) north of Heredia in Barva (signposted from Heredia center), this theatrical, highly-entertaining happening takes visitors through the entire coffee process, from growing the coffee cherry to correctly tasting the final product. Combining elements of professional theater, a multimedia show, a farm visit, plant tour and tasting session, Cafe Britt whirls the visitor through the world of coffee in about two hours. You must reserve your tour in advance by telephoning 260-2748.

PLACES

A detailed guide to the entire country, with principal sites cross-referenced by number to the maps

Costa Rica may be a relatively small country, but don't think that means there's little to see or do here. Its beaches rival the best of the Caribbean for their crystal waters and white sand. Inland, lush forests and towering volcanoes attract walkers and nature lovers from all over the world. Indeed, national parks comprise a greater proportion of national territory than other country in the world, amply justifying Costa Rica's reputation as the home of eco-tourism.

We begin the places section in the capital, San José, the small but bustling metropolis that acts as the international gateway to Costa Rica. It's not a beautiful city, but like most capitals it has a buzz and is worth staying a day or so to visit some fascinating museums (from the underground Gold Museum to the Serpentarium in a skyscraper). It is also a good base for exploring the country, and there are some excellent lodges in the nearby mountains, offering activities from horseback riding to whitewater rafting.

Next we focus on the Central Valley. By contrast, this is the country's green and fertile heartland. It is an area of agricultural towns, coffee farms and many cultural treasures. From here it's a short hop to the beaches of the Central Pacific. These are some of the best in the country and particularly famous is Manuel Antonio whose perfect white sands are the stuff of tropical dreams.

Many visitors regard the north as the true Costa Rica. This is almost a country in itself with the wonderful beaches of the Nicoya Peninsula, the great cattlelands of Guanacaste, and the natural riches of Monteverde and the Sarapiquí. By night, Arenal Volcano, belching sulfurous smoke and hot boulders is an unforgettable sight.

By contrast the Caribbean Coast presents Costa Rica's laid-back face: its tall palms, radiant sunshine and aquamarine waters, beckoning visitors to share in its indolent lifestyle.

Our tour ends in the south, off the beaten track, amid a wild region of vast inaccessible forests and Central America's highest peak. And in special picture features we'll tell you more about Costa Rica's volcanoes – mountains of fire, its traditional handicrafts, and its spectacular birdlife including its proudest natural treasure, the aptly and exotically-named Resplendent Quetzal.

All the sites of interest are numbered on specially drawn maps to help you find your way around, but don't worry about getting lost. Everyone does, but then just getting there is half the fun of enjoying this remarkable country. ❑

PRECEDING PAGES: Atlantic coastline; páramo, an unusual ecosystem seen on the summit of Mount Chirripo; Basilica de Nuestra Señora de los Angeles in Cartago.
LEFT: a *campesino* ponders the origin and significance of this giant stone ball.

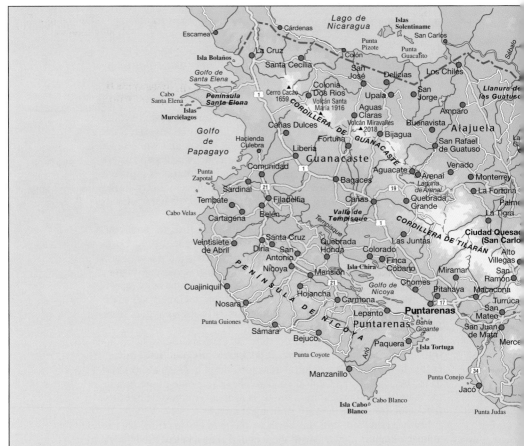

Lago de Nicaragua · Islas Solentiname · Escamea · Cárdenas · San Carlos · Punta Pizote · Punta Guacanito · Sabalo · Isla Bolaños · La Cruz · Santa Cecilia · Colón · San José · Delicias · Los Chiles · Golfo de Santa Elena · Cabo Santa Elena · Península Santa Elena · Cerro Cacao 1659 · Colonia Dos Ríos · Volcán Santa María 1916 · Upala · San Jorge · Amparo · Llanura de los Guatuso · Islas Murciélagos · Cañas Dulces · Aguas Claras · Volcán Miravalles 2018 · Bijagua · Buenavista · Alajuela · La · Golfo de Papagayo · Hacienda Culebra · Liberia · Fortuna · San Rafael de Guatuso · Venado · Monterrey · Comunidad · Guanacaste · Aguacate · Arenal · La Fortuna · Punta Zapotal · Bagaces · Laguna de Arenal · Sardinal · 21 · Filadelfia · Cañas · 19 · Quebrada Grande · Palme · Tempate · Belén · Valle de Tempisque · La Tigra · Cabo Velas · Cartagena · Temisque · Cordillera de Tilarán · Ciudad Quesada (San Carlo · Veintisiete de Abril · Santa Cruz · Quebrada Honda · Colorado · Las Juntas · Alto Villegas · Diria · San Antonio · Finca Cóbano · Miramar · San Ramón · Nicoya · Isla Chira · Chomes · Macacona · Cuajiniquil · Mansión · Golfo de Nicoya · Pitahaya · Turrúca · Nosara · Hojancha · Carmona · **Puntarenas** · 17 · San Mateo · Punta Guiones · Lepanto · **Puntarenas** · Bahía Gigante · San Juan de Mata · Merce · Sámara · Bejuco · Paquera · Isla Tortuga · Manzanillo · Punta Conejo · 34 · Punta Coyote · Arió · Jacó · Isla Cabo Blanco · Cabo Blanco · Punta Judas

PACIFIC OCEAN

Isla del Coco

0 — 2 km
0 — 2 miles

Punta Agujas · **Isla Manuelita** · **Isla Pájara** · Bahía Chatham · Bahía Wafer · Cabo Barreto · **Parque Nacional Isla del Coco** · Cabo Atrevida · Cerro Yglésias 634 · Cerro Jesús Jiménez 430 · Cabo Lionel · **Isla Muela** · Cabo Dampier

CARIBBEAN SEA

NICARAGUA

Indio
Caño Negro
Deseado
San Juan del Norte
Punta Castilla
ucitas
San Juan
Trinidad
llanura de San Carlos
Boca Sahino
Heredia
Las Medias
Puerto Viejo de Sarapiquí
Llanura de Tortuguero
Suerte
Pital
La Virgen
Las Horquetas
Cariari
Limón
Venecia
Volcán Cacho Negro 2150
Rita
Roxana
Río Jiménez
Parismina
inchona
Guapiles
CORDILLERA CENTRAL
Jiménez
Florida
Siquirres
Batán
Matina
ecia Charrizal
San José de la Montaña
Santa Cruz
Peralta
Puerto Limón
Isla Uvita
Alajuela
Volcán Irazú 3452
Petróleo
Heredia
Pavas
San José
Turrialba
Pavones
Limón
Finca Banaga
Escazú
Desamparados
Tucurrique
Cahuita
Tabarcia
Aserrí
Cartago
Platanillo
Vesta
Punta Cahuita
San Gabriel
Orosí
Pejibaye
Valle de la Estrella
angrejal
San Andrés
Cartago
Bibrí
Punta Uva
Punta Mona
San José
San Marcos de Tarrazú
CORDILLERA
Shiroles
Valle de Talamanca
Bratsi
Parrita
San Lorenzo
Cerro Urán 3333
Telire
Coén
Sixaola
arenas de Parrita
Naranjito
DE
I. Colón
arrita
Río Nuevo
Rivas
Teribé
Changuinola
I. Cristóbal
uepos
Savegre
San Isidro
General Viejo
Cerro Ení 3097
Almirante
Barú
Cajón
San Pedro
TALAMANCA
Cerro Kamúk 3549
PANAMÁ
Pejibaye
Volcán
Buenos Aires
Punta Uvita
Cerro Fábrega 3336
Valle de El General
Colinas
Boruca
Potrero Grande
Valle de Coto Brus
Santa Elena
Bahía de Coronado
Cortés
Palmar Sur
Valle de Diquis
Chánguena
Alturas
Puntarenas
San Vito
Isla del Caño
Bahía Drake
Drake
Limoncito
Río Sereno
Boquete
Punta San Pedrillo
Agua Buena
Sabalito
Hato del Volcán
Punta Llorona
Golfo Dulce
Golfito
Neily (Villa)
Pueblo Nuevo
Península de Osa
Puerto Jiménez
Canoas
Portón
La Concepción
Gualaca
Punta Salsipuedes
Carate
Punta Banco
La Cuesta
David
Cabo Matapalo
Puerto Armuelles
Península de Burica
Bahía de Charco Azul
I. Sevilla
Yerbazales
I. Boca Brava
Punta Burica
Isla Burica

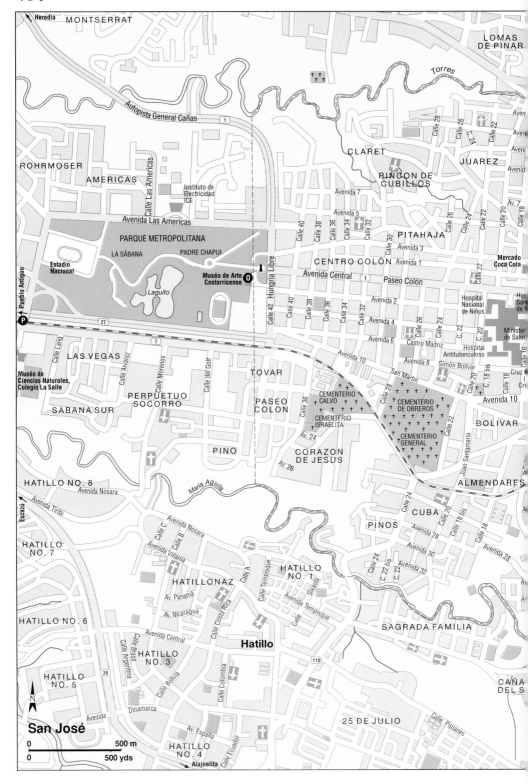

San José

San Juan
de Tibás

Llorente, Guápiles

**Calle
Blancos**

SAN GABRIEL

PINOS

San Isidra de
Coronado

IGLESIAS
FLORES

SANTA
TERESA

VOLIO

San Francisco

COLONIA FLORIDA

UNION

Centro Comercial
El Pueblo
(Shopping Center)

COLONIA
DEL RIO

SO DE
VACA

Penitenciaria
Central/Muséo
de Niños

TOURNON

Spyrogyra Jardín
de Mariposa
(Butterfly Garden)

Asilo
Carlos María
Ulloa

LOMAS
ESCALANTE

PARQUE
ZOOLÓGICA
SIMÓN
BOLÍVAR

Torres

Muséo de Jade,
Instituto Nacional
de Seguros
INS

Casa Amarilla
(Min. of Foreign Aff.)

Iglesia de
Santa
Teresita

Radiográfico
Costarricense

ercado
e Borbón

Correos,
Muséo de
Postal

PARQUE
ESPAÑA

Fábrica Nac.
de Licores

Ferrocarril
al Atlántico

Mercado
Central

Banco Nacional
de Costa Rica

Club
Unión

Iglesia
El Carmen

PARQUE
MORAZÁN

Biblioteca
Nacional

PARQUE
NACIONAL

Presentes

Banco
Central

Palacio Nacional,
Asamblea Legislativa
(Parliament)

Aduana Theatre

Banco
de Costa
Rica

PARQUE
CENTRAL

Teatro
Melico
Salazár

Muséo
de Oro

Plaza
de la
Democracia

Iglesia
La Merced

Teatro
Nacional

ITC

Gran
Hotel

Centenario

Av. 2

Paseo Ruben Dario

Dirección
General
de Estadística
y Censos

Teatro
Rex

Catedral
Metropolitana

Inst. de
Turismo
Costarricense

Iglesia La
Soledad

Tribunales
de Justicia

Dirección General de
Migración, Departamento
de Extranjeros

Archivos
Nacionales

Estación General
de Bomberos
(Fire Station)

Muséo de
Criminología,
Corte Suprema
de Justitia

Servicio de
Parques
Nacionales

Iglesia
La Dolorosa

Rep. de Chile

San
Martin

Paseo Sarmiento

DOS
FINOS

MANGOS

Republica de Panamá

CERRITO

MONTE
ALEGRE

Ministerio de
Obras Públicas
y Transportes

Plaza
Gonzales
Viques

Ferrocarril
Eléctrico al
Pacífico

Instituto
Geográfico
Nacional IGN

Dr. Carit

Autopista Estado de Israel

CORDOBA

MONGITO

INVU

UJARRAS

LUNA PARK

COLOMBARI

SAN
DIMAS

EL TREBOL

Calle Alemanes

LUISAS

CARMEN

Calle Moreno Cañas

Río María Aguilar

BRASIL

MENDEZ

**San
Sebastian**

Laguito

PARQUE
DE LA PAZ

SANTA
MARTA

HISPANO

San Rafael Abajo

Desamparados

SAN JOSE

With modern high-rises ranked alongside tin-roofed, faded colonial villas, Costa Rica's capital may seem a jumble at first. Yet it possesses a certain Tico charm

Map on pages 130–131

San José

The growth, some might say the flowering, of San José, began on that day, sometime during the first half of the 19th century, when Europe decided to have its daily cup of coffee.

By the 1850s, San José had been transformed from a humble village to a boom town. Everything had to be the best, the most modern, the most European. With every bag of coffee that was exported, there was a proportionate enrichment of the economic, social and cultural life of the Josefinos. And as the city became wealthy, so its inhabitants became more refined, more sophisticated and more worldly.

The golden age

By the end of the 19th century, San José was booming from the profits of its coffee exports. It was the third city in the world to have public electric lighting, one of the first to have public telephones, the first in Central America, perhaps in all of Latin America, to initiate free and compulsory public education to all of its citizens, and the first to allow women to attend high school. Admittedly, the roads were unpaved, but most upper-class homes had pianos.

Through much of the first part of the 20th century, San José continued to prosper and build: a national library, schools, bank buildings, parks and plazas, ministries, hotels, theaters, a sumptuous post office building, bookstores, hospitals, churches, a magnificent Palace of Justice, an international airport.

And then, in 1956, Costa Rica's population passed the 1 million mark. The international focus of influence had shifted and the people ceased coveting things European and became heavily influenced by North American standards and sensibilities.

The modern city

Cars and trucks began to appear where there had only been the gentle horse and buggy, ox carts, pedestrians and bicycles. The population doubled over the next two decades.

By the mid-1970s, the air in San José had become noticeably dirty and the once civilized, narrow streets had become overwhelmed with a relentless rush of cars and people, all seemingly in a big hurry to get somewhere. Graceful, ornate old buildings were torn down and replaced with harsh, ugly copies of North American modern architecture. San José, the civilized 19th-century city, could not adapt its physical limitations to meet the demands of its raucous 20th-century people. And today, the realization of this conflict is a city that, by any standards, is traffic-clogged and unimpressive.

PRECEDING PAGES: a section of ceiling in the National Theater. **LEFT:** political exposure at a tender age. **BELOW:** the National Youth Symphonic Orchestra.

Oases of calm

Fortunately, amid the stench of diesel fumes, and the hordes of people, there are still some islands of repose where you can rest and refresh yourself as you search to find the heart of this city. The National Theater is probably the most beautiful building in the country and its coffee shop is a favorite place; quiet, elegant, yet alive. And to relax, sipping a *refresco natural* on the veranda of the Grand Hotel, while listening to marimba bands and the burble of 20 different languages as other people rush around the Plaza, should not be missed.

The National Museum and the Gold Museum are worth seeking out; there are souvenir shops, good theaters, many decent, if unremarkable restaurants, an abundance of cabarets and night clubs, and a few interesting art galleries. There are also, tucked here and there, some extraordinary remnants of old San José, hints of what a handsome, delightful place this used to be, not so long ago.

Getting your bearings

Before you embark on the following tour of the city, or indeed go looking for any address within San José, sit down with our map (*see pages 130–131*) and familiarize yourself with the way it is laid out. The city is organized on a grid system of numbered streets (*calles*), which run north to south, and avenues (*avenidas*), which run east to west. The southern and eastern streets have even numbers, the northern and western streets use odd numbers.

Confusingly, however, buildings are not numbered and, for the most part, only in downtown San José do streets have names. Addresses are often given in the following format: Metropolitan Cathedral, Calle Central, Ave 2–4, meaning that it is on the Calle Central between Avenida 2 and Avenida 4. Alternatively

BELOW: a bustling downtown shopping street.

and more commonly, addresses are given in terms of distance in meters (metros), north, south, east or west from known landmarks. It's as well to know, however, that Ticos often equate a city block with 100 meters (no matter how big or small it really is). The end result of all this is that Ticos and visitors alike can be seen wandering the city streets perpetually stopping one another to ask for directions. The good news is that people are generally happy to help and, if nothing else, it gives you a chance to talk to the locals.

The best time to walk in San José is on a Sunday morning, when there is less traffic on the streets. Or go early or late in the day, perhaps just before twilight, when the rush and roar of the city has quietened down somewhat.

Plaza de la Cultura

The Plaza de la Cultura marks the heart of the city. This large square is a popular meeting point for traders, artisans, street musicians, painters, actors, in fact just about anybody and everybody. The pride of the square is the **Teatro Nacional** , without doubt the finest building in San José, if not all Costa Rica. Its construction was financed by 19th-century coffee barons, who, embarrassed that there was no appropriate venue for the world renowned opera star, Adelina Patti, to perform in Costa Rica (she had snubbed San José on her 1890 tour of Central America), offered to pay a tax on every bag of coffee exported.

Modeled after the Paris Opera House and Neoclassical in style, the theatre was opened in 1897 with a production of *Faust*. It is on four levels, with a very well-equipped stage system and its main audience seating floor is adjustable to different heights. The floor plan is in the form of a horseshoe, and the acoustics are excellent. The detailing was done by Spanish and Italian artisans. Ironi-

Map on pages 130–131

ABOVE: mountains of fruit for sale at the Central Market. **BELOW:** quiet Sunday morning on the Paseo Colón.

City Buses

Buses are ubiquitous in San José. They go everywhere throughout the city and its surrounding areas. Some downtown streets are clogged with them: shiny new Mercedes models, freshly washed and festively painted with murals on their rear windows; sooty, rusty wrecks emitting thick black smoke; re-cycled school buses from the US, scrupulously cared for and graced with fanciful names to give them new life.

Whether new and slick or decrepit and smoky, the buses have a common trait. They are wonderful windows into Costa Rican life. Most everyone uses them: students on their way to classes, women in heels, dressy clothes and impeccable make-up on their way to work, country folk coming into town to do business of one kind or another, young mothers taking children to doctors' appointments at the social security hospital, men with briefcases and neat slacks and shirts. They're all on the bus, heading this way or that.

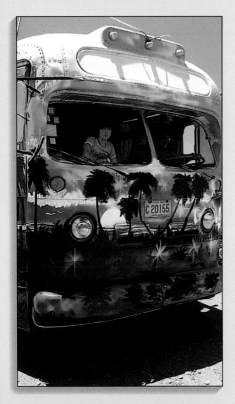

And for a fistful of colones, you can climb aboard and join in the great comings and goings of life on the Central Valley. A bus ride in San José is not particularly comfortable, especially during peak hours, but there's no better or more enjoyable way to make quick and often delicious observations on Tico life and character.

For one thing, chivalry is still alive. Or is it a simple sense of decency, of caring for others, a quiet courtesy? Young men will assist older men or women up the steps, a seated passenger will offer to hold your packages while you stand, someone will always offer his or her seat to an older person or a pregnant woman. The bus driver will wait for someone making a last-minute dash.

A *young boy, known to the bus driver by name, boards on Paseo Colón, and for a few stops, becomes the bus's official door-opener. Then the boy tires of the game and, saying goodbye to the driver, leaps off at the next stop.

A wizened old campesino, returning from a trip to the city, takes a long time to board. He carries with him, a heavy burlap bag, redolent of coffee beans and *pejibaye*.

A small girl in a rumpled pink dress enters the parked bus, waiting for its scheduled departure at the Coca Cola bus stop. She speaks to the driver, then stands at the front of the bus, singing a mournful song about love. When she finishes, she moves down the aisle with an open hand, into which we drop our small change.

Take at least one bus ride in San José. Board near the beginning of the line, when you can still get a seat, and watch the rush of humanity come aboard, pausing to place their fare in the driver's hand, pushing past the turnstile, greeting friends and neighbors as they make their way down the aisle, more passengers stop after stop, until it isn't possible to squeeze another body on.

It's a good idea to take a ride outside the city too. The best trip is the Periferica Bus, which as the name suggests goes around the periphery of the city, and allows you a glimpse of some of San José's most desirable suburbs. ❑

LEFT: traveling "a la Tica" is a quick way to get an insight into local life.

cally, Adelina Patti never did come to Costa Rica, but performances by Costa Rica's top-quality National Symphony Orchestra are given each Sunday morning. There are also daily tours where you can admire the magnificent main hall, foyer and central staircase, decorated with marble, gold, bronze, tropical woods, crystal chandeliers, velvet drapes and statuary. The ceiling fresco is famous and features a bucolic scene of coffee and banana pickers (*see pages 128–29*).

The **Cafe del Teatro Nacional** features changing art exhibits and is a very popular place, serving excellent salads, snacks, desserts and speciality coffees.

On the north side of the square, opposite the National Theatre. **The Gran Hotel Costa Rica ❸** is an unremarkable building, but is renowned as a meeting place for tourists and foreign residents who fill out its charming outdoor cafe where musicians often entertain with marimbas. Inside is a 24-hour casino.

Below the Plaza de la Cultura is the capital's best museum, the **Museo de Oro ❹** (Gold Museum). On the east side of the square in cool cavernous rooms this collection has recently been remodelled and features over 2,000 brilliant pre-Columbian artefacts made by the indigenous peoples from the southwestern part of the country. Highlights include tiny figures half-man, half-bird, and erotic statuettes (open Tue–Sun; entrance fee). The museum also contains the National Coin Collection and exhibitions of modern art.

Before leaving the Plaza de la Cultura pay a visit to the Costa Rica Tourist Office (ICT) for news of what is on in town.

More museums

A short walk west of the Plaza de la Cultura along Avenida 2 is the **Parque Central ❺** (Central Park), another great place for people watching. Ticos com-

Map
on pages
130–131

TIP

On the Avenida Central side of the Plaza de la Cultura is a branch of Pop's Ice cream parlor, generally agreed to be the best in Costa Rica. It is always crowded.

BELOW: the National Theater.

At the northern end of the Parque Central, look for the neo-Classical facade of the Teatro Popular Melico Salazar. A folklore show is staged here every Tuesday.

BELOW: the Central Market is one of the most colorful and dynamic places in the city.

plained when most of the park's trees were cut down in the 1980s, leaving only a few Royal Palms, but at least it is now a safer place. The Gaudí-like kiosk in the center of the park was donated by the Somoza family of Nicaragua and sometimes hosts open-air concerts on weekends.

Directly in front of the park is the huge columnar **Catedral Metropolitana** ❺ (Metropolitan Cathedral). It is of little architectural merit, but do notice the finely wooden carved ceiling of the Chapel of the Holy Sacrament; also its walls, so carefully adorned with flower motifs that it almost looks as if they have been tiled. The cathedral provides a refuge of peace from the hot bustling city and midday masses are well attended by local people.

Due north of the Parque Central, along Calle 2 is the **Correos** ❻ (Central Post Office) in a grand old building which also houses the **Museo de Postal** (Post Office Museum, open Mon–Fri 8am–5pm, Sat 8am–noon).

Two blocks west of the Post Office on Avenida 1 is the **Mercado Central** ❼ (Central Market) the city's best market, dating from 1881. There are over 200 stalls selling everything from old kitchen utensils to saddle bags, fresh fish, coffee and spices by the kilo, to religious icons. The prices are some of the cheapest in the city. At the centre of the hall are the snack stands, a good place to find real Tico food at real Tico prices. Keep your hand on your wallet as pickpockets operate here (and just love tourists), but don't be deterred from diving into this den to witness gritty Tico life at first hand (open daily; 6.30am–6.30pm).

If you have children in tow, you might at this point like to make a diversion a few blocks north to the old Penitenciaria Central (city jail) to the **Museo de Niños** ❽ (Children's Museum), which has lots of interesting interactive exhibits

and is entertaining for adults, too. There is a good summary of the Ticos' historical developments, with models of Indian huts, Caribbean wooden shacks and modern housing (open daily; entrance fee). It is in a rough part of town, however, so take a cab, rather than walking there.

On Avenida 7, on the north side of the Parque España, is the excellent **Museo de Jade** ❾ (Jade Museum). It can be found on the 11th floor of the National Insurance Institute, better known as the **INS Building**, a useful landmark which also offers great views over the city. Alongside the museum's carefully crafted jade pieces (*see page 28*), most of which are *colgantes* (amulets or pendants), are masterpieces of pre-Hispanic sculpture from all regions of the country.

Opposite the Jade Museum is one of the capital's most interesting old buildings, the **Iron School**, shipped here in 1892 from Belgium to house 1,000 students. Next door to the museum is the **Casa Amarilla** (Yellow House), now the home of the Foreign Ministry, but built in 1816 as the Court of Justice. You can take a look inside its foyer.

Nature in the city

A block north of the Jade Museum is the **Parque Zoológico Simon Bolivar** ❿ (Simon Bolivar Zoo), at present a rather sorry excuse for a zoo with small cages and compounds. Plans are under way, however, to turn it into the sort of natural showcase of which Costa Rica will be proud so, depending on progress, it may be worth a visit. The park makes for a pleasant stroll especially on a weekday morning, when you may have it all to yourself (open daily 9am–4.30pm; entrance fee).

Immediately north, at the back of the park, is the **Spyrogyra Jardin de Mariposa** ❸ (Spyrogyra Butterfly Garden). It's not far as the butterfly flies, but the entrance is a long way off on foot, so you will need to take a cab from the zoopark to get there. Among the few remaining forested areas in the capital, one of the main aims of Spyrogyra is to help rural women find alternative sources of income from laboring in the fields by exporting butterfly cocoons to Europe and the US (open daily 8am–3pm; entrance fee). In addition to the many colorful butterflies, there are gardens and hummingbirds to enjoy.

Arts, history and culture

Also close to the INS building is the **Fábrica Nacional de Licores** ❶ (National Liquor Factory) also known by the initials FANAL. Founded in 1856, it has been turned into an arts and cultural center. which is somewhat confusingly also known as the Centro Nacional de la Cultura y la Ciencia or CENAC (National Center of Culture and Science). Pop into the pretty courtyard and amphitheater which leads to another part of the complex; the **Museum of Contemporary Art and Design** which has changing exhibitions of art, sculpture and photography. FANAL is open Tues–Sun; entrance free, check the *Tico Times* for what's on.

A few blocks east of here is the **Parque Nacional** ❶ (National Park). This is the largest of San José's parks, where lovers drape themselves over park benches and bureaucrats eat their lunches under the shade of the 50 or so native

Map on pages 130–131

ABOVE: crested iguana at the zoo.
BELOW: central post office (*Correos*) and Post Office Museum.

Map on pages 130–131

tree species. It's a very pleasant place by day, but is dangerous by night. In the center of the park is a monument depicting victory in the war against the hated *filibustero*, William Walker (*see page 45*).

Two blocks south of here, on calle 17, is the **Museo Nacional**  (National Museum), housed in the old Bellavista fortress, which still bears the bullet marks from the Civil War. Constructed in 1870, the building served as a barracks until the abolition of the army in 1949. The collections provide an overview of Costa Rica's history and culture, and include displays on burial ceremonies, a treasury of gold pieces, and rustic furniture from the Colonial period. In the courtyard are cannons and some of the mysterious stone spheres found in the south of the country (*see pages 28, 251*). (The museum is open Tues–Sun; entrance fee.)

From the terrace of the building there are fine views down onto the city and the amphitheater-like Plaza de la Democracia where open-air concerts are sometimes held. Artisans congregate to sell handicrafts and souvenirs, and even if you don't find too much from Costa Rica there are generally bargains to be had in handmade clothes from Guatemala and El Salvador.

ABOVE: gold plate, Museo de Oro.
BELOW: potatoes make a change from rice and beans.
RIGHT: foxgloves.

Sabana Park and Pueblo Antiguo

The large grassy area of **Parque La Sabana** occupies what was Costa Rica's first international airport. The Spanish-style building, housing the departure hall and control tower, has been converted into the **Museo de Arte Costarricense**  (Museum of Costa Rican Art). This features revolving exhibitions of works by the country's finest 19th- and 20th-century painters and sculptors as well as that of international artists (open Tues–Sun; entrance fee).

In the *Salon Dorado* (upper story), French artist Luis Ferrón has immortalised Costa Rican history in a striking-looking stucco and bronze mural. *

In the south east corner of the park is the Museum of Natural Sciences, also known as the **Museo La Salle**. The main attraction is a huge collection of stuffed animals from Costa Rica and beyond. With pickled snakes, toads and fish, a stuffed swan suspended from the ceiling, and even a scale model of a US space shuttle, the place has a faintly eccentric air (open daily, entrance fee).

Sabana Park is a popular weekend retreat for Tico families who come here to picnic, ride their bikes, skate, play and feed the ducks in the park's many lakes. Kite vendors also do a brisk trade on breezy days. Sporting facilities include soccer fields, tennis courts, a swimming pool (only occasionally open) and jogging trails. The park should be avoided after dark, however.

A short bus ride west of Sabana Park in the district of La Uruca is the **Pueblo Antiguo**  (literally "Old Village"), an idyllic re-creation of old Costa Rica. Actors demonstrate traditional craft skills and bygone agricultural techniques, and there are other shows plus restaurants serving local food (open Mon–Sat 9am–5pm; Sun and public holidays 9am–9pm; entrance fee). Sunday is the best day to visit, when a fiesta is always enacted. ❑

Map on page 146

THE CENTRAL VALLEY

The heartland of Costa Rica is home to 60 percent of the nation's people. It is the center of government, agriculture and commerce, and has the oldest cities and many cultural treasures

The Central Valley *(Valle Central)*, or Central Plateau *(Meseta Central)*, as it is often called, is neither, strictly speaking, a valley nor a plateau since it contains both kinds of landscape. The Central Highlands might be a more apt name for this area, only 24 km by 64 km (15 miles by 40 miles), where two mountain ranges meet. You'll find rich, volcanic hills and river-filled valleys, with altitudes reaching up to 1,500 meters (4,500 ft).

The good life

The countryside is beautiful and variable. The climate is salubrious. The air is sweet and soft. The people are generally friendly, dignified and independent. Volcanoes, some still active and smoking, others dormant or extinct, rise up above the hills around the valley, and above them, a big sky is constantly changing – dark, charcoal rain clouds; intense, searing patches of blue; fluffy white cumulus; and occasional rainbows; all come and go in quick succession.

There are misty, almost enchanted places like the Orosí Valley or dusty farm towns like Santa Ana, adobe villages that sing of old Costa Rica, such as Barva, and crowded, noisy, relentlessly vital cities, like San José or Cartago. And they're all easily accessible. Daytrips by bus or rented car, or with tour groups can easily be arranged.

Passing through the small, highland towns and villages, you see what in Central America is the unusual and impressive sight of people living in houses on plots of land that they themselves own and farm. Neighborhoods are often a hodgepodge of larger, fancy homes and small, humble ones. Housewives in housedresses and aprons chat in front yards as they watch their babies. Children in school uniforms talk and play together as they walk up the road for lunch at home. Produce from back yard fruit trees and gardens is for sale on little tables or stands in front of houses: strawberries and berry preserves, homemade farmers' cheese and sour cream, oranges, candied, stuffed grapefruit, mangoes and tomatoes. Visitors to shops and stands, restaurants and parks are accepted with a mild, easy curiosity. No one seems especially surprised to have a *gringo* walk into the local *soda* and order *arroz con pollo* (chicken and rice).

San José, Alajuela, Cartago and Heredia are the largest and most important cities of the Central Valley. Radiating out from San José are busy towns and suburbs, each with its own flavor and identity: international Escazú, bland Rohrmoser, exclusive Los Yoses with its lovely old residences, San Pedro, home of the University of Costa Rica, the largest shopping mall in Central America, and many good restaurants. There are also four national parks to explore, several volca-

PRECEDING PAGES: grazing in the hills above Heredia. **LEFT:** Central Valley coffee plantation. **BELOW:** the parish church is the focus of every Costa Rican village.

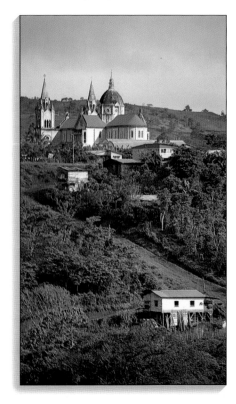

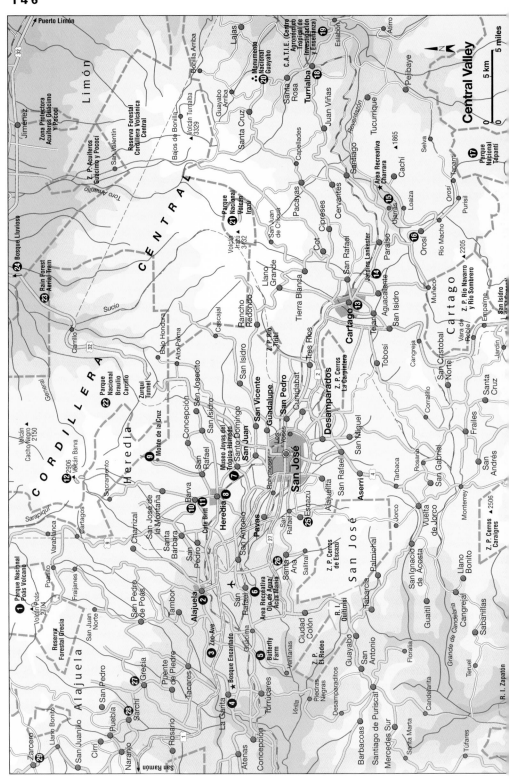

Central Valley

5 km
5 miles

↑ Puerto Limón

L i m ó n

C E N T R A L

C O R D I L L E R A

H e r e d i a

A l a j u e l a

S a n   J o s é

C a r t a g o

San José

Alajuela

Heredia

Cartago

Turrialba

Desamparados

Zona Protectora
Acuíferos Guácimo
y Pococí

Reserva Forestal
Cordillera Volcánica
Central

Z. P. Acuíferos
Guácimo y Pococí

Monumento
Nacional Guayabo

C.A.T.I.E. (Centro
Agronómico Tropical de
Investigación y Enseñanza)

Parque Nacional
Braulio Carrillo

Parque Nacional
Poás Volcano

Reserva
Forestal Grecia

Rain Forest
Aerial Tram

Bosque Lluvioso

Parque Nacional
Volcán Irazú

Área Recreativa
Charrara

Jardín Lankester

Parque
Nacional
Tapantí

Z. P. Río Navarro
y Río Sombrero

Z. P. Cerros
La Carpintera

Z. P. Cerros
de Escazú

Z. P. Cerros
Caraigres

Z. P.
El Rodeo

R. I.
Quitirrisí

R. I. Zapatón

Área Recreativa
Ojo de Agua /
Acua Manía

Butterfly
Farm

Bosque Encantado

Museo Joyas del
Trópico Húmedo

Monte de la Cruz

Zurquí
Tunnel

Café Britt

Zoo-Ave

Volcán Poás
2704

Volcán
Cacho Negro
2150

Volcán Barva
2906

Volcán Turrialba
3329

Volcán Irazú
3432

① Parque Nacional Poás Volcano
② Alajuela
③ Zoo-Ave
④ Bosque Encantado
⑤ Butterfly Farm
⑥ Área Recreativa Ojo de Agua / Acua Manía
⑦ Museo Joyas del Trópico Húmedo
⑧ Heredia
⑨ Monte de la Cruz
⑩ Barva
⑪ Café Britt
⑫ Volcán Barva
⑬ Cartago
⑭ Jardín Lankester
⑮ Área Recreativa Charrara
⑯ Orosí
⑰ Parque Nacional Tapantí
⑱ Turrialba
⑲ C.A.T.I.E.
⑳ Monumento Nacional Guayabo
㉑ Parque Nacional Volcán Irazú
㉒ Parque Nacional Braulio Carrillo
㉓ Rain Forest Aerial Tram
㉔ Bosque Lluvioso
㉕ Escazú
㉖ Santa Ana
㉗
㉘ Sarchí
㉙ Zarcero

Map on page 146

noes to climb and Guayabo National Monument, the country's most important archaeological site.

Though most travelers come to the Central Valley between December and March to escape the winter chill of North America and Europe, these months are Costa Rica's dry season, its "summer." Frequent travelers to the area know that it is the rainy season in Costa Rica, with its afternoon downpours and dramatic displays of lightning, when the Central Valley is at its magnificent best: lush, green, bursting with life and color. Best of all the air and San José itself is kept clean by a daily bath.

Poás Volcano National Park

The most developed of all the parks is **Parque Nacional Volcán Poás ❶**, a popular attraction. It is only 37 km (25 miles) from San José on good roads leading through the city of Alajuela. Poás can become crowded and cloudy, so it's best to visit early in the day when views are better and before the throngs arrive. The cool freshness of the air as you ascend the mountain is invigorating, but it can get chilly and rainy, so dress appropriately.

A map of the nature trails is available at the Visitors' Center, where there is a gift shop, an insect exhibit, and a cafe. From a lookout point above the crater, there is an overview of the volcano, which in May 1989 shot ash a mile into the air. The main crater, which is 1.5 km (1 mile) wide and 300 meters (1,000 ft) deep, is one of the largest in the world. Poás, unlike the volcanoes of Irazú and Arenal, rarely has violent eruptions and is one of the more accessible active volcanoes on the continent. It is active in 40-year cycles and is currently producing acid-like rain and sulphurous gases. It is therefore not advisable to stay for more than 20 minutes near the active crater. Just a 20-minute hike away is another crater, which is filled with a jewel-like lake.

ABOVE: mangoes in Alajuela.
BELOW: a streambed in Braulio Carrillo National Park.

Well-maintained trails lead through a vivid landscape rich with wildflowers and with a multitude of mosses, bromeliads and ferns. An additional attraction: the famed quetzal (*see page 206*) can even be seen here at certain times of the year.

After wandering through this wonderland, descend from the park to one of the nearby restaurants for lunch and enjoy the local speciality of *fresas en leche*, strawberries blended with milk, or stop at one of the many roadside stands to buy strawberry preserves and cookies made by local women. To spend more time in the fresh, mountain air consider an overnight stay at La Providencia Ecological Reserve.

Alajuela and environs

As you descend some 200 meters (660 ft) into **Alajuela ❷** (population 165,000), it becomes noticeably warmer. To relax, you can join old-timers in the central park, amidst an orchard of mango and other mature trees. Here the colorful Festival of Mangoes is held for nine days in July.

Alajuela is the birthplace of Juan Santamaría, the young Costa Rican whose courage was responsible for the routing of William Walker and his *filibusteros* from Costa Rica in 1856 (*see page 45*). **The Museo**

Juan Santamaría in the former jail, one block from the central park, tells his story (open Tues-Sun; entrance free).

From Alajuela take the old highway towards the Pacific, La Garita, en route is **Zoo-Ave ❸**, which has over 60 species of Costa Rican birds, as well as monkeys, deer, crocodiles and giant tortoises (open daily; entrance fee). **La Garita ❹** which, among several other places in Costa Rica, is said to have the best climate in the country, is expansive and green, filled with lovely homes and gardens, fields of dark green coffee bushes and plant nurseries (*viveros*). Stop at a nursery and walk through rows of magnificent ferns, palms, ficus and flowering plants. The restaurant La Fiesta del Máiz, open on weekends, is an interesting experience. It features the near-endless variety of tasty dishes that Ticos make from corn. Customers can sample them all.

A few kilometers southeast near Guacima is **The Butterfly Farm ❺**, a breeding farm for over 500 different kinds of exotic butterflies, which are exported by the tens of thousands to waiting markets in Europe. The Butterfly Farm is full of interest, with its waterfall, extensive tropical plantings, and the endless color variations of the butterflies themselves (open daily 9–6pm; tours 9–11am and 1–3pm; entrance fee). The Blue Crowned Motmot Restaurant, on the same site, is recommended.

Water holes

If it's a warm day and you feel like cooling down and splashing around, then stop on the way back to San José (6 km/4 miles before town) at the **Area Recreativa Ojo de Agua ❻** (open daily 8am–5pm; entrance fee). Thousands of gallons of water pump out of this natural spring every hour of the day and around

The most spectacular of all Costa Rica's butterflies is the Blue Morpho, a veritable giant which grows to between 13–20 cm (5–8 inches) long.

BELOW:
Volcán Poás in an active phase; signs warn visitors not to linger too long near the summit.

it has been created swimming pools and a boating lake. Though it may sound a paradox, the wet season is the best time to go, when the spring is in full flood. At weekends, however, Ojo de Agua is very busy with locals. The water isn't just used for recreational purposes, it is also pumped to Puntarenas to use as a major part of its water supply.

Map on page 146

Coffee country

A day trip to the province of Heredia, the center of Costa Rica's coffee production, quickly takes you away from the heat and clatter of San José. Just 24 km (15 miles) from the city, you can walk in an evergreen forest or cloud forest reserve rivaling those of much more remote and inaccessible areas.

En route to Heredia, around 5 km (3 miles) from San José, up the hill from Rio Villa Bridge at the entry to Santo Domingo is the **Museo Joyas del Trópico Húmedo** ❼ (Jewels of the Rainforest Museum) also known as the Whitten Collection. Here you can see some 50,000 specimens of butterflies, beetles and insects from all over the world, ingeniously displayed on walls and stands in the rooms of a large house (open daily; entrance fee).

Heredia ❽ (population 75,000) lies 9 km (6 miles) north of San José, and is known as *La Ciudad de los Flores* (The City of Flowers). The city was first settled in 1706 by Spaniards, and is famous for having the largest number of blue-eyed people in Costa Rica. Many stores full of merchandise suggest that this coffee-rich area is affluent, and, indeed, by Costa Rican standards, it is. **The National University** is located in Heredia; it turns out the nation's teachers and has one of the best veterinarian schools in Latin America. It also features a **Marine Zoological Museum** which exhibits over 2,000 examples of Costa

ABOVE: the lovely church of Sarchi.
BELOW: after church on Sunday; spectators at a soccer match.

Rica's varied marine life (closed lunchtimes and weekends; entrance free). The old town center, with its colonial Casa de Cultura and lovely church, is a pleasant place to stroll. The **Inmaculada Concepcion**, constructed in 1796, is adorned with bells brought from Cuzco, Peru and its "seismic baroque" construction has enabled it to survive many earth tremors.

The newer section of Heredia looks like many modern Developing World cities, with dangling wires, and electrical signs hanging across the streets advertising the global spread of American brands such as Lucky Strike and Pepsi.

TIP

After a hike in the Bosque del Río, pay a visit to the Hotel Chalet Tirol, where top-quality French cooking refreshes weary walkers.

Alpine scenery

Take the road to **San Rafael** and begin the ascent into the mountains from there. Villas above the town are architecturally alpine, often down to Tyrolean paintings on the shutters. Driving through here, you get the feeling of having suddenly entered into an Austrian watercolor landscape. Wealthy Ticos of earlier generations were traditionally educated in Europe and returned to their country with a great appreciation for the architecture of Northern Europe, which is evident in this cool, mountain area. Now, many young Ticos go to graduate schools in North American universities, and with this shift in academic background cultural affinities are changing.

Above San Rafael the temperature drops dramatically and you will pass a sign to El Castillo Country Club (open to members only). The road beyond El Castillo continues to **Monte de la Cruz** ❾ where a small shrine sits in a private cloud forest reserve. For Sunday hikers from San Rafael, far below, this is a favorite destination.

BELOW: the coffee crop, all picked by hand, earns Costa Rica over US$200 million in exports each year.

Proceed downhill to the fork and turn back uphill to El Tirol. People stroll the roads of Costa Rica, especially on Sundays, the traditional day for visiting with family. Bus services are reduced on Sundays, further necessitating walking. Tico drivers are used to sharing the roads with pedestrians, but some foreigners in rental cars can find such driving conditions unnerving. Before El Castillo, look for a sign indicating **Bosque de la Hoja**. Here, you can hike along a lovely road bordered by graceful trees, for a mile or so, to the Heredia Water Works, and from there, walk to other unpopulated areas that are perfect for hiking.

Tell the guard at El Tirol gatehouse that you are going to **Hotel Chalet Tirol** and drive through a residential area of weekend cottages and retirement homes set in alpine fields. A good road leads through a cypress forest where sun filters warmly through branches and dapples meadow wild flowers.

Hotel Chalet Tirol sits in the middle of a cloud forest reserve bordering Braulio Carrillo National Park. A fern-choked trail winding under orchid and bromeliad-laden old trees allows visitors to hike several hours through the cloud reserve to the border of the national park. A grove of A-frame wooden cottages awaits those who choose to spend the night.

As you descend, the warmth of the valley below is welcome. The road to San José de la Montaña is lined with flowers grown for export. On the road above San

José de la Montaña, in wonderfully fresh, cool mountain air, is El Pórtico Hotel, offering conference rooms, a comfortable bar and dining room and acres of green hills with good hiking trails.

Map on page 146

Barva and environs

In **Barva de Heredia** ⑩, founded in 1561, colonial-era adobe houses surrounding the central park are being restored, giving the entire area the atmosphere of a colonial town. If you stand on the steps in front of the adobe **Basilica de Barva,** which dates back to 1767, and look out over the red tile-roofed adobe houses to the mountains beyond, you will get a sense of what the Central Valley must have looked like in the 18th century. The Basilica de Barva was built on an ancient Indian burial ground. Close by is the small grotto of the **Virgin of Lourdes** (1913).

In the hills just outside Barva is the lively and entertaining *Aventura de Café* tour at the **Cafe Britt** ⑪ coffee farm. This includes an informative tour of the plantation, a very amusing bit of live theater, and the opportunity to sample their gourmet coffee. Aficionados can sign on for a full-day organic coffee-farming tour. Ask, too, to taste the ripe, red fruit which surrounds the coffee bean. It is surprisingly sweet and good, though beware eating too many of them at once as they act as a mild laxative. (Tours daily 9am, 11am, last approximately two hours. During the dry season, there is an additional tour at 3pm; entrance charge. Transport to and from San José available.)

Artisans from Barva produce wonderful baskets: shopping baskets, baskets used by coffee pickers, and fruit and bread baskets. You will see them on sale by the roadsides.

ABOVE: Spanish fort, Heredia.
BELOW: Lankester Gardens.

In **Santa Lucía de Barva**, 4 km (2½ miles) north of Heredia, the **Museum of Popular Culture** has renovated the charming and graceful Gonzaléz house, a 19th-century home, built just around the time that coffee cultivation was beginning to change Costa Rican life forever (closed Mon; entrance fee).

Barva Volcano

Vásquez de Coronado wrote to the Spanish king of Cartago: "I have never seen a more beautiful valley, and I have laid out a city between [its] two rivers."

There is a road to **Volcán Barva**  that runs just above the town of Barva de Heredia, and then through San José de la Montaña and on towards Sacramento. The volcano is actually on the western side of Braulio Carrillo National Park. The approach road is in terrible condition and cars must be left 4 km (2½ miles) from the park entrance, where you will see camping facilities. From here it's a good and enjoyable hike through pasture land and cloud forest to the crater lake. An alternative one-hour hike will take you to the **Laguna Brava** (2,900m/ 9,514 ft), a green lake in an extinct crater rimmed with trees.

If you are still feeling energetic, there is the smaller Laguna Copey to explore, another 40-minute walk away. You may be rewarded by sighting a quetzal there – but don't bank on it. Wherever you hike on Volcán Barva, bring raingear, a compass and waterproof shoes or boots – even in the dry season – and whatever you do keep to the designated paths.

The roads in this area criss-cross and are not at all well-marked. Even *Josefinos* taking Sunday drives have to stop passersby and ask for directions.

Cartago and south

BELOW: flowering bougainvillea in front of the 17th-century ruins of Costa Rica's oldest church at Ujarrás.

Cartago  (population 100,000) is located 23 km (14 miles) south of San José. It was the capital of Costa Rica until 1823, when it lost its status to San José. Its

Map on page 146

illustrious colonial past is obscured, however, since repeated earthquakes and eruptions of Irazú Volcano have destroyed most of the colonial buildings. Throughout their history, Cartagans have attempted to build a temple to Saint James the Apostle, patron saint of Spain. The first church, begun in 1562, was finished in 1570, and was one of only two in the entire country. When it was destroyed, a stronger building was erected in 1580 on the same site. This, too, was leveled by the trembling earth. Subsequent churches met the same fate and when Cartago's massive cathedral, begun early in the 20th century, was toppled by the 1910 earthquake, all efforts to rebuild were abandoned. The roofless walls with their empty Gothic windows still stand. The site, called **Las Ruinas** (The Ruins), is now a garden with a small pond and is a popular and romantic spot.

Cartago, once the center of Costa Rican culture, is still her religious center. The enormous **Basilica de Nuestra Señora de los Angeles** (Basilica of Our Lady of the Angels), a Byzantine structure that dominates the landscape for miles, was built in honor of Costa Rica's patron saint, *La Negrita*.

From Cartago it is a short trip to the **Jardines Lankester ⓮** in Paraíso de Cartago. It is said that Paraíso (Paradise) was named by weary Spaniards moving inland from the Atlantic coast who found its cooler weather and lack of malarial mosquitoes paradisical. English botanist Charles Lankester, sent to Costa Rica by a British company to work with coffee planting, arrived in 1900 at the age of 21. The coffee venture failed, but he decided to stay and bought 15 hectares (37 acres) of land to preserve local flora, especially orchids and bromeliads, and to regenerate a natural forest. Today, Lankester Gardens is run by the University of Costa Rica. Hundreds of species of orchids attract large numbers of birds, particularly in the peak flowering months of February through April (open daily 8–4pm; entrance fee).

The Sanchiri Lodge, not far from Lankester Gardens, is a good place to stop for a light snack. The open dining room offers guests stunning views across the Orosí valley.

Ujarrás

South of Cartago the landscape becomes green, misty and almost magical, especially during the verdant rainy season. At **Ujarrás ⓯**, in a beautiful site, are the ruins of Costa Rica's oldest church, Nuestra Señora de la Limpia, dating from the 17th century.

The first place of worship constructed in this region was not the church, but a shrine in honor of the Virgin del Rescate de Ujarrás, who, in 1565, appeared to an Indian fishing on the banks of the Reventazón River. The apparition came from inside a small trunk. The Indian carried the trunk to the center of Ujarrás, but by the time he got there, the trunk had become so heavy that even a dozen men could not lift it. The phenomenon was interpreted by the Franciscan fathers as a sign that the virgin wanted them to construct a shrine on that spot to be used by the Indians and the Spanish, and so it was constructed.

A hundred years later, in 1666, so the story goes, a band of pirates led by the notorious Mansfield and Henry Morgan landed on the Atlantic Coast of Costa Rica with the intention of sacking the country. The

BELOW: raging torrents flood the spillway of the dam at Cachí *(see p154)*.

Spanish governor, Juan Lopez de la Flor, assembled all available fighting men and sent everyone else to the mission to pray. The pirates came inland as far as Turrialba and then, mysteriously, abruptly turned back. Some say the pirates were tricked by de la Flor, who had posted the few men and guns they were in possession of at strategic points in the hills and then leaked the word that there was an ambush awaiting the pirates. A few gunshots from different points caused them to believe the ruse and retreat. Other accounts say their retreat was a miracle worked by the Virgin.

The grateful townspeople built the church of Ujarrás to commemorate the miracle, though sadly it was destroyed 100 years later by an earthquake. Its remains stand among gardens and trees draped with Spanish moss.

The Orosí River Valley

A few kilometers beyond Orosí, the **Cachí Hydroelectric Dam** channels waters from a reservoir on the Reventazón and Orosí Rivers into an immense spillway. The concrete dam structure contrasts sharply with the lush natural terrain around it, as does the power of the rushing water with the peace of the river.

Just up the road towards Orosí, some 5 km (3 miles) north of the Motel Río restaurant, on the bank of the river, is **La Casa del Soñador** (the House of the Dreamer), a simple two-story cane structure surrounded by primitive wood sculpture. Here Macedonio Quesada, a famous Costa Rican primitivist artist lived and worked until his death in 1995. His work can be seen in galleries around San José, but it is best viewed in this charming cane building where his sons now work, producing melancholy campesino and religious figures from coffee wood. Visitors are welcome.

TIP

Near Orosí is the Casona del Cafe, a restaurant set in the hacienda of a large coffee plantation. After lunch here you can rent a boat for a ride on its lake.

BELOW: the Basilica of Our Lady of the Angels is one of the country's most sacred sites.

LA NEGRITA

The origins of Cartago's Basilica of Our Lady of the Angels are rooted in the miraculous. In 1635, a young girl walking through the forest that once grew on the site of the basilica discovered a dark-skinned statue of the Virgin Mary. A priest carried the statue, called La Negrita, to the parish church, but it mysteriously returned, twice, to its location in the forest.

In 1926, the Catholic Church built a basilica on the spot to house the statue. Today in the shrine room, cases full of abandoned crutches, plaster casts and votive offerings (some made of gold) representing various parts of the body testify to the cures effected by La Negrita, Costa Rica's patron saint. Water from the spring behind the church is also said to have healing powers and the faithful fill their bottles from there.

On the saint's day, August 2, thousands of pilgrims gather at the basilica. Many walk the 22 km (14 miles) from San José; devoted penitents making the last part of the journey on their knees. Some walk from as far afield as Panamá and Nicaragua. On that day, the image of the black virgin is carried to another church in Cartago and then, in a solemn procession, through the city and back to its shrine in the basilica.

The town of **Orosí** ⑯ is untouched by the earthquakes which have leveled the colonial structures of Cartago and retains the look of an earlier Costa Rica. Make your first stop Orosí Turismo, in the center, where you can pick up useful information on the town. Visit the colonial church of San José de Orosí and the former Franciscan monastery, now the **Museum of Religious Art**, just north of the church, which features artefacts from the colonial era (open Tues-Sun; entrance fee). Take a walk around town and have a snack at one of the *sodas*.

Just above the valley, there is a lookout site (*mirador*) and park, maintained by the ICT (Costan Rican Institute of Tourism). Its large area of sloping, well-trimmed lawns provides spectacular views of the Reventazón River with Cachí to the left and Orosí to the right. It is a perfect spot for a picnic and a walk.

Tapantí National Park

The upper part of the **Orosí Valley** has enormous rainfall, rendering it unsuited for agriculture: thus it still has magnificent virgin rainforest. **Parque Nacional Tapantí** ⑰ protects the rivers which supply San José with water and electricity. It also offers great birdwatching, fishing and river swimming. Bird-watchers will want to get an early start and arrive in Tapantí when the park opens at 8am. The drive from San José is especially beautiful in the dawn. Past the coffee plant, turn right and drive for 10 km (6 miles) over poor roads.

Trails are well-marked in the lower part of the refuge. Oropendulas, black, raven-sized birds with golden tail feathers and stout ivory-colored bills, nest in colonies within the park. Clusters of 30 or more pendulous nests hang from branches high in the trees. Two eggs are laid by the oropendula females, but parasitic giant cowbirds, like the cuckoo, steal a spot in the nest for their own eggs,

Map on page 146

ABOVE: Orosí's church, the oldest in Costa Rica.
BELOW: the late sculptor, Macedonio Quesada.

letting oropendula females raise their chicks. An exchange is affected, however, as the baby cowbirds, which feed on botflies, keep the baby oropendulas free from these parasites. Park visitors usually hear oropendulas before seeing them. The males let out a gurgling, liquid song and then bow to the females in courtship displays.

The creek running parallel to Oropendula Trail is filled with smooth, warm boulders which invite hikers to sit, cool their feet in the water, and perhaps lie back for a mid-morning snooze in the sun. However, it is always advisable to take raingear and warm clothes on the trails.

Turrialba

Turrialba ⓲ is a busy town, its streets and parks bustling with people of all ages, talking, yelling, buying, selling. The open fruit and vegetable market which lines the sidewalk in front of the railroad station features some of the freshest and best-looking produce available in Costa Rica, most of it grown in the hills above town. Turrialba's reputation as a whitewater river rafting center is growing, and rafters and kayakers from all over the world are discovering the Reventazón and Pacuare Rivers (*see pages 98–99*).

Just a few miles beyond the town of Turrialba on the highway is CATIE, the **Centro Agronómico Tropical de Investigación y Enseñanza** ⓳ (Center for Tropical Agronomy Research and Teaching). On this 800-hectare (2,000-acre) research plantation, scientists are experimenting with the introduction of more than 5,000 varieties of 335 species of crops with economic potential. Over 2,500 varieties of coffee, 450 varieties of cacao, as well as many varieties of bananas and pejibaye palms are part of the seed bank of CATIE. Work is being

ABOVE: Turrialba is becoming a popular rafting center.
BELOW: the symbiosis of oxen and egret.

Map on page 146

done here on the critical problems of deforestation, overgrazing and the sensitive ecology of the river basins. Guides demonstrate the cultivation, processing and care of palms, coffee, cacao, and orchids. (If you are not with a group, call ahead to arrange a tour, tel: 556-6431.)

Visitors to Catie and the surrounding areas usually stay at the Hotel Wagelia or at the basic Hotel Interamericano. About 3 miles (5 km) out of town on the road toward Siquirres is the very luxurious Casa Turire, a lavish plantation-style hotel in the grounds of a sugar cane, coffee and macadamia nut plantation. In the mountains above the valley, not far away, are the Turrialtico and the Pochotel, which has cabins with lovely views to the Caribbean Coast.

Guayabo National Monument

The **Monumento Nacional Guayabo** ❷⓿ is the site of a large pre-Columbian city, located on the slopes of Turrialba Volcano, 18 km (11 miles) from Turrialba. It is thought that 10,000 people lived at the Guayabo site from 1000 BC to AD 1400, when they abandoned it for some unknown reason.

Visitors can take a self-guided tour through the excavated area, which contains a complex system of stone aqueducts, house foundations and roadways amidst a setting of guava trees, wild impatiens and clusters of oropendula nests. Stone-lined graves, now empty, served as the first indication to archaeologists that a city site was nearby. In addition, there are several large petrographs, the significance of which remains a mystery.

Not far from the park is the Guayabo Lodge, which is owned by the presidential Figueres family, and is a pleasant inn located on a dairy farm about 19 km (12 miles) from Guayabo.

Around Guayabo grow the best pejibaye *in the country. Look out for houses selling the fruit, they must be cooked, as you cannot eat them raw.*

BELOW: volcanic farmlands on the Meseta Central.

On the way back to Cartago stop for rest and refreshment in the village of Cervantes at La Posada de la Luna.

Irazú Volcano National Park

Easily accessible from Cartago is **Parque Nacional Volcán Irazú** ㉑. From the 3,800-meter (11,000-ft) summit, it is possible on a clear day to see both the Atlantic and the Pacific. Irazú, Costa Rica's highest volcano, also known as El Coloso, broke a 30-year period of silence with a single, noisy eruption on December 8, 1994. It previously erupted on March 19, 1963, the day of the arrival of President John F. Kennedy in Costa Rica on one of his last visits to a foreign country before his assassination.

For two years Irazú continued to shower ash over much of the Central Valley. People carried umbrellas to protect themselves. Ash piled up on the Reventazón River causing it to flood and destroy 300 homes. Roofs caved in from the weight of the ash and San José was temporarily turned to black.

A visit to Irazú is a relatively easy half-day tour from San José. Visitors can go to the top ridge, walk along the rim of the main crater and look across an other-worldly landscape consisting of a brilliant green lake and black-and-gray slopes, punctuated with plumes of white steam jetting into the air, escaping from fissures in the rock.

Braulio Carrillo National Park

Only 45 minutes from downtown San José is **Parque Nacional Braulio Carrillo** ㉒. Take the highway to Limón and turn off before the Zurqui tunnel at signs to the park. Or alternatively, you can take the entrance located 17 km

TIP

Braulio Carrillo Park suffers from security problems. Don't leave anything of value in a parked car, and if you intend hiking, check first with the park authorities as to the security situation.

BELOW: relaxing at a lookout point over the beautiful Orosí Valley.

(11 miles) beyond the tunnel at La Botella trail, where the grade is not so steep and strenuous. The trails are often muddy and snakes are sometimes sighted; be sure to wear sturdy boots and mosquito repellent.

Occupying 445 sq. km (170 sq. miles) of mostly primary forest, Braulio Carrillo National Park was founded in 1978 at the urging of environmentalists who feared that the opening of a highway between San José and Guápiles would provide loggers and developers with access to rapidly vanishing virgin forest. Deforestation had followed the opening of many other roads throughout the country. A compromise was reached: the road would go through, but the 32,000 hectares (80,000 acres) of virgin forest surrounding the highway would be preserved as a national park. The park thus embodies some ideals of enlightened progress.

Braulio Carrillo contains five distinctly separate forest habitats, dominated by the wet tropical forest. Hundreds of varieties of orchids and ferns, and a majority of the bird species native to Costa Rica are found here. In order to understand the life cycles, to spot the camouflaged wildlife and avoid missing hidden spectacular vistas, it is essential to arrange for a guide through the National Parks service or an eco-tourism agency. A circular trail begins behind the kiosk. The lingering impression of Braulio Carrillo is of vastness: huge canyons, misty mountains and the ubiquitous broad-leaf plant, the Poor Man's Umbrella, covering the hillsides.

Rainforests made easy

For a bird's-eye-view of the forest canopy adjacent to Braulio Carrillo, take a ride on biologist Don Perry's **Rainforest Aerial Tram** ㉓, a 90-minute, 1.3-km

Map on page 146

ABOVE: Costa Rica's national orchid.
BELOW: all aboard for the Rainforest Aerial Tram.

(1-mile) trip through the forest's treetops, 35 meters (100 ft) above the forest floor, the first such ride of its kind in the world. The "tram" allows visitors to experience the forest canopy up close: to breath the steamy air, to catch the unforgettable tropical smell of damp, mossy tree trunks and, if you are lucky, to spot the elusive wildlife. It is located about 5 km (3 miles) north of Río Sucio on the road to Puerto Limón, about 50 minutes from San José (open daily, reservations recommended, tel: 257-5961. Entrance fee includes tram ride, video and a short hike).

The **Bosque Lluvioso** ㉔ (Rainy Forest) is a pleasant and gentle day trip for those who are not up to negotiating the demanding, roughly-hewn trails in national parks and reserves. Located on the highway to Limón, just before the town of Guápiles, about one hour's drive from San José, Bosque Lluvioso has neatly manicured, well-maintained paths which can be walked by almost everyone, including the very young and the elderly. These beautiful walks, which require very little effort, range from 30 minutes to 4 hours. There is also a small orchid garden, a tropical flower and fruit plantation, a short spice trail and a restaurant.

San José suburbs

On the west side of San José are the suburbs of Pavas, Rohrmoser, Escazú, and Santa Ana. The rather colorless, modern suburbs of **Rohrmoser** and **Pavas** are chiefly of interest to travelers due to the presence of the Embassy of the United States of America. Owing to this, many diplomatic personnel live along the wide, nearly treeless streets of Rohrmoser, in modern houses protected by wrought-iron grillework.

TIP

The San José suburb of San Pedro is one of the capital's liveliest areas thanks to the presence of the university. It features several good restaurants, bars and nightspots.

BELOW: Escazú and the Central Valley from the air.

Escazú ㉕ was originally a crossroads on trails between Indian villages. Because water was abundant there, the Indians found it a good place to spend the night on their journeys, and gave it its name, which in their language meant "resting place."

Spanish settlers were also attracted to Escazú: they settled in the hills and began farming. It was during these early days that Escazú became known as the city of the witches and today there remains a tradition of metaphysical and mystical arts practiced clandestinely in the village, hidden away from the fierce disapproval of the orthodoxy.

Escazú is an interesting if sometimes chaotic blend of old Costa Rica and a modern, international community. The town center has adobe buildings, an attractive, Ravenna-style church and, of course, a soccer field. Altogether, it has the atmosphere of a sleepy *campesino* town where neighbors have known each other for generations. Just outside of town, however, are enclaves of fancy homes owned by North Americans, Europeans and wealthy locals, drawn to Escazú by the agreeable climate and superlative views.

In the hills to the east of Escazú, in an area called **Bello Horizonte**, are many fine old residences with lovely gardens. It is worth a drive through the hills of Bello Horizonte to visit **Biesanz Woodworks**, the studio/workshop of Barry Biesanz, an accomplished artist who works with Costa Rican hardwoods. Wooden bowls and boxes, remarkable for their grace and fluidity, are on display in his light-filled studio overlooking the city.

San Rafael de Escazú is a newer section of town along the highway to Santa Ana. It has several shiny commercial centers where the town's glamourous inhabitants do their shopping, with international stores, supermarkets, restaurants and glitzy interior decoration shops.

Turn left onto the road that leads to Il Pomodoro restaurant and continue a short distance to El Rincón. Almost directly across the highway from the bookshop there is a large walled compound with lights, guards and surveillance paraphernalia. It isn't a high-security penitentiary: it's the residence of the United States ambassador to Costa Rica.

Halfway to Santa Ana on the old highway is the luxurious Alta Hotel.

Map on page 146

ABOVE: Central Valley adobe house.
BELOW: Escazú celebrates its heritage of witches.

Santa Ana

There is a distinctly rural atmosphere in **Santa Ana** ㉖, a town famous for its onions, which hang braided on the lintels and eaves of restaurants and stands along the road. On the west side of town, toward the freeway entrance, are stands selling pottery, baskets, local fruit and onions.

Above Santa Ana is the small village of Salitral, where mineral springs bubble and there is an **Oxcart Museum** (*see pages 164–65*).which features displays of *campesino* life from the 19th century (open Tues–Sun, entrance fee payable).

Rancho Macho, high in the hills above Santa Ana, has sweeping views of the valley below. Sit under the stars, overlooking the city lights, enjoy the balmy breezes, sip a cold beer and partake of delicious grilled onions, barbecued chicken and beef. To get to

Rancho Macho continue on the old highway through the town of Santa Ana, past the huge red cross and continue straight for about half a kilometer until you see a Rancho Macho sign indicating you should turn left. From here just follow the signs up the hill.

Near Escazú, at the village of San Antonio de Escazú, an annual oxcart festival, Día de los Boyeros *is held in March. It attracts around 100 painted antique carts and the great oxen that pull them, plus thousands of visitors.*

If you are in search of more ordinary pursuits, look for **Multiplaza**, one of the largest shopping malls in all of Central America. It is just off the freeway on the way to Santa Ana, across the road from El Camino Real Hotel.

Ciudad Colón can be reached by backroads from Santa Ana, through rolling hills, or by way of the freeway. It's best known perhaps to those who have come to inspect the **University for Peace**, which is on a well-marked road not far out of town. The University for Peace, sponsored by the United Nations to study the ways of peace, and to offer a counter to the teachings of the war colleges which predominate in many other countries, offers graduate courses to students from all over the world.

Returning to Santa Ana via back roads, you will come to **La Cabriola**, a popular weekend restaurant and picnic site where horses can be rented. The food at La Cabriola is nothing special, but the gently rolling hills above it are beautiful and perfect for horse-riding.

Sarchí and surrounding villages

BELOW: Grecia's metal church was imported from Belgium in 1897.

For a half-day excursion of craft shopping and sightseeing around typical Central Valley village-towns head north through Alajuela towards Sarchí, stopping en route at **Grecia ㉗**. Once known as the pineapple capital of Costa Rica, this tidy little place has also been voted the cleanest town in all Latin America. It is definitely worth a stroll and is well known for its unusual dark-red, all-metal church.

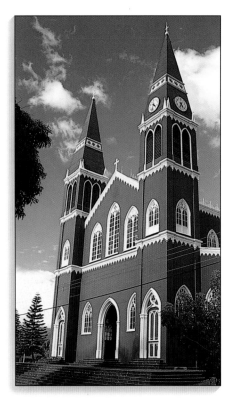

The approach to the mountain town of **Sarchí ㉘** is unmistakable. Distinctive and colorful Sarchí decorative designs can be seen on bus stops, bars and bakeries, restaurants and houses.

Sarchí is a crafts center heavily geared towards the tourist trade where you can see artisans painting traditional ox-cart designs (*see pages 164–165*) and creating household furnishings out of tropical hardwoods. Around the year 1910, as legend has it, a *campesino* was crossing the Beneficio la Luisa when it occurred to him to decorate his ox-cart wheels with colorful mandala-like designs derived from ancient Moorish influences. The art form caught on. Originally each district in Costa Rica had its own special design and locals could tell just by looking at the cart where the driver lived. It was also said that each cart had its own distinctive "*chirrido*", or song of the wheels, which could identify who was passing by, without even glancing upward.

As late as 1960, the most typical mode of transportation was the ox-cart. It was the only vehicle which could transport agricultural products through the rugged Costa Rican terrain. The father of former president Oscar Arias Sánchez made his original fortune hauling coffee by ox-cart to Puntarenas. The painted carts, pulled by oxen, are still in use today in villages as close to the capital as San Antonio de Escazú.

There are pleasant little roadside stalls on the outskirts of Sarchí, selling homemade candied fruits, and honey and fudge. In comparison to the large commercialised furniture shops which predominate in Sarchí, a visit to these small stands is very friendly and personal, as though stepping into a Costa Rican home for a chat.

About 15 km (9 miles) up the road is the town of **Zarcero** ㉙. Should you arrive on a day when the highland clouds are swirling through the town or when a drizzling fog is bathing everything in soft, diffused light, you might feel that you have just walked into a fantasy dreamland.

Unique in Costa Rica, and possibly the world, is the **Parque Central** in Zarcero, a museum of topiary. For over two decades, Evangelisto Blanco, the park gardener, has been clipping and pruning cypress bushes and hedges into a whimsical garden of amazing creatures: bulbous elephants with lightbulbs for eyes, a bull ring complete with spectators, matador and charging bull, a cross-bearing Christ, and a cat with tail flying, riding a motorcycle along the top of a hedge. Evangelisto has been sculpting the hedges alone for over 25 years, 7 days a week, including holidays. The energetic compulsion of his work has been compared to the creations of Antonio Gaudí, in Barcelona in Spain, and of Simón Rodía, who created the Watts Towers in Los Angeles. Unable to afford marble or stone, Evangelisto works with the plants as his medium of self-expression.

After the highway turnoff to Zarcero is the 200-year-old colonial town of **Palmares**. This lovely area used to be a tobacco-growing center. Unaffected by the vicissitudes of modern tourism, it is a model town through which to stroll and view typical Tico life. ❏

Map on page 146

BELOW: taking a break from planting new coffee bushes.

POTTERS, SCULPTORS AND GOLDSMITHS

The indians of Costa Rica left behind gold, pottery and stone artifacts. Most of their traditions were destroyed by the conquistadores

A cultural and commercial meeting point for ancient civilizations in the Americas, native Costa Ricans absorbed and modified known techniques in ceramics, gold and jade work, weaving and stone carving. Early inhabitants, especially in the pre-Colombian port of Nicoya (in the province of Guanacaste), traded with travelers from as far away as Ecuador and Mexico. They also developed their own style of decorating pottery: beasts that are half bird, half man and people with exaggerated genitals, suggesting a fertility-rites culture. Examples of the pottery, which was also traded, can be found throughout Central America.

Visitors to the Museum of Gold, the Jade Museum and the National Museum, can see early pieces and learn more of their history and uses.

CRAFTSMEN AND ARTISTS

While the Spanish never found the gold deposits that inspired them to name the land "Rich Coast", early Costa Ricans worked with both gold and jade (not found in the country) to make statuettes and other decorative pieces. Although these traditions – along with stone work and the southern Pacific tradition of making fine white cloth – have been all but lost, pottery and the more modern craft of ox-cart decoration have been revived by the tourist dollar. For pottery, visit Guatil and Nicoya, for other crafts try Sarchi.

Other examples of Costa Rica's crafts, less compromised by modern tourism, are found in the wild south of the country; *molas* (hand-sewn appliqué) pieces are produced around Drake Bay, and grotesque balsawood masks are made by the Boruca Indians.

▷ **"HOUSE OF THE DREAMER"**
Self-taught sculptor Macedonio Quesada, who died in 1997, whittled charming statues depicting Costa Rican life. His two sons continue the tradition, sculpting in coffee wood in the Orosi Valley. Some of the pieces are for sale.

▽ **COTTAGE INDUSTRY**
Costa Rica's clay-rich soils provide excellent material for pottery, most of which is shaped without the aid of a potter's wheel. Many Guanacaste families have outdoor ovens for baking.

◁ **EARLY STONE WORK THE HARD WAY**
Early Costa Ricans used granite andesite and sedimentary stone to fashion stone figures with wooden tools. It is thought that they may have split the rocks by inserting wooden dowels into cracks and soaking them with water. The expanding wooden dowel would then have cracked the stone.

ORNAMENTED OX-CARTS

Used exclusively to transport coffee and other agricultural products until well into the 20th century, wooden ox-carts are unmistakably Costa Rican, and symbolize the self-reliance of the small farmer (much like covered wagons do in the US).

Ideally suited for the country's mountainous conditions and rutted dirt roads, ox-carts are still common in many parts of the country. The carts, which come in all sizes (including a miniature about the size of a toy car), are made in Sarchi, the wooden crafts capital of the country. There, master carvers began painting the carts in the early part of the 20th century. Originally adorned with bright colors and geometric patterns, these days ox-carts are being decorated with jungle scenes, wild animals, flowers and other non-traditional designs.

Visitors to Sarchi can have a go at painting the carts themselves with fine-tipped brushes, or alternatively they can leave it to the experts and order a custom-painted cart; these are often used as decorations at hotels and the country estates of the wealthy.

◁ **BRILLIANT BIRDS, MAGNIFICENT MEN**
Reproductions of pre-Columbian gold figures make excellent gifts.

▷ **LIVING TRADITIONS**
Boruca indians make their woven goods and carved gourds according to traditional designs.

◁ **PAINTED POTS APLENTY**
Although the Chorotega culture no longer exists, their descendants use water-based paints to decorate inexpensive pottery with whimsical animals and other pre-Columbian images.

▷ **SONG OF THE WHEELS**
Neighbors can recognize the distinctive sound of each other's ox-cart in motion.

THE CENTRAL PACIFIC

Map
on page
170

*The Central Pacific beaches are among the best in Costa Rica,
and Manuel Antonio is the stuff of tropical dreams. There is plenty
to see en route to the coast, with a host of natural wonders*

W hen the chaos of San José becomes just a bit too much – then take a day trip to the Pacific Coast and get away from it all at the beach. The nearest is Jacó, one of the country's most lively and popular seaside destinations, a little less than two hours away. The country's finest beaches, at Manuel Antonio National Park, are over an hour's drive south of here, but if you don't want to drive, there are inexpensive flights from San José to Quepos (adjacent to Manuel Antonio). Buy tickets well in advance during the dry season.

The Road to the Coast

If you go by car, and want to take the fast route to the coast (as opposed to the old scenic route, *see page 174*), turn off the highway towards Atenas, past the Juan Santamaría International Airport, then head through La Garita de Alajuela. One of the first lowland towns that you'll approach is Orotina. The road to Orotina winds through coffee plantations built on precariously steep slopes. Driving along the ledges of these mountains, the views are often of rich green farms and rolling valleys; and looking up at the almost horizontal *fincas*, you may find it difficult to imagine how the coffee can possibly be harvested here.

Near Orotina, Dagmar Werner, a German herpetologist, operates his **Iguana Park ❶**. The park, or ranch, as it is also known, is a surrealistic dream. Brilliantly colored turquoise green iguanas appear to be everywhere, sitting silently in rows, observing you as boldly as you observe them. It is said that iguana meat tastes much like chicken, and is referred to as *gallina de palo* (literally, tree chicken). Moreover, these large lizards grow faster than cattle, reaching up to 6 feet (2m) in length, including the tail, and they produce a much higher yield of meat per acre than beef. Werner and the Pro Green Iguana Foundation are hoping that the iguanas they release will provide local people with a source of food and income that will encourage them to maintain the forest, or even to reforest it, rather than slashing and burning their land, and clearing it for cattle grazing.

Guided tours of the Iguana Foundation's private reserve are available, as are forest canopy tours, which allow visitors to sail through the treetops via a system of pulleys and cables (open daily 9am-3pm; entrance fee). There is also a gift shop, where you can eat iguana meat, or even buy one (as a pet).

The **Carara Biological Reserve ❷** straddles the highway between Playa Jacó and Puntarenas. One of the closest reserves to San José, Carara lies in a transitional zone between humid and dry land forest, and sustains wildlife from mountainous terrain, primary and secondary forests, lagoons, and marshlands of the

PRECEDING PAGES:
Manuel Antonio
National Park.
LEFT: cascade
waters the plants.
BELOW: scarlet
macaw at Carara
Biological Reserve.

Tárcoles River. The vegetation in Carara covers a similarly broad range: from shady evergreens to clustering epiphytes and strangling vines. Among the birds most commonly spotted here are vultures, toucans and guans, ducks and macaws. Squirrel, howler, white-faced, and spider monkeys are often seen, and, more rarely, wildcats such as margays, jaguarundis, ocelots and jaguars. There are also sloths, coatis and agoutis, as well as a variety of reptiles and morpho butterflies. Guides, available by advance request (contact the National Parks Service), are invaluable in interpreting the ecological complexity of this reserve.

It is said that only 1,000 macaws are left in the wild, while there are some 1,500 in captivity.

Nearly 100 scarlet macaws are the great glory of Carara. These enormous red, yellow and blue parrots mate for life and live for over 30 years. A small staff patrols the park and is continually on the lookout for poachers of these highly prized birds. The macaw nests in December and by January the young are strong but still in their nests. They make easy prey at this point for thieves who sell them on the black market. It is said that only 1,000 macaws are left in the wild in Costa Rica, while there are some 1,500 in captivity.

Like most birds, macaws are easiest to spot during the hours of dawn or dusk. In the evenings, when the lowlands cool, pairs of macaws fly down from their daytime feeding areas in the mountains. At sunset, park your car near the bridge over the Tárcoles River along the highway outside of the park entrance and listen for their raucous squawking as they fly to their roosting areas in the nearby coastal mangroves. And while waiting for the macaws to fly by, watch for shorebirds and waders which frequent the estuary. Roseate spoonbills, with their startling pink plumage, are spectacular at sunset. Crocodiles look like inanimate logs as they bask on the river banks, apparently comatose, but waiting for such a prize as one of the spoonbills.

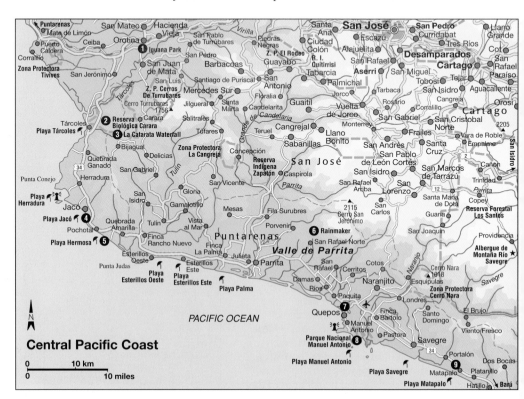

Central Pacific Coast

The beaches

If you are anticipating the white powder beaches washed by gentle, clear waters of tourist brochures, then the beaches of the Central Pacific could be something of a disappointment (Jacó is actually a dirty grey). The attraction of these places is their proximity to San José, their big waves for surfers, and their lively atmosphere, not their picture-postcard perfection. However, with a bit of exploration off the main road, and once away from the density and hustle of the central beach scene, you will find some clean and appealing beaches and secluded coves.

Playa Herradura lies 5 minutes north of Jacó, its waves are gentle, and there is shade and trees for stringing hammocks. **Playa Esterillos** is a huge 11-km (7-mile) stretch of mostly deserted beach, but beware strong riptides. Avoid Playa Tárcoles,which is polluted. Crocodile tours run along the Tárcoles River, but don't use or encourage irresponsible operators who get their clients to feed the crocs with pieces of meat. Once a crocodile associates a person with food, then that is one very dangerous animal.

Several kilometers from the Jacó-San José highway, before Jacó Beach, is **La Catarata Waterfall** ❸, a 200-meter (650-ft) high falls of awe-inspiring proportions (open daily*). Be warned, though, the 45-minute hike to La Catarata is strenuous. Hikers must be in good physical shape and should bring plenty of water with them.

Jacó Beach

Jacó Beach ❹ has a party-time, beach town ambience, with plenty of cold beer and hammocks slung between coconut palms. Cabinas are inexpensive to

ABOVE: birds also make colorful T-shirt designs.
BELOW: captive iguana at Orotina.

rent and readily available. They are usually clean and often situated right on the beach. In addition, there have recently been constructed several hotels with swimming pools, full bars, air conditioning and tour packages to other points of interest in this coastal province. Perhaps the hotel pool is the best place to swim in Jacó as the water is not very clean and there are also dangerous undercurrents.

True to its nature nonetheless as a resort/party town, Jacó has no shortage of amusements: horses, bikes, scooters and kayaks are available for rent. Salva la Selva rents surfboards, offers lessons and provides free information on surfing conditions. There is even a small miniature-golf course right in the middle of town and a US-style giant screen sports bar on the beach. Jacó also has a lively nightlife. Try Disco La Central, Foxy's Disco or the disco at the Hotel Jacó Beach.

Along the coast some 3 kms (2 miles) from Playa Jacó is **Playa Hermosa** ➎, one of the best surfing spots on the coast with very strong beach breaks. It is an easily accessible place where there is also a variety of wading birds to observe: great white herons and snowy egrets, great blue, little blue, tricolor and little green herons. You may also see *jacanas*, walking on lily pads with huge yellow feet, and black-bellied whistling ducks.

Rainmaker

Head east on the coastal highway for around 40 km (24 miles) to the small plantation town of **Parrita**, dominated by an enormous African oil palm development, which was established in 1985 by United Brands Fruit Company. Oil palms do very well here. Unfortunately, palm oil is much higher than other oils in saturated fats, and thus is declining in popularity. Palm oil workers live next to the highway, in plantation villages of two-story, brightly painted-homes, set in a "U" around what is the focal point of every Tico village: the soccer field.

Around 10 km (6 miles) east of Parrita is the tiny village of Pocares from where you should turn inland and continue for around 6–7 km (4 miles) to reach **Rainmaker** ➏, the most exciting recent eco-project to come to this region. Rainmaker is the first suspended walkway project in Central America and allows visitors to explore the rainforest canopy with the minimim of environmental disturbance. Boardwalks link six suspension bridges, one of them spans 90 metres (300 ft) and at the highest point of the trail you will be a dizzying 25 stories above the jungle floor. Visits must be booked in advance with operators in Quepos and Manuel Antonio (see below).

Manuel Antonio National Park

Once an important banana shipping port, **Quepos** ➐ is now something of an inexpensive dormitory town to its famous neighbor, Manuel Antonio, 7 km (4 miles) away. There is a regular bus service, some very acceptable accommodations, restaurants, shops and nightlife, while still retaining the flavor of an old-time Costa Rican fishing and banana town. Its beaches are polluted, however. Regardless of where you stay, reservations are essential during the holiday season at both Manuel Antonio and Quepos.

BELOW: driving in Costa Rica is rarely without interest.

It is a little-known fact that the first mission in Costa Rica was established near here, in 1570. It was abandoned in 1751 and its ruins are located up the Naranjo River. The cemetery is still visible, as are remnants of the fruit orchard, which has regenerated from the original stumps. The folks at the Buena Nota gift shop, located just to your left as you enter Quepos, are long-time residents of the area and can provide information concerning the mission, as well as most things related to Manuel Antonio. Just north of the Catholic church, pop into La Botánica, which sells huge cinnamon, glossy vanilla beans, bags of peppercorns, herbal teas and fragrant spice mixtures.

Parque Nacional Manuel Antonio ❽ is Costa Rica's most famous beach area, composed of three long strands of magnificent white sand, fringed by jungle on one side, and by the Pacific on the other. The beaches are clean and wide. Above them are tall cliffs covered in thick jungle vegetation. In fact, this park is one of the few places in the country where the primary forest comes down to the water's edge in places, sometimes allowing bathers to swim in the shade. In order to protect the eco-system of the park, rangers allow a maximum of 600 visitors on weekdays and 800 on weekends.

Playa Espadilla Norte is the first of the beaches, very beautiful, but also dangerous because of its unpredictable riptides. Accessible across a sand spit, which may be submerged at high tide, are **Playa Espadilla Sur** and **Playa Manuel Antonio**. Both provide safe swimming and good diving.

There is plenty to do in the National Park. On the the beaches you can sunbathe, surf, swim, snorkel or perhaps rent horses from Equus Stables and go on a jungle trail horseback ride. *La Mamá de Tarzan*, a 19-meter (62-ft) catamaran, offers a 3-hour sightseeing tour of the coast. If you're lucky, you'll have an

Map on page 170

TIP

Beware over-tame monkeys in search of a free lunch at Manuel Antonio. Don't feed them as you not only create a begging colony, but risk catching diseases should they bite you.

BELOW: one of the advantages of flying to Manuel Antonio is the bird's-eye view.

Map on page 170

ABOVE AND BELOW: beachside and poolside at Manuel Antonio.

RIGHT: pavoncillo flower.

escort of local dolphins. There are trails for hiking and wildlife sighting – various species of monkeys can be seen, including capuchin, spider and white-faced monkeys, as well as marmosets, the smallest species of monkey in Costa Rica. Birdlife includes many seabirds such as boobies, frigate birds, pelicans and terns. Snakes and iguanas are often seen and, if you are sharp-eyed, sloths. Within the park are primary forest, swamps and tropical woodlands, containing hundreds of species of plants. Other options include mountain biking, white-water river rafting or sea kayaking tours, available from Ríos Tropicales.

Just outside the park to the north, in the hills that rise up from the beach, there is a garish profusion of signs advertising an ever-growing number of hotels, international restaurants and cabinas. With rare exceptions, most accommodations on the ocean side of the road are built on the cliffs above the beach and offer views of the ocean rather than direct access to beaches.

You can get to Manuel Antonio by car, bus or plane. The road is paved as far as Parrita, after which it is good, but loose and dusty, gravel as far as Quepos. You pass through some beautiful countryside, although the flat coastal section runs through endless green corridors of palm plantations, which soon becomes monotonous. It's about a 3-hour trip by car, some 4 hours by bus and 20 minutes by plane. SANSA and Travelair fly daily to Quepos. A final word about Quepos/Manuel Antonio: theft is on the increase. Be attentive. Don't leave your belongings unattended on the beach and keep valuables in your hotel's safe.

The old highway to the Pacific

The road less-traveled to Manuel Antonio heads west of San José, through Ciudad Colón and Puriscal. It was once *the* highway to the Pacific coast. Today, most traffic heads through Orotina, leaving the old route for those interested in a much more relaxed drive, through unspoiled mountain terrain. Renovated farmhouses offer rooms for those who want to break their journey.

About 6 km (4 miles) west of **Ciudad Colón**, the old highway passes through the Guayabo reserve of the Quitirrisí indians, who sell woven vine baskets, and other handmade goods at roadside stands.

Santiago de Puriscal, a vital farming town with a beautiful church, is the last outpost of city life before reaching Quepos, on the Pacific coast. Soon after Puriscal the road is unpaved and winds its way through stunning mountains and valleys, carpeted with coffee, sugar cane and banana plantations, rows of orange groves, populated only by small farms and settlements. This is untouched Costa Rica. Aside from one bumpy stretch just outside of Puriscal, the gravel road is generally in good shape, and there is little traffic. After the village of La Gloria the road quickly descends to sea level, south to Parrita, and onward to Quepos and Manuel Antonio.

Matapalo ❾ is a beach town 25 km (16 miles) south of Manuel Antonio on the Costanera Sur road (15 km/9 miles north of Dominical). The beach is long and quiet, the surf is large. To north and south respectively are **Playa Savegre** and **Playa Baru**, seldom visited but beautiful beaches. Visit both at low tide. ❑

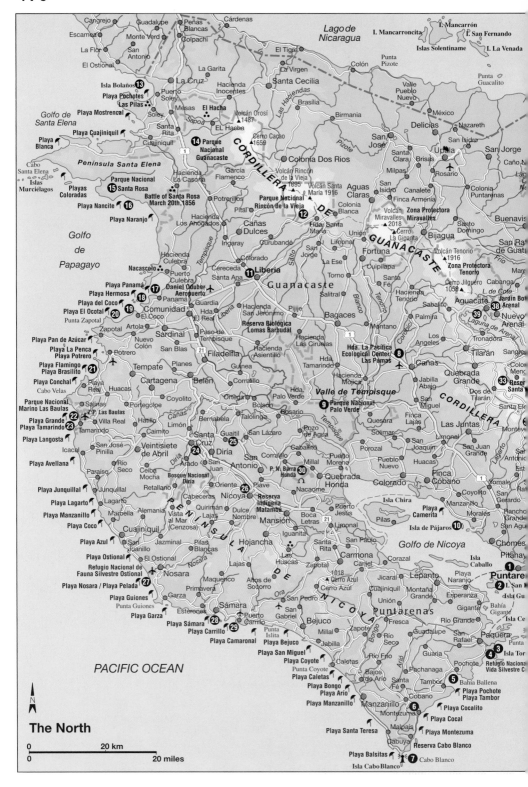

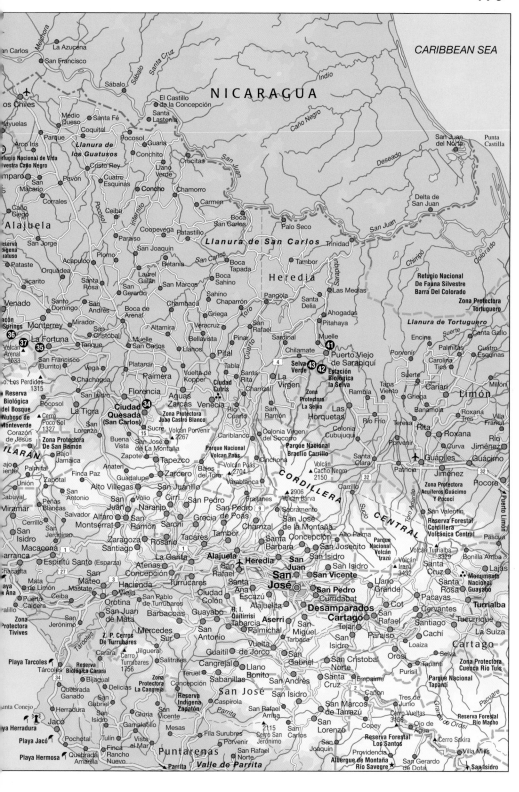

CARIBBEAN SEA

NICARAGUA

CARIBBEAN SEA

Llanura de los Guatusos

Alajuela

Llanura de San Carlos

HEREDIA

Refugio Nacional De Fauna Silvestre Barra Del Colorado
Zona Protectora Tortuguero

Llanura de Tortuguero

Limón

CORDILLERA CENTRAL

Río Limón

San José

Cartago

CARTAGO

Puntarenas

Valle de Parrita

THE NORTHWEST

Almost all aspects of Costa Rica are to be found in this large and rewarding region; miles of beaches, acres of steamy rainforest, punctuated by cattle pastures and cowboy towns

Map on pages 178–79

San José

he northwest of the country is split into two provinces. The larger part is **Guanacaste** – a vast tract of land stretching endlessly towards the horizon. During the dry season much of it is covered in wild savanna grasses that float over the land like lakes of gold. During the rainy season the land itself appears to be alive with thick, green tropical forest growth. This is Central America's state of Texas, the Big Country, where vast grasslands are dotted only by huge, spreading trees and white Brahma cattle.

Though traditionally cattle country, Guanacaste is nowadays also known for its sunny, wide beaches, many of which have been developed as part of major resort complexes. The international airport outside Liberia now brings sun-starved tourists from northern countries directly to their beach destinations.

Puntarenas province, which straddles the Gulf of Nicoya and takes in the South Nicoya Peninsula, is also becoming a vacation paradise of broad sandy beaches, turquoise waters, shady palm trees and some controversially large hotel resort developments.

Also just within this region (though it actually belongs to Alajuela province) is the highly-popular **Monteverde Cloud Forest.**

PRECEDING PAGES: the Tabebria tree. **LEFT:** getting down and dirty. **BELOW:** Guanacaste cowboy.

The *Guanacastecos*

The *Guanacastecos*, as the residents of this province are called, are an independent people. Many are descended from the dark-skinned Chorotega indians with skin the color of tortoise shell, eyes a warm brown, black wavy hair, and an easy, friendly grace.

In 1787, the Captaincy General of Costa Rica,, which then governed the country from Guatemala, decided that Guanacaste should be part of Nicaragua and there it stayed until 1821 when the Captaincy General was dissolved and the people of Guanacaste were asked to decide their own national identity. Opinions were divided: the Northerners around Liberia wished to be a part of Nicaragua and the Southerners on the Nicoyan peninsula wished to revert to Costa Rica. A vote was held and, as we know today, the majority elected to be a part of Costa Rica.

Puntarenas

Many people think that **Puntarenas** 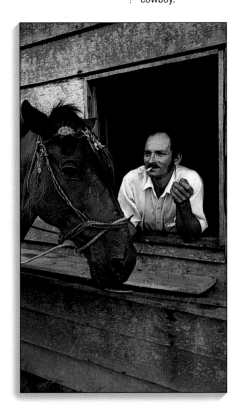 (population 45,000) is simply a place to pass through so that you can get somewhere else: you pass through Puntarenas en route to the islands of the Gulf of Nicoya, or when taking the ferry to Bahía Ballena, Tambor and Montezuma. However, if this is your view, it's worth reconsidering – slow down a bit and take some time to explore this port town.

Puntarenas used to be a bustling, noisy place, filled

with longshoremen, sailors on leave, prostitutes and businessmen. Wealthy merchants from San José had homes here where they went to conduct business and escape the city. But the growth of the port of Limón and, more recently, the opening of the modern deepwater port of **Puerto Caldera** have made Puntarenas something of an anachronism.

Puerto Caldera handles the cargo of over 360 major ships a year and is Costa Rica's second largest port, after Puerto Limón. Cars from Japan, rice and corn from the United States, and coffee, bananas and pineapples from Costa Rica pass through here. Cruise ships dock to allow passengers their parsimonious one day in Costa Rica.

Today, fishing is the main industry of Puntarenas. The tourism industry is small, though recently spruced up large new hotels, such as the Fiesta, have opened south of town. With its views of the long, arching coastline, the beach along the gulf is beautiful, and the sun setting over Nicoya is spectacular. Though the ocean waters were until quite recently badly polluted, they have now been declared safe to swim in by the Costa Rican Ministry of Health. The estuary and rivers, however, should be avoided.

Take a trip into the glorious waters of the Gulf of Nicoya aboard the Lohe Lani *catamaran, which sails from the Water Sports pier of the Hotel Fiesta.*

Downtown

The crowded center of Puntarenas, three blocks back from the beach, bustles in the morning as the townfolk conduct business. Everyone seems in a hurry, perhaps to accomplish what they need to before the onset of the afternoon heat. Though, like San José, an architectural victim of excessive concrete, Puntarenas still retains many of its older buildings: plank structures with latticework below the roof to permit the breeze. The wooden buildings are painted in such color

BELOW: beach goers at Puntarenas.

combinations as bright turquoise and red, and together with the few remaining mansions of the merchants and the Church, they convey the flavor of a Puntarenas in its prime.

Map on pages 178–179

Visit the museum in the **Casa de Cultura** (House of Culture), formerly the city's jail, where exhibits feature the area's history, geography, natural history, and indigenous crafts (open Mon–Sat, closed 12–1pm; entrance free).

Evening is perhaps the best time to catch Puntarenas. Enjoy a late afternoon *refresco* at one of the *sodas* on the **Paseo de Turistas** and watch the sun sink below the mountains of Nicoya across the bay. The *sodas* offer a chance to try some native Costa Rican drinks. This is perhaps the only place in the country to get *maté*, a type of milkshake with a lingering, nostalgic aftertaste. Try a cold, creamy *pinolillo* made with toasted, ground corn, or a "Churchill", a cold and refreshing fruit drink.

Seafood restaurants and hotels line the oceanfront. Most are airconditioned or adjusted to catch the ocean breezes. The Tioga and Las Brisas are recommended. On the estuary is the Portobello, a good hotel, which offers privacy, gardens and birdwatching. The hotels along the estuary also offer free mooring and facilities to cruising sailboats. The Yacht Club here is extensive, well protected, professionally managed, and one of the very first stops a trans-oceanic yacht makes on the first leg of a trip from the West Coast of the US to more distant ports of call.

Just south, down the coast, from Puntarenas is **Playa Doña Ana**. Here the Tourist Institute (ICT) has developed a beach resort with bar, restaurant, showers and parking, on a cove well situated between two spectacular rock headlands. The Costa Rican world invitational surfing championships are held here.

ABOVE: crushed ice fruit drinks stand.
BELOW: paddling a kayak in the Gulf of Nicoya.

If you like a game of golf or fancy a spot of horseriding, there are resorts on the Nicoya Peninsula which specialise in both activities.

BELOW: tumbling waters at La Catarata La Cangreja, near El Rincón de la Vieja.

The Gulf of Nicoya

A ferry crosses from Puntarenas to Playa Naranjo and the **Nicoya Peninsula**. The two-hour trip across the Gulf of Nicoya passes among small lush islands. There is also a ferry service to Paquera, near the Tambor Resort.

In the midst of the gulf, among 40 or so other islands, is **Isla San Lucas ❷**, Costa Rica's former prison island. The prison was closed in 1991 and the island deserted, except for the guards posted there to prevent vandalism. There are no restrictions preventing visits to the island, however, and visitors who are so inclined can view numerous disturbing reminders of the life prisoners endured here. It is possible to arrange tours to San Lucas from Naranjo.

Calypso Tours offers a cruise on its 21-meter (70-ft) catamaran and visits to the islands in the Gulf of Nicoya. It crosses the waters of the Gulf and visits **Isla Tortuga ❸** (Turtle Island), where, in an idyllic setting of white sand and turquoise waters, you can enjoy what is perhaps the best seafood buffet in the country, as well as folk music and entertainment. There is also adequate time for swimming and sunbathing. Calypso,one of the oldest tour operators in Costa Rica,.also offers other excellent tours, including fishing trips.

The South Nicoya Peninsula

The ferry ride across the Gulf of Nicoya brings you to a different world from that of the area around Puntarenas. It is one of seasonally-dry grasslands, gigantic spreading trees, rolling cattle ranches, memorable bays and beautiful beaches.

From the ferry landing at Paquera, Tambor is just a short drive, and Montezuma is about an hour away. There are no road signs along the way, but the local people are used to giving visitors directions. There are no buses leav-

ing from Playa Naranjo; but there is a service from Paquera, to Cóbano, the last stop before Montezuma.

The drive along the peninsula, although rough, is rewarding. It traverses small towns and villages, miles of vast pastureland, past dwellings of every description, people on horseback, and every now and again startling views of the blue bays of the Pacific.

South of the town of Paquera, some 7 km (4½ miles), lies the **Refugio Nacional de Vida Silvestre Curú ❹** (Curú National Wildlife Refuge). Although small, the park encompasses five habitats and offers sanctuary to a surprisingly large and diverse number of plants, animals (including the white-faced monkey), and over 220 species of birds. It has three beautiful beaches, ideal for swimming and diving. There are no facilities, but hiking is excellent. The refuge is private property, owned by the Schultz family, so you must call in advance; tel: 661-2392 to arrange a visit.

Bahía Ballena

A large, wide bay, **Bahía Ballena ❺**, which means Whale Bay, is a place of surprising beauty and tranquility. The waters are gentle and warm, with large flocks of pelicans diving for fish. January is an especially good time for sighting whales. The bay shelters two beaches, **Playa Pochote** and **Playa Tambor**. Recently, however, its tranquil face has been irrevocably and controversially transformed by the construction of the enormous Hotel de Playa Tambor. The project inspired a passionate debate about what kind of tourism is best for Costa Rica: mammoth projects such as this, or small, privately-owned businesses which reflect the character of their communities. In the end, big business won.

Map on pages 178–179

BELOW: a Costa Rican bullfight, where only the *toreros* get hurt.

In the village of **Tambor**, inexpensive lodgings and good local-style meals can be found, and you might just get a sense of life as it was before the arrival of big-time tourism. Continuing southeast to the town of Cóbano the road leads to Montezuma.

Montezuma

Montezuma **❻**, in many ways, feels like the end of the line. The dirt road rolls bumpily down a hill and ends abruptly in front of a row of funky hotels and cantinas on the beachfront. Here, young North American and European travelers outnumber the local people, who have accepted them with seeming good grace, building a variety of small, inexpensive cabinas, *sodas*, extra bedrooms and camping places to accommodate visitors. Places fill up quickly everywhere in Montezuma during the dry season, so reserve well ahead.

Downtown, the Hotel Montezuma overlooks the beach, and serves cold beer, loud music and good fish *casados*. Chico's Bar serves local food and drinks, and the shiny white El Sano Banano features great fruit drinks, hearty, vegetarian fare and big screen videos of popular foreign films three nights a week.

While most lodging and dining in Montezuma ranges from basic to acceptable, the beach-going is exceptional. To the north of town there are wide, sandy beaches, with beautiful clear water, some with great shelling. A walk up a scenic path leads to a dramatic waterfall and river. To the south are beaches with surf crashing against volcanic rock – and, just a short hike away, another waterfall with a pool for swimming. The first couple of rocky bays north of Montezuma have strong currents, but Playa Grande is safe for swimming.

Bikes and boogie boards can be rented at El Sano Banano, and horses through

BELOW: Young *Guanacastecos* get in the saddle at a very early age.

the Hotel Los Mangos and Finca Los Caballos, outside of town, but most visitors to Montezuma seem to spend their time swimming, sunning or simply hanging out in this laidback place that seems expressly designed for the youthful, low-budget traveler.

Map
on pages
178–79

Cabo Blanco

It is almost 11 km (7 miles) from Montezuma to **Cabo Blanco Wildlife Reserve** ❼ along a little-used, unpaved road which runs parallel to the beach. Property owners along the road rent basic rooms and camping spaces.

The reserve was established in 1963 through the inspiration and tireless efforts of Swedish immigrant Nils Olaf Wessberg, and is Costa Rica's oldest protected wildlife region. Sadly, Wessberg was murdered while trying to establish a similar reserve in the Osa Peninsula and he is fondly recalled as an important pioneer of the parks system in Costa Rica.

Originally, Cabo Blanco allowed no public access: all life there was to be protected, without any interference from humans. Today, however, approximately one-third of the reserve is open to visitors. It encompasses a wet, tropical forest on the tip of the peninsula and is one of the most scenic spots along the whole Pacific coast. There is a large population of marine and shore birds and mammals. In addition, there is a small museum, picnic areas, well maintained trails and a lovely remote beach, where you may swim but not snorkel.

Strict rules guide the behavior of all visitors beginning with registration and a briefing at the reserve's administration center. To enter the reserve you have to cross two small streams and a 4-wheel drive vehicle is recommended. Note the reserve is closed on Mondays.

Beyond Cabo Blanco, the road is rough and unpaved. During the rainy season it is muddy and some of the rivers and creeks without bridges can become impassable without a 4-wheel drive vehicle. During the dry season things don't get any more comfortable as along the roadway a fine, brown dust coats plants and road travelers.

The Interamericana northbound

From San José the Interamericana highway, route C1, cuts northwest straight through the heart of Guanacaste, via its capital, Liberia, and northwards onto Nicaragua.

At **Cañas** you first get the sense that this part of the immense Guanacaste is more like a separate country, caught somewhere between Costa Rica and Nicaragua, than it is a province of Costa Rica.

Cañas, which was named for the fields of white-flowered wild cane which covered the countryside, is a cowboy town, with a frontier feeling, not unlike a village in Mexico. There is a fine hermitage a few kilometers north, just before the highway crosses the Corobicí River.

Four kilometers (2½ miles) north of Cañas on the highway is **La Pacífica Ecological Center** ❽. This private reserve with comfortable cabins, beautiful pool and grounds has extensive trails which run parallel to the Corobicí River, which provide excellent

ABOVE: spiky agave in Cabo Blanco.
BELOW: waiting for the tide to turn in the Nicoya Peninsula.

vantage points for bird-watching. Over 220 different species have been identified here. One of them is the boat-billed heron, an exotic-looking bird with a wide, ungainly bill, the use of which has never been scientifically explained. **Las Pumas**, adjacent to La Pacífica, provides a shelter for some of Costa Rica's large cats which, for various reasons, are not able to live in the wild (open Tues-Sun; donations requested).

The Rincón Corobicí Restaurant, overlooking the Corobicí River on the highway adjacent to La Pacífica, is a pleasant place to rest and take refreshment. **Safaris Corobicí** offers guided "floats" down the Corobicí on its 6-meter (17-ft) Avon rafts, a wonderful opportunity to observe the river habitat, especially the birds – laughing falcons, herons, trogons, wood storks, mot-mots, parrots, osprey, and, of course, egrets. Plan for an early morning trip to enjoy the best birding.

Palo Verde National Park

Parque Nacional Palo Verde ❾ is one of Central America's largest protected wildlife areas. It is situated near the mouth of the Tempisque River. To get there take the road from Bagaces to the west, off the Inter-American highway. Four-wheel drive is recommended, especially during the rainy season. If you are travelling independently, note that the southern entrance to the Park, from Cañas, may be closed; be sure to call the National Parks Service office to find out which routes are open and which are the most navigable. Alternatively, book a tour with one of the many operators who visit here.

Palo Verde encompasses lakes, swamps, woodlands, grasslands and forest and is a major sanctuary for migrating waterfowl in Central America. Tidal fluctuations and seasonally overflowing rivers attract 300 species of terrestrial

Las Pumas is owned by the Swiss-born Haganauer family who emigrated here in 1950. To raise revenue to help with the upkeep of the big cats that they rescue they also breed various birds.

BELOW: father and son at a rodeo near Liberia.

and waterbirds, including herons, whistling ducks, ibises and the immense jabirú stork. Large mammals and reptiles are also abundant and can easily be seen during the dry season when they gather at waterholes. Deer, coatimundis, armadillos, iguanas and crocodiles measuring up to 5 meters (15 ft) long are not uncommon here.

Only 25 years ago, currents and sediment runoff from Guanacaste formed a sand bar, which then became stabilized as an island in the middle of the Tempisque River near the head of the Gulf of Nicoya. Today, it is known as **Isla de Pájaros** ⑩. From the park a boat and guide can be chartered to this island, alternatively you can ask to go along with the park rangers on their visits to Pájaros. This quiet place provides the isolation which is favored by many water birds. While the white ibis and a species of egret are the only birds which regularly nest here, roseate spoonbills, wood storks and snake birds also occasionally make their homes on Isla de Pájaros.

Liberia

The capital city of Guanacaste province, **Liberia** ⑪ was established over 200 years ago. It is also known as *Ciudad Blanca*, the White City. Original residents carried white volcanic earth and gravel from the nearby slopes of Rincón de la Vieja and Miravalles volcanoes and constructed traditional white adobe homes in the *Puertas del Sol* – "Doorway of the Sun" – style, designed to let both morning and afternoon sunlight into north-facing corner houses.

ABOVE: Sunday-best cowboy tack.
BELOW: bubbling mud pots at Rincón de la Vieja.

Many of these lovely old adobe homes can still be seen, off the city's narrow streets, just south of the park. Some of them are being restored, and the owners may welcome visitors to see the work in progress. Inside many of the houses are classical courtyards, and grand rooms with high ceilings and 19th-century murals. The kitchens, to the rear of the house, open onto courtyards, where corn and other grains were dried.

Early morning is an ideal time to take a walk through the center of Liberia. Visit **Agonía Church**, an adobe structure built in 1852 and one of the oldest Catholic churches in the country. Talk with the helpful people at the Tourist Information Center, located in the **Casa de Cultura** (House of Culture) which is also home to the small **Museo de Sabanero** (Cowboy Museum). It is open Mon-Sat 8am–12pm, 1–4pm; entrance free. There is a lively daily farmers' market near the bus station.

Rincón de la Vieja National Park

Continuing upcountry from the city of Liberia is the **Parque Nacional Rincón de La Vieja** ⑫ with four complete ecosystems contained within its 14,000 hectares (35,000 acres). The name, which applies to both the park and the volcano it protects, derives from the legend of an old woman who once lived on its slopes. Her house was referred to as the old woman's corner – hence Rincón de la Vieja. Access is difficult because of poor roads, but the adventurous will find it virtually untouched. Hiking is excellent, but trails are not marked. Rainfall can be heavy so bring waterproof gear. April and May are normally the best times to visit.

Map on pages 178–79

At the junction of the Inter-American Highway just outside Liberia is the Bramadero restaurant. It is rich with the smell of leather tack and beef cooking in the kitchen. Dark-tanned cowboys sit at heavy wooden tables drinking beer.

BELOW: four-wheel drive vehicles are a good option if you can afford it.

The "official access road" to the park station at Rincón de la Vieja winds bumpily 27 km (17 miles) east out of Liberia. Appearing strangely snow-covered, it traverses an area of white chalky earth that gives Liberia its nickname of the White City. At the ranger station at the end of the road, you can climb to a lookout point for a view down the slopes of the volcano, across grassy plains, and all the way to the ocean. The station offers a bunkhouse and a good camp-site next to the ruins of an old sugarcane-processing plant. It is about a two-hour walk from there to the hot springs, which offer a place to soak weary bones. A cool pond nearby is refreshing afterwards. Horses can be rented from local tour companies.

The most extraordinary area, located at the foot of the volcano, is **Las Pailas** or the Kitchen Stoves. Here 8 hectares (20 acres) of hot springs, boiling mud pots, sulfur lakes and vapor geysers that color the surrounding rocks red, green and vivid yellow, offer a bizarre geological phenomenon unique to Costa Rica. It is said that the mud from the so-called Sala de Belleza (Beauty Salon) boiling pots makes an excellent facial beauty mask. Visitors must exercise extreme caution, however, since breaking through the brittle ground surface of the area can result in severe burns. It is much wiser to go with a guide.

Lodging is available at a number of inns. Closest to the Las Pailas entrance is the Albergue Rincón de la Vieja. Call in advance to let the owner know that you are coming. Then go north from Liberia, approximately 5 km (3 miles), and turn right onto the gravel road which leads to the village of Curubandé. From there go approximately one mile to the entrance to Hacienda Guachipelín, then enter through the gate and continue until you see a sign saying "Albergue."

The Albergue Buena Vista is more difficult to reach, but it is worth the effort. Take the Inter-American Highway 14 km (9 miles) north of Liberia, then turn right at Cañas Dulces and travel 17 km (11 miles) on a rough road.

To the Nicaraguan border

A good base from which to explore the area north to the border is the **Hotel Hacienda Los Inocentes**, a former ranch, now travelers' lodge, off the Inter-American highway on the road to Santa Cecilia. This scenic byway is bordered by streams with waterfalls and acres of saplings being used in reforestation pro-grams. Well-trained horses are available for visitors and the *sabanero* guides will match one to a guest's riding ability. Along streambeds, through forests and fields at the base of Orosi Volcano, the guides point out monkeys and sloths, iguanas and rare birds, enriching your experience considerably.

At the end of a day in this region, consider making a short trip east to the village of Santa Cecilia to watch the sun set over **Lake Nicaragua**.

During the recent war in Nicaragua, many of the local young men from this area were drawn into the battle, either for or against the US-backed Contra forces who were trying to overthrow the ruling San-dinistas. Near here, in the northern addition to Santa Rosa National Park, a clandestine CIA airstrip was constructed to bring in supplies to aid the Contra effort, in violation of Costa Rica's neutrality laws.

Built with the blessing of ex-president Alberto Monge, it was torn up under the administration of Oscar Arias. Arias' destruction of the CIA airstrip caused great chagrin to the Reagan administration, and resulted in a drastic decrease in US aid money for Costa Rica.

A rise in the bumpy road about 8 km (5 miles) beyond the center of Santa Cecilia brings the vast inland sea that is Lake Nicaragua into view. William Walker (*see page 45*) planned to conquer Nicaragua and to use the Nicaraguans as a labor force to build canals from Lake Nicaragua to the Pacific. He envisioned a waterway to transport goods by boat across the isthmus from the Pacific to the Atlantic. Wealthy investors in the United States backed this plan. But the defeat of Walker in Costa Rica, and later in Nicaragua and Honduras, put an end to the venture.

A trip to the bay at **Puerto Soley**, the northernmost Pacific beach of Costa Rica, passes through the small town of La Cruz, a stopping place for those traveling north through Central America, and for migrant laborers from Nicaragua crossing back and forth, seeking work in Costa Rica. A left turn in the center of La Cruz goes to the *mirador* built by the Costa Rican Tourist Institute, a pleasant place to rest and view the valley and bay below. Winding down the hill, past a ranch established by Somoza, the ex-dictator of Nicaragua, is serene Puerto Soley. The beach here is empty and breathtakingly beautiful.

Isla Bolaños

In the bay, the National Wildlife Refuge of **Isla Bolaños** ⓭ thrusts its rocky ledges 81 meters (267 ft) above the surface of the sea. An almost vertical island, it is the only nesting site in Costa Rica for the frigatebird and one of very few

Map on pages 178–79

BELOW: a park ranger, cycling to work on Playa Nancite.

TIP

In Parque Nacional Santa Rosa there are fine views from the lookout point at the Monumento a los Héroes – a large concrete arch which commemorates those who fell in battle at Santa Rosa in 1856.

for the brown pelican. You can visit Isla Bolaños by asking for Gustavo, almost certainly to be found among the houses near Puerto Soley, as he has been for many years. He will take up to five people to the island at a time and guide them around it. The 25-minute ride in his fishing boat gives a magnificent view of the shore.

The frigatebirds make nests in the dense thickets of woody vines on cliffs 40 meters (131 ft) above the sea. It's not just for the isolation and protection of the remote island that they nest here. Because of their wide wingspan and small bodies and feet, they find it difficult to take off from a standing or running start, like other birds, and therefore have to throw themselves into the air from a high ledge to catch the wind updrafts. In the dry season, when the frigatebirds mate, you can see the males puffing out brilliant scarlet sacs on their throats to attract the females.

It is an enjoyable walk around Isla Bolaños and the return to Puerto Soley, over transparent blue water, watching the magenta sun setting behind shimmering evening clouds, makes the perfect end to the day.

Guanacaste National Park

Parque Nacional Guanacaste ⓮ was created in 1989 with foreign funds donated to Costa Rica's Neotropica and National Park foundations in order to protect the migratory paths of animals living in the adjacent protected area of Santa Rosa National Park *(see opposite)*.

Guanacaste Park encompasses a wide band of largely deforested land which extends from Orosi and Cacao Volcanos to the Pacific Coast. Dry tropical forest dominates this vast land, but habitats ranging from mangrove swamps and

BELOW: poolside perfection at El Ocotal.

beaches to rain and cloud forest are also within the park's boundaries. Over the past several hundred years, complex patterns of cutting, grazing, burning and farming have dissected Guanacaste into a complex mosaic of life zones.

Dan Janzen, the visionary ecologist whose life work is the preservation and reforestation of Guanacaste, feels that this park will ultimately be restored to its original state. "Dry forests have been destroyed," Janzen says, "but they are tough, able to withstand six months of drought a year and are very regenerable." With the acquisition of Guanacaste National Park, the large tracts of land necessary for successful forest regeneration are now protected and under national park management. The park sustains large populations of many animal species which are able to find refuge during summer droughts and migrate freely between "islands" of forested areas.

Animals eat and disperse seeds from the trees, and have created these forest islands. Rain forest insects, important in pollinating dry forest plants, are attracted from nearby mountain slopes. In 20 years, significant canopy forest will have developed. And, in 200 or 300 years, full-grown tropical dry forests may again dominate Guanacaste.

Map on pages 178–79

Santa Rosa National Park

Parque Nacional Santa Rosa ⓯ encompasses virtually all of the environmental habitats of the region. A nearly infinite system of trails takes visitors through zones of deciduous tropical hardwoods, to arid mountains with deserts of cactus and thorny shrubs, and along rivers lined with forests to mangrove swamp estuaries near the beach. Two of its beaches, Nancite and Naranjo, are important turtle nesting sites. Elsewhere, many mammals, including monkeys and peccaries (wild pigs), plus over 20 species of bats live in the park.

ABOVE: pestle and mortar, La Casona.
BELOW: A Guaitil potter at work

During 20 years of scientific work at Santa Rosa, Dan Janzen has taught two generations of local people an intelligent appreciation of the forest. Through his work, residents of Guanacaste now have experience and expertise in firefighting, maintaining horses and managing cattle, identifying plants and dealing with "biotic challenges" like ticks, diseases, thirst and wounds. Jobs as research assistants, guides and reserve caretakers provide many with skills and a stable, long-term source of income.

Along Santa Rosa's **Naked Indian Path**, like many of the park's trails, you pass through forest which, during the dry season, loses many of its leaves, making wildlife viewing easier for the tropical naturalist. Enormous multi-colored iguanas are commonly seen in the trees bordering the trail. Hiking toward Duende Creek and the bat cave, look for them sunning on tree branches.

Santa Rosa's significance as the location of the historic battle against William Walker (*see page 45*) was a primary factor in the government's decision to make it a national park. The final battle against Walker took place at the hacienda **La Casona** ("The Big House"). By coincidence, on the three occasions that Costa Rica has been invaded, it has been here that the invaders were eventually turned back.

Today, a different kind of battle is fought in Santa Rosa. The rangers at the station tell of their encounters with hunters. Though hunting is outlawed in the park, the law is virtually unenforceable due to inadequate numbers of rangers. Armed hunters are frequently met by unarmed rangers who often must fight them to remove them from park boundaries. The low-paid rangers often risk their lives in these skirmishes.

The beautifully-restored hacienda of La Casona (open daily; entrance free) provides a window into the life of Costa Ricans during the Colonial period. The stone corrals are 300 years old. The house itself, with its beautiful weathered wood, has on display original pieces of furniture and artifacts. A trail leads to a memorial to the heroes and martyrs of the battle, and an historic plaque contains President Juan Rafael Mora's famous speech in which he exhorted his countrymen to defend Costa Rica against William Walker.

Wartime secrets

The northern section of the park was expanded to include the ranch of former Nicaraguan dictator Somoza, who lived there so he could move easily and clandestinely back and forth across the border. The Costa Rican government was interested in expanding Santa Rosa Park to make possible a stable population for some of the park's species. It also felt that its best interests were not served by the presence of an ousted military dictator near its border. So, in 1979, the **Murciélago Hacienda**, owned by the Somoza family, was expropriated and made part of the national parks system. The hacienda, which lies on **Saint Elena Bay** with access to **Playa Blanca** and its untouched white sand beach, is now a part of Santa Rosa Park. It can be reached from the entrance at the northern end of

BELOW: a deserted Pacific Coast beach.

Map on pages 178–79

the park. A sign on the Inter-American highway past the main entrance to Santa Rosa indicates the way.

A recent addition to the park is the land which was occupied by the formerly secret **Santa Elena Airstrip**, used by Oliver North and his cronies in their - Iran-Contra activities, and finally put out of operation in 1986, by President Oscar Arias.

Santa Rosa National Park beaches

A rugged 13-km (8-mile) hiking trail, or four-wheel drive road during the dry season (inaccessible during the wet season), leads from the Santa Rosa ranger station to **Playa Naranjo.** White sand and clear water with excellent surf breaking near **Witch's Rock**, a monolith 2 km (1 mile) offshore, make Naranjo a popular, though remote, surfing destination. Primitive campsites at Argelia House and Estero Real have outhouses and a windmill pumping fresh water for showers. Campers should, nonetheless, bring their own fresh drinking water.

Playa Nancite ⓰, one of Costa Rica's most pristine beaches, is northwest from Naranjo. Each month, usually on a waxing three-quarter moon, turtles come ashore here to nest. Tens of thousands may participate in the event, called an *arribada*, one of Costa Rica's grandest natural spectacles (*see pages 240–41*). Exact times are unpredictable, as they are with most biological phenomena. Even though a full-scale *arribada* may not be taking place, solitary turtles can usually be seen nesting on Nancite and Naranjo beaches.

Playa Panamá to Playa Ocotal

Playas Panamá, Hermosa, Coco and Ocotal are beaches some 30 to 40 km

The Santa Elena Airstrip was financed by a bogus Panamanian company set up by Oliver North. Its seizure by the Costa Rican government is a source of friction between Costa Rica and the United States even today.

BELOW: an idyllic beach scene on the Nicoya peninsula.

(15 to 20 miles) from Liberia, at the end of winding roads, most of which are paved but pocked with mudholes and ruts during the rainy season.

Playa Panamá , on a beautiful bay at the end of the road, is the site of a controversial Costa Rican Tourist Institute development called Papagayo, which had planned to bring a vast hotel complex – similar in style to the one that has transformed Cancún in Mexico – to the area. In the wake of fierce and long-running legal battles, however, the scale of the project has diminished considerably*.

Just south is **Playa Hermosa** ⓲, a sparkling cove with gentle surf. Cabinas Playa Hermosa, in a setting of beach almond trees, was one of the first hotels on the beach. Next door to the Cabinas Playa Hermosa, on the sand, are *campesino*-run restaurants that usually offer a fresh fish dinner for a few dollars. And at the other end of the cove and the economic spectrum is the Condovac luxury hotel and condominiums, which entertains its guests with toys ranging from jet skis to windsurfers.

The first view of the ocean coming from Liberia is of **Playa del Coco** ⓳, a honky-tonk little town of open-air bars, tiny restaurants, beachfront hotels, boardwalks, and teenagers on vacation. The large cove and wide sandy beach bustle with activity. Skiffs filled with fish are brought ashore and offloaded onto trucks parked on the sand. Radios playing in the seafood restaurants help to put people in the party mood with infectious Latin *salsa* and raucous rock 'n' roll.

South of Coco Beach, at **Playa El Ocotal** ⓴, a luxury hotel rests serenely on a hilltop overlooking the pounding surf, sandy coves, rocky capes and islands of the Nicoya coast. El Ocotal commands incredible views. Its circular restau-

Hotel El Velero on Playa Hermosa is named for the sailboat which brought its French-Canadian owners all the way from Quebec to Playa Hermosa. It is available for cruises to secluded beaches and other trips.

BELOW: handsome craft at Playa Flamingo marina.

rant perched on the edge of the cliffs is open to the general public. There is a road to the quiet beach, near the entrance to the hotel and a shady cove provides good sheltered swimming. Diving expeditions, to local waters, or as far away as Isla del Coco, can be arranged at El Ocotal Hotel, with Diving Safaris.

Though difficult to drive to, **Bahía Pez Vela** has a nice black-sand beach and a big game fishing resort, offering excitement in the form of world record-breaking blue marlin and sailfish. It is a bit on the pricey side. You can, for somewhat less, fish the same waters with local guides and boats.

Continuing south there are other pleasant, less-visited beaches. It may seem as though it is an impossibly complicated maze of dirt and gravel roads, but remember that the ocean is to the west and the highway is to the east and you should never get too lost!

Punta Zapotal to Cabo Velas

Turn off the highway at Comunidad and then head toward Belén. From there it is a short distance to **Playa Brasilito** and **Playa Potrero**. Or you can backtrack from Ocotal to Playa Coco and then drive on for another 15 km (9 miles) to the main highway. From there turn right to Filadelfia. Five km (3 miles) south of there, head right toward the coast and follow the signs to Flamingo. **Playa Conchal**, once a deserted slice of beach composed of bottomless drifts of pink, orange, mauve and sunset-colored sea shells, lies just south of Flamingo. To get there pass through Brasilito, a small town on a grey-sand beach with a few cabinas and a hotel, and then head south to the end of the road. An opulent resort which includes an 18-hole golf course, the **Hotel Meliá Conchal** has been constructed there on 360 hectares (900 acres) of land.

Map on pages 178–79

ABOVE: the taste of the tropics.
BELOW: shooting green turtles the ecological way.

Head back again to Brasilito, five minutes to the south, and you will come to **Playa Flamingo ㉑**, one of Costa Rica's more exclusive beaches, with its own marina and landing strip, or head up the hill to the Villas Pacífica Condominiums and Restaurant for fine dining and deluxe accommodations.

Development is proceeding apace on the beautiful beaches of Flamingo, which may owe its name to an early developer who mistook the pink-plumed roseate spoonbills who frequent the area for flamingoes.

Several kilometers up the coast, just inside Punta Salinas, **Flamingo Marina Resort** dominates a spectacular, white-sand beach, and looks out on rocks and islands dotting the horizon a few miles from shore. Wildlife, such as caimans, monkeys and wading birds have not yet deserted the nearby estuary, but they soon may, with the completion of the Flamingo Marina, the first fuel dock and full service marina on the Pacific coast south of Acapulco. Presently, it provides service for transient yachts heading north or south and has dock space for 80 vessels. Fishing tours can be arranged.

To the north is **Playa Potrero**, a cove of coconut palms and calm water, which is an excellent place for a picnic and a secluded dip in the ocean. The views get better, although the roads get worse, as you continue north along this picturesque coastline toward **Playa Pan de Azúcar**.

When you arrive at Pan de Azucar, it is obviously the last resort. Stop in at the **Hotel Sugar Beach** for incredible views, loud guffaws from the pet macaw, and enjoy a drink, lunch or a swim in the cove.

South of Cabo Velas

Go through Brasilito to Huacas and continue for 13 km (8 miles) south, where you will make a right turn for **Playa Grande ㉒** and **Playa Tamarindo ㉓**. Tamarindo is a national wildlife refuge, though you would scarcely realize it. The wildlife seems more concentrated at Henry's Third World Bar on the south end of town than it is in the nearby forest.

BELOW: away from the beaches and resorts, everyday life trundles on at a slow pace.

The luxurious Hotel Jardín del Edén, with pink-tiled roofs, is in the hills above the beach. The friendly, Swiss-owned Capitan Suizo is also luxurious. Relatively inexpensive lodging is available in the village of Tamarindo, at the Cabinas Zullymar, and other small hotels and *pensiones*. Or you can simply ask around about private beach houses for rent.

Tamarindo is a favorite surfers' haunt and has its own surf shop, Iguana Surf, where you can rent boards, kayaks and snorkeling equipment. Windsurfing is also becoming popular. Iguana Surf offers tours: one of itsmost popular is a 2-hour guided paddle through the estuary – a great way to see birds and wildlife.

Playa Grande is a 40-minute walk north on the beach at low tide, but is separated by chest-high water at high tide. Or it is a one-hour drive over dirt roads. Like Tamarindo, it has excellent surf.

Playa Grande is also a major leatherback turtle nesting habitat, and the site of environmental conflicts between conservationists and developers. When ultimately resolved, they may well define Costa Rica's policies of eco-tourism.

Las Baulas National Marine Park, which incorporates Playa Grande, was created in 1991 to protect the world's most important leatherback hatching area, was expanded in 1995. It was estimated at that time that there were only about 35,000 leatherbacks left in the world and approximately 900 of them come to Playa Grande to lay their eggs each year. During the long nesting season from August to February, as many as 80 turtles a night have been counted. On the beach at Playa Grande is Hotel Las Tortugas, a congenial, turtle-friendly hotel. Catch the Guanacastecan breezes from a comfortable hammock near the turtle-shaped swimming pool, chat with the charming owners of the hotel, or take a guided tour of the mangrove estuary on a pontoon boat whose motor is covered and nearly silent, ensuring a peaceful trip for riders and the birds they observe.

Playa Langosta, immediately south of Tamarindo across an estuary which is chest-deep at high tide, is also frequented by turtles, and by surfers who ride waves just in front of the estuary.

Head inland from Tamarindo for some 18 km (11 miles) and, at the junction of the 27 de Abril School, turn toward the coast and proceed for approximately 12 km (8 miles) to lovely **Junquillal Beach**. Junquillal is a paradisical, wide beach with high surf which gives you the sense of having found a secret place. Beware, all is not rosy in this Garden of Eden, however – there are rip currents and sharks to contend with.

Inland to Santa Cruz

Heading inland from the coast at Paraíso, few populated areas disturb the unbroken beauty of the rolling hills and valleys. An occasional cluster of three or four houses indicates a village. Here chickens, ducks and the lone cyclist claim

TIP

For more on turtles, see the features on page 202 and pages 240–41.

Map on pages 178–79

BELOW: a glorious Nicoya sunset.

The Vampire Bats of Guanacaste

There are over 100 kinds of bats in Costa Rica. From the shrilling flutterings of millions of these creatures, which rises up from the deep caves of Barra Honda, to a quiet few hanging in the cool, darkened corners of La Casona in Santa Rosa Park they are to be found throughout the country. Most of them are benevolent, curious-looking animals, who feed on nectar, fruit and insects. But within Santa Rosa Park, in Guanacaste, inside of a cave near Naked - Indian Path, lives a group of *Desmodex Rotundum*, or vampire bats.

Bats are beneficial, even necessary, as significant pollinators and disseminators of seeds, especially in deforested areas in Costa Rica. Researchers know them to be clean, docile – even friendly. Nectar bats are gregarious and hang from the ceilings of caves in tight clusters. In the evening, they feed on

insects along roads or dry river beds. At night, they search for nectar from white, night-blooming flowers which they pollinate. Bats do much to control insect populations; it is reported that a colony of one million bats would consume over 10,000 pounds of insects a night.

Three of the species drink blood. Hollywood and Victorian novelists have done their part in creating the myth of the vampire who lives on the blood of innocent humans. And there are certain other factors which contribute to the legends that surround this creature: the vampire bat has large thumbs which protrude from the wings, appendages used for stealthy crawling towards the prey. A flat, red, pig-like nose, large eyes, prominent front teeth and relatively small and pointed ears make this one of the least appealing creatures of the night.

The caped and fanged, black-haired fictional figure from Transylvania no doubt rose up, fully-formed, in the imagination of early movie makers who had heard of the nocturnal activities of these animals. For it is true that this species feeds mainly during the darkest hours, before the moon is out, quietly alighting upon a sleeping victim and making a painless incision with razor sharp teeth. Contrary to the myth, the blood of the victim is not sucked out, but rather lapped up, much as a cat drinks milk.

A bat does not drink its victim dry. Instead, rabies and other infections, introduced through the wounds, kill the prey. More than a million animals a year die this way. Humans are sometimes prey as well, and sleeping people have been infected by the bat with the dreaded paralytic rabies.

Cattle ranchers are striking back against the vampire bat. Methods of extermination have included gassing their caves with toxic substances and dynamiting. Such methods, often born of an irrational aversion to the bat, do not specifically target the vampire variety. Unfortunately, anything and everything in the area is harmed or killed. A more precise, but equally extreme, system involves trapping the bats and coating them with poisons. When released, each bat will then fatally infect up to 20 others. ❏

LEFT: vampire bats inflict huge financial damage each year by infecting farm animals.

the road. The miles are marked by the infrequent passage of herds of noisy Brahma cows, turning traffic into a cattle drive, followed in their leisurely journey by *sabaneros* on horseback. These *Guanacasteco* cowboys don't direct the animals out of the road; they let the automobile wend its way through them. The cattle, with their sensitive faces, seem neither concerned nor curious.

Santa Cruz ㉔ (population 15,000) is a small, friendly town. In the central plaza, the modern church, built when the old one was destroyed by an earthquake in 1950, stands beside the original colonial clock tower. The central park is a quiet shady place for sitting and viewing the life of a Guanacaste town.

Map on pages 178–79

Hungry visitors to Santa Cruz should not miss the experience of eating indigenous food at the **Coopetortilla**, 500 meters west of the church. In a huge single-room building of tin and screen, an open wood fire is used to prepare the large, handmade *tortillas Guanacastecas*, rice and beans, and other local dishes. A sign says "*ambiente familiar*," or family atmosphere.

For visitors wishing to spend the night in Santa Cruz, the Diriá provides air-conditioned rooms and a pool, and many cabinas are available around the town offering basic but adequate facilities.

Guaitil

One of the main visitor attractions in this part of Guanacaste is the small town of **Guaitil** ㉕, where you will find ceramic pots in the style of the pre-Columbian inhabitants of this part of Costa Rica. After the Conquest, pottery-making died out here, possibly because the images adorning pots were considered pagan by the Catholic Church. The craft has been reawakened in recent years and today the popularity of these giant, luscious ceramic pots is

ABOVE: Chorotega pottery. **BELOW:** golden sands and mangroves at Tamarindo.

obvious from their presence in the lobbies and dining rooms of many hotels in Guanacaste.

It seems as though almost every house in the neighborhood of Guaitil has a kiln and pots for sale in the yard. The widest selection, however, will be found next to the soccer field in front of the church. You may possibly see so-called pre-Columbian pottery for sale, though these pieces, if in fact they are pre-Columbian and not fakes, are taken from Indian burial grounds and as historical artifacts are prohibited by the 1982 Patrimonial Law of National Archaeology from being taken from Costa Rica. Their purchase also creates a market, which encourages desecration of burial sites.

Nicoya

From Guaitil it is a scenic, bumpy 50-minute drive on the old road to the town of **Nicoya** ㉖, considered to be the cultural capital of Guanacaste. (An alternative is to return to Santa Cruz and make the 20-minute drive on the highway.) The pride of Nicoya is its central park and colonial church, now a museum (open 8am–12pm, 2–6pm, closed Sun and Wed; entrance fee).

Three hours off the Inter-American highway towards the Pacific from Nicoya, and 7 hours from San José, on bad, bumpy roads, is the seldom-visited **Ostional National Wildlife Refuge** (*see below*).

Playa Nosara

The beaches of Nosara and nearby Sámara are becoming increasingly popular destinations for North American and European holidaymakers. **Playa Nosara** ㉗ is a splendid long wide beach with white sand and good surf, backed by rolling

If you don't already find that Nosara is the sort of place where you can totally unwind, try seeking out the Nosara Retreat, which specializes in physical and spiritual rejuvenation.

BELOW: against mighty odds, a baby turtle makes it to the ocean's edge.

THE ARRIBADA

Created to protect the endangered Olive Ridley turtle, the Ostional National Wildlife refuge is witness to the spectacular phenomenon known as the *arribada*, when tens of thousands of turtles come to the beach to lay their eggs. It is estimated that during these brief periods as many as 100,000 Olive Ridleys may come ashore to this isolated beach, and leave behind over ten million eggs. *Arribadas* generally occur at two to four-week intervals between the third quarter and full moon from April to December, peaking during July through September.

Presently, there is a controversial program of egg collecting at Ostional, which gives the people of the nearby village the right to legally gather as many of the Ridley turtle eggs as they can during the first 36 hours of every *arribada*.

If you wish to view the amazing sight of thousands of these creatures laboriously coming ashore to thump the sand with their flippers and dig their incubation holes to lay their eggs, then check in at the guard station on your journey down to the beach. And please remember to watch the activities as unobtrusively as possible.

green hills.The roads from Nicoya are nearly impassable during the rainy season, and many visitors fly here from San José.

Many of the 100 or so residents of the Nosara Beach community are willing to rent out their homes by the week or month, and if you drive through the windy roads of this striking international community, along the lush, wooded hillsides above the beaches, look for "*Se Alquila*" (To Rent) signs.

A large part of Nosara is protected as a reserve, and as a result it is more forested and richer in wildlife than other parts of the region. Coatimundis, armadillos, parrots, toucans and monkeys are plentiful. There is also excellent snorkeling, tide pool exploring, and camping in the area.

The Hotel Playa Nosara is on a point above the beach, and offers inspiring views from its cabins overlooking Playa Guiones and Playa Pelada. Here, also, the Nosara Retreat offers idyllic instruction in yoga. Apartments and *cabinas* are available for rent; camping on the beach is also an option.

In the town of Nosara, Monkey Business sells fresh whole wheat bread and good sandwiches. It also rents boogie boards.

Playa Sámara and south

Playa Sámara 28, nearly an hour south of Nosara, has a beautiful white-sand beach and a good reef for snorkeling, which also protects the beach from direct waves. Swimming is safe in crystalline, warm, shallow waters with minimal surf. Windsurfers have recently discovered this area, but at present there is the minimum of activity. Off season, there is a feeling of dramatic isolation and escape. During the high season, Playa Sámara is popular with Costa Ricans and many Ticos have summer homes here.

Map on pages 178–79

ABOVE: statuesque white egret.
BELOW: another lazy day on the Nicoya peninsula.

Rip tides are a danger in Costa Rica, and kill several visitors every year. Ask around first whether a beach is safe for swimming. If you are caught by a rip tide, don't panic and do not swim against it. Try to swim parallel to the shore, and eventually the breaking waves will carry you back in.

Villas Playa Sámara, located on the beach, is a rambling village of over 50 red roofed, privately-owned villas which are often available for rent. Diving, snorkeling, fishing, and bicycle and horse-back trips can be arranged. On the south side of the beach is the exceptional Hotel Las Brisas del Pacífico, with a pool fronting the ocean. The German restaurant manager impresses guests with excellent rich food. To the north of the beach are smaller, basic *cabinas* and hostels, with camping permitted.

There are regular flights to Sámara which cut out the long and tiring drive. Driving is particularly difficult during the wet season, as you have to cross a shallow river between Nosara and Sámara.

A little way south of Sámara is **Playa Carrillo** **②**, yet another near-flawless white-sand beach protected by an offshore reef. The Guanamar fishing facility is located here, as are a few very basic *cabinas*. Driving to Playa Carrillo requires crossing the Río Ora, which is impassable if the tide is high. Beyond Carrillo are other extraordinary beaches, isolated, lonely places, sometimes with fresh water available, sometimes not. **Playa Caletas,** just a little way south of Carrillo on unpaved, almost non-existent roads has large surf with offshore breezes. And further south still is **Punta Islita.** Located in the heart of a picturesque valley, the Punta Islita Hotel has wonderful ocean views, a beautiful blue-tile pool, private porches with picture windows and hammocks.

Parque Nacional Barra Honda

BELOW: the aptly-named elephant's ears plant.

About 16 km (10 miles) from the town of Nicoya is **Barra Honda National Park** **③**, a vast network of caves. Along the road to the Tempisque Ferry are national park signs showing the way to this seldom-visited place. On the flat

ridgeline, 300 meters (1,000 ft) above the caves, is a *mirador* (lookout) that can be reached via marked paths. Standing there along the high ridge, with the sounds of an enormous waterfall, amongst screeching tropical birds, howler monkeys, and iguanas in the trees, looking out across the vast Nicoya peninsula can be a humbling experience.

You don't have to be a dedicated spelunker to enjoy Barra Honda, though some of the caves are quite deep and require steep vertical drops to enter. With names such as *La Trampa* (The Trap), and *Terciopelo* (Fer-de-Lance viper), they may not sound inviting, but the fragile cave formations are dazzling. One such formation, called The Organ, produces melodic tones when gently touched. Ancient human remains, blind salamanders, vampire bats and strange birds share the world of darkness in the Barra Honda caves, which, have escaped vandalism and exploitation because they lack an easily accessible horizontal entrance. Barrio Cubillo is the closest town to the park where you will find a community group led by Luis Alberto Díaz which provides cave tours. Simple lodging and good *campesino* food (try Las Delicias) are also available. In the dry season, it gets *hot* so be sure to bring a wide-brimmed hat and a canteen.

The ferry across the **Tempisque River** is the preferred passage back to the highway to San José. Pedestrians and hitchhikers are always grateful for a ride to the ferry, and in exchange you might possibly hear a good story or two.

The Tempisque ferry is able to carry 40 cars and innumerable passengers for the 20-minute ride across the river. On Sundays, the wait to board can be a long one, as Ticos from San José return home after a weekend at the beaches near Liberia and Santa Cruz. Small restaurants selling food and beer line the road near the ferry crossing. Vendors near the gate to the ferry sell hot tortillas, shish-kabobs, and peeled oranges.

When the ferry arrives, the cars and buses roll aboard, laden with souvenirs of the weekend: stalks of coconuts and bananas fill rooftop luggage carriers. And, in season, children and adults alike carry home bags of the eggs of endangered species of turtles, still considered by many to be aphrodisiacs. Some of the eggs have been excavated by adventurers, others have been purchased at *sodas* near the beach and are the booty of *hueveros*, who make an illegal business of raiding the turtles' nests. Others are part of a cache of eggs taken legally by those who are given permits by the government to take the eggs during the first 36 hours of an *arribada* (*see page 202*).

It is another 185 km (115 miles) up the coast and through the mountains back to San José. Along the highway, dozens of fruit stands offer an opportunity to load up on tropical fruit, honey, and homemade candies before returning to the hustle and bustle of the capital.

Monteverde Cloud Forest

Lying atop the Continental Divide, some 180 km (110 miles) northwest of San José is the **Reserva Biológica del Bosque Nuboso de Monteverde ③**. It is a difficult place to get to and you should allow 4 hours' driving time from San

Map on pages 178–79

BELOW: with around 760 cm (300 inches) of rain per year, there are plenty of waterfalls in Monteverde.

The Resplendent Quetzal

The Resplendent Quetzal is rightly acclaimed as the most magnificent bird in the western hemisphere. Some 40 species inhabit the tropics worldwide and ten are found in Costa Rica. It is one of the country's greatest natural treasures.

The pigeon-sized male owes his elegance to the intensity and brilliant contrasts of his colors, the sheen and glitter of his plumage, the beauty of his adornments, and the great dignity of his posture. The rich crimson of his underparts contrasts with the shining, iridescent green of his head, chest, and upper parts. His head is crowned with a narrow crest of upstanding feathers that extends from his small yellow bill to his nape. The pointed tips of the long, loose-barbed coverts of his wings project over the crimson of his sides in beautiful contrast. Most notable are his central tail coverts, which stretch far

beyond his tail and, like two slender green pendants, undulate gracefully when he flies.

As may be seen on many an ancient sculpture and modern painting, the long tail coverts were highly valued as personal adornments by the Aztec and Mayan nobility. As Guatemala's national bird, the peaceful quetzal contrasts with the fierce predators and firebreathing monsters that other nations have chosen for their emblems. Guatemalans one believed that their symbol of liberty would die if deprived of freedom, but modern aviculturists have learned how to keep it alive in captivity – a hard negation of a beautiful myth.

The quetzal's song is eminently worthy of a bird so splendidly attired. Fuller and deeper than those of any other trogon, they are not distinctly separated but slurred and fused into a flow of soft and mellow sound that is unforgettably beautiful.

Monogamous pairs of quetzals nest in the holes of trees located in mountain forests or in nearby clearings. The hole, like that of a woodpecker, extends straight downwards from the opening at the top. Usually it is deep enough to conceal all of the sitting birds except the ends of the male's train. On the unlined bottom of the chamber, the female lays two light blue eggs. She incubates through the night and the middle of the day. The male takes a long turn on the eggs in the morning and again in the afternoon. His train arches over his back and projects through the doorway, fluttering in the breeze. On an epiphyte-burdened trunk, the ends might be mistaken for two green fern fronds.

Sometimes, when his partner arrives to relieve him of his long spell in the nest, he soars straight upward, right above the treetops, loudly shouting a phrase that sounds almost like "very-good very-good." At the summit of his ascent he circles, then dives into sheltering foliage. These "joy flights" seem to express the bird's great vitality.

Resplendent Quetzal are still abundant in the tracts of unspoiled mountain forests. So long as such forests are preserved, they are in no danger of becoming extinct, but if they are destroyed, then Central America will lose its most magnificent bird. ❑

LEFT: the quetzal with its favorite food, *aguacatillo*, a type of small avocado.

José. Head for some 36 km (22 miles) past the turnoff to Puntarenas, on the Inter-American highway, and just before crossing the Lagarto River there are signs to Monteverde. Turn right at kilometer marker 149 and continue on the gravel road into the Cordillera de Tilarán mountain range for 43 km (26 miles) of very poor road conditions, all the way to Santa Elena and then Monteverde. The last 90 minutes of the drive is especially rough.

Even so, every year tens of thousands of people visit the preserve. In order to protect the flora, and fauna and the trails themselves, visitors are now limited to 100 at any given time – which means you may have to wait your turn. You should book at least one night's accommodation in advance and to get the best out of the area a total of three days is recommended.

More visitors are attracted to Monteverde Cloud Forest than to any other forest reserve in Costa Rica, and usually for one purpose only: to sight the Resplendent Quetzal, the most colorful and spectacular bird in the tropics.

Though listed as an endangered species throughout Central America, it is estimated that nearly 1,000 quetzals make their home in Monteverde. Be warned, however, it is a difficult bird to spot. With the exception of their almost luminous crimson breast, they are cloaked in radiant green plumage and easily disappear among the rich colors of the cloud forest. The best time to spot them is January to September and especially during the mating season, which runs from April through May.

Monteverde is much more than just an opportunity to spot a quetzal, however. This misty verdant high-altitude cloud forest is home to a multitude of diverse creatures: 400 species of birds, 490 species of butterflies, 2,500 species of plants and 100 species of mammals. There are jaguars here, too, though they prove

Map on pages 178–79

ABOVE: Monteverde flora.
BELOW: sunrise mist rises above the forest canopy.

even more elusive than the quetzal. Pick up a checklist and map at the Visitors Center. Guided tours are available.

Before leaving the forest, visit the **Hummingbird Gallery**, across the road from the entrance. Owners Michael and Patricia Fogden, biologists and pre-eminent nature photographers, have spent two decades shooting the fauna of Monteverde and their remarkable work is shown here.

Mayan kings prized the iridescent green tail feathers of the quetzal more than gold itself. They also believed the bird could not live in captivity, and it was therefore the supreme symbol of freedom.

Monteverde's Quaker community

The community of **Monteverde** ❷ was established by a group of Quakers who, wanting to escape the obligations of US military service, moved here from Alabama in 1951. To support themselves the Quakers began making cheese from milk brought to their primitive processing plant each morning by Tico dairy farmers. Today, the Quakers produce tons of cheese daily, it has become a proud Costa Rican speciality, and it can be found in markets throughout Central America. En route to the reserve, stop in at their cheese processing plant, **La Lechería**, for a tour (open Mon–Fri, Sat am; entrance fee), or watch the production through windows in the plant. Don't expect to see too many Quakers elsewhere in Monteverde, however. They keep themselves to themselves on their farms and generally avoid the commercialised town that Monteverde has now become.

Just north of here look in at CASEM (Comité de Artesanías Santa Elena-Monteverde) an arts and crafts cooperative founded by eight women in 1982. Today, over 140 artisans contribute their work, which is on sale at less-than-downtown prices at the CASEM shop. Across the road is the popular coffee shop of Stella's Bakery and Meg's Stables which offers horse-riding tours.

BELOW: a timid tapir, rarely seen in the wild.

Other Monteverde attractions

Adjacent to Monteverde Cloud Forest preserve are two much smaller reserves. There is usually good wildlife viewing at the **Reserva Sendero Tranquilo** (Quiet Path Reserve), which is open for guided tours only from December through August. You must book ahead (tel: 645-5272).

Opposite the Hotel Heliconia, on the road to Santa Elena, turn off left (heading west) to the **Monteverde Butterfly Garden** (El Jardin de las Mariposas) which exhibits all the butterfly species of the region (open daily 7am–4pm; entrance fee). Guided tours take you through the various stages of a butterfly's life and into a screened garden where hundreds of species flutter freely. There is also a leaf-cutter ant colony exhibition.

Adjacent to the Butterfly Garden is the **Monteverde Eco-Farm** (Finca Ecologica) which is a small private reserve with four loop trails. The longest only takes 2½ hours at a leisurely pace so is quite accessible to all visitors. Agoutis, coatis and sloths are often spotted, and porcupines and monkeys are also frequent visitors. The birdwatching is also good – quetzals are seen here – and the finca provides a list and an information kiosk where you can find out the best locations. Tel: 645 5222 to reserve your place.

Another new Monteverde attraction is **The Sky Walk**. This comprises a series of hanging bridges suspended Indiana Jones-style from platforms in the tree canopy. It's a wonderful way of getting a bird's-eye-view of the forest. For the truly adventurous there is a two-hour trail which involves donning mountain-climbing harnesse and zipping through the trees suspended on thin wires.

Santa Elena Reserve and around

Around 5 km (3 miles) northeast of Monteverde village is an outstanding local initiative, the **Reserva Santa Elena ㉝**, or Santa Elena Rain Forest Reserve. It was created in 1992 as a local high school project and includes several kilometers of well-kept paths. Tours are well-organised and cheaper than Monteverde, yet the flora and fauna (including quetzals, jaguars and howler monkeys) is every bit as impressive as that of its famous neighbor. You also avoid the crowds here. The most exciting way of exploring the reserve is by joining a Canopy Tour. You are pulled up to the treetops by pulleys, then go from platform to platform on horizontal cables. Tours last two hours and depart daily from the Canopy Tour Base Camp in Santa Elena (7.30am, 10am, 2pm).

Some 3km (2 miles) north of Santa Elena at **El Trapiche** is the chance to see a traditional sugar mill, driven by ox power. There is a coffee plantation adjacent and also a rather sad so-called Eco-Park.

A little further out, on the Atlantic slope, east of Monteverde Cloud Forest, is the **Children's Eternal Forest** (El Bosque Eterno de los Niños). Back in 1987, a group of Swedish school children raised and donated enough money to purchase 6 hectares (15 acres) of forest. Now, with support from young people from all over the world, they have bought over 16,000 hectares (40,000 acres). A small section of the forest is open to the public. ❏

Map on pages 178–79

ABOVE: visitor and resident at Monteverde's Serpentario.
BELOW: false eyes ward off predators.

COSTA RICA'S WINGS OF WONDER

With over 850 species of birds, Costa Rica is one of the world's foremost destinations for professional ornithologists and amateur birders

Despite its small size, Costa Rica has roughly the same number of birds as the whole of North America, and significantly more than Europe or Australia. This tremendous diversity is explained partly by the fact that the country is in the tropics, and partly by its position on one of the world's great bird migration routes, which links North and South America.

For most birders Costa Rica's resident species – rather than its migrants – are the ones that hold the most interest. The most sought-after sighting of all is undoubtedly the Resplendent Quetzal, a high-altitude fruit-eater that lives in the cloud forests of the Central Highlands. Quetzals are generally shy and quiet, and it takes patience to locate them. Toucans are much more vocal, while the scarlet macaw is garrulous and noisy, skimming over the treetops in fast-flying raucous flocks.

NECTAR FEEDERS

Costa Rica boasts about 50 species of tiny but pugnacious hummingbirds, which feed largely on a diet of sugary nectar. They are often lured to artificial feeders and make an unmissable spectacle of color and whirring wings.

▷ **MID-AIR REFUELLING**
A hummingbird, which can be surprisingly pugnacious for its size, feeds on a "hotlips" flower at Monteverde. Although hummingbirds live largely on nectar, they also catch insects to feed their young.

▽ **RESPLENDENT QUETZAL**
Rich and lustrous when seen in the open, the quetzal's iridescent green plumage provides effective camouflage against a background of leaves. The male's tail streamers are up to 1 meter (3ft) long, and have to be folded around the body when the bird enters its nesting hole.

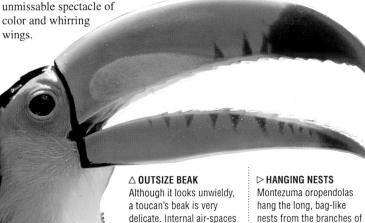

△ **OUTSIZE BEAK**
Although it looks unwieldy, a toucan's beak is very delicate. Internal air-spaces help to reduce its weight.

▷ **HANGING NESTS**
Montezuma oropendolas hang the long, bag-like nests from the branches of tall, isolated trees.

ENDANGERED SPECIES

Despite Costa Rica's notable efforts to protect its forests, habitat destruction has had a serious effect on some of its birds. A handful of species, such as the cattle egret and roadside hawk, have actually benefited from man-made changes to the environment, because they need open ground to feed. However, for many others, the steady shrinkage of forest cover has been very bad news.

The quetzal is particularly vulnerable because it depends on undisturbed cloud forest for survival. The three-wattled bellbird, famous for its extremely loud call, shares this habitat, and is equally threatened by its conversion to pasture. For species like these national parks and private reserves, such as Monteverde, are a lifeline to survival.

As in other parts of the American tropics, large parrots have also fared badly, and only the colonies in Carara and Corcovado are likely to survive. Even higher on the critical list is Costa Rica's biggest flying predator, the awe-inspiring American harpy eagle. This giant monkey-eating bird is known to have bred in the forests of the Osa Peninsula, but sightings of it have become extremely rare.

△ **WATCHING ON WATER**
Open waterways – such as the canals at Tortuguero – make good places to see birds when they set off at dawn to find food, or settle down to roost at dusk.

▽ **SUBMERSIBLE SWIMMER**
An anhinga or darter with its catch. Anhingas feed in lakes and coastal lagoons, and often swim with just their head and neck visible.

△ **INSECT-EATER**
The blue-crowned motmot lives in forests and coffee plantations, and spends most of its time watching for food from its perch. Its diet consists mainly of insects.

THE NORTHEAST

*Volcán Arenal is the star of the region, though the Sarapiquí River
and the lodges of Rara Avis and La Selva are also becoming
popular with more environmentally conscious visitors*

Map
on pages
178–179

San José

The region to the northeast of San José corresponds roughly to the area
known as the Northern Zone. The landscape is lush and agricultural and,
with the exception of Volcán Arenal, has traditionally only been the haunt
of hardy independent travelers. These days, however, more and more visitors are
discovering the magnificent rainforests of this region.

Around Ciudad Quesada (San Carlos)

At the foot of the Cordillera Central, **Ciudad Quesada ㉞**, often called by its
former name San Carlos, is the gateway to the north and is the agricultural and
commercial heart of the region. Its chief products are cattle, citrus and sugar
cane. It's a pleasant, clean, bustling town of around 40,000 people and in the surrounding areas are several good places to stay. Some 15 km (9 miles) north of
Ciudad Quesada just beyond Planatar, and overlooking the Planatar River, is
La Garza, a large working cattle and horse ranch, which has charming *cabinas*
set among beautifully-landscaped gardens and expanses of lawn. Guests are
invited to go horseback riding, tubing, swimming or fishing for *guapote* on the
river and they can learn about the dairy, cattle and horse operations of the ranch.

   The Tilajari Hotel Resort, near Muelle, around 22 km (14 miles) north of
Ciudad Quesada, is a luxurious spread, set on several
acres of rolling lawns overlooking the wide, muddy
San Carlos River. It makes a good base for exploring
this region, and offers tennis, swimming, racquetball,
horseback riding, and hiking in 300 hectares (750
acres) of rainforest. Further afield you can take fishing trips, and jungle river tours to Caño Negro Wildlife Reserve *(see page 220)*.

   The Tilajari is also one of the lift-off points for an
enchanting hot-air balloon ride over the **San Carlos
Valley**. (Rides are also available at other sites.) Standing in a traditional wicker balloon basket, under a
multi-colored balloon, in the quiet time just after
dawn, you rise up, as if in a dream, over a forest preserve and look down into the tree tops at the howler
monkeys and toucans who are just waking up. Moving on, over pasture lands, sugar cane and pineapple
fields, over grazing cattle and horses, the sun rises
and the countryside comes alive.

La Fortuna and Tabacón Hot Spring

From Muelle it's around 25 km (16 miles) west to **La
Fortuna ㉟**, (also known as Fortuna de San Carlos).
It's a pleasant village located near the base of Arenal
Volcano, and functions as a gateway to the volcano
with all sorts of tours and accommodation available.

   Some 5 km (3 miles) east of La Fortuna is the turn-
off to the **Río Fortuna Waterfalls**. They are accessi-

PRECEDING PAGES:
Volcán Arenal.
LEFT:
Sarapiquí waterfall.
BELOW:
white ibises.

ble in an hour's easy horseback ride from La Fortuna through pastures and fields of ginger, corn, bananas and peppers. The ride by car requires 4-wheel drive. Once at the falls, a muddy hike down a slippery slope to the swimming area at the base of the falls makes the clear, fresh water all the sweeter.

Tabacón Hot Springs

Moving ever closer to the volcano, between La Fortuna and Lake Arenal, is the **Tabacón Hot Springs Resort and Spa ㊱**. From here you can look directly up the small valley to the slopes of the volcano, and to cascades of glowing hot boulders. It appears dangerously close, yet the volcano also has a benign effect. Arenal heats Tabacón's therapeutic waters to a perfect temperature. Tiled slides, waterfalls and pools of varying temperatures are surrounded by tumbling warm water creeks and lush gardens. You can even have a jacuzzi, or a massage. Enjoy a meal in Tabacón's dining room and watch the erupting volcano from a quiet pool under the starry sky. And should you be there when the full moon waxes over Arenal, then that single experience is worth the trip to Costa Rica in itself.

Just across the road from the spa is a cheaper more basic springs complex where you can still luxuriate in warm mineral-rich waters in sandy-bottomed pools, though here there is no view of the volcano.

Down the highway, past the Tabacón Hot Springs Resort, is a dirt road going to the left and the **Arenal Observatory Lodge**, formerly a research facility for the Smithsonian Institution and Costa Rica's Universidad Nacional. It is the only lodge in the National Park, located on its own huge estate with primary and secondary forest, waterfalls, hiking and horseback trails. To get to the lodge follow the gravel road for 9 km (6 miles), crossing two rivers on the way. From

BELOW:
an active Volcán
Arenal is an
unforgettable sight.

here Arenal is only 1 km away and by night the air is rich with the sounds of howling monkeys and the glow of fireflies.

Arenal Volcano

Until early July 1968, Arenal was a heavily-wooded low hill, similar to many others in the area, near the village of La Fortuna. Then one morning the people there began feeling a few earth tremors. Suddenly, the forest started smoking and steaming. Women washing their clothes marvelled at the sudden warm water which flowed in the creeks. Then, on July 29, all hell broke loose and **Volcán Arenal** ㊲ exploded. Rolling clouds of gas and fountains of red-hot boulders and molten lava hit the countryside like a bomb. Official estimates put the death toll at 62, but local people claim that many more were killed. Over 5 sq. km (2 sq miles) of land near the volcano was abruptly changed from pastoral farmland to a landscape out of Dante's *Inferno*.

Since then, Arenal has been continuously active. It is everyone's preconception of a volcano: conical, rising abruptly out of flatland vegetation. But do not attempt to climb it. The molten lava running down her western slope has a temperature of 926°C (1,699°F), not to mention an unpredictable spew of rocks, intense heat and poison gases. Sadly, every couple of years there is a visitor who disregards the warning signs and then the volcano claims another life.

The road west to **Nuevo Arenal** is dreadful and a four-wheel drive vehicle is recommended. This New Arenal is a town reborn from the old village of Arenal, which was flooded in 1973, to create the lake. Nuevo Arenal has a good number of friendly and inexpensive restaurants and small hotels – and a variety of pleasant accommodations are available along the road to Tilarán. A few kilo-

Map on pages 178–79

A sign at the base of Arenal Volcano reads "Volcano influence area. If you notice abnormal activity, run away from the area and report it to the nearest authority."

BELOW: beautifully landscaped grounds of the Tabacón Hot Springs Resort.

meters east is the **Jardín Botánico Arenal** ❸ (open daily, closed Oct; entrance fee), which are the work of Michael Le May, an indefatigable amateur horti-culturist. It features over 1,000 native and exotic species and is a magnet to humming birds and butterflies. Late afternoon is the best time to visit, though visitor numbers are limited, so the gardens are never too busy.

Lake Arenal

Laguna de Arenal ❹ offers some of Costa Rica's most challenging freshwater fishing. The *guapote* is the favorite of fishermen there *(see page 105)*. Wheth-er you choose to fish or not, charter a boat and guide to take you sightseeing on the lake. It is preferable to go in the early morning, when, for much of the year, the lake's surface is like glass and the volcano can be viewed as a crystalline reflection. A few local fishermen will probably be out in the middle of the lake, sitting on chairs perched on a pair of floating balsa logs, fishing for *guapote* with simple handlines.

From December through March, usually in the afternoons, northeasterly winds blow almost daily, and the lake is anything but calm and glassy. Between 40 and 50 knots of sustained breeze is not uncommon and whips Arenal into a sea of whitecaps. Latterly, attracted by these conditions, it has become a favorite destination for experienced windsurfers. Tico Wind, in Nuevo Arenal, rents a full range of windsurfing equipment and offers lessons. It is open from December 1 through to the end of April.

The west end of the lake is the best for short board sailing and a number of windsurfing resorts have opened near **Tilarán,** an old-time Costa Rican town with a population of less than 6,000, whose name comes from the Chorotega

ABOVE: cattle at la Fortuna.
BELOW: naturalists on a bridge over the Sarapiquí near Selva Verde.

words for "wind and rain." Whether or not you are a windsurfer, it is a good place to spend the night as it is situated in the hills above the Guanacaste lowlands and is refreshingly cool. The countryside around the town is pastoral, the upland meadows spotted with dairy cattle. Villagers will arrange for boats and fishing guides on Lake Arenal.

It is perhaps predictable that such a myth-inspiring lake as Arenal would find a resident monster. A few years ago, some local fishermen were out on their raft early one evening and felt a strange rumbling in the water. Suddenly, right in front of them an enormous, hairy serpent with horns broke through the surface with a belching roar and a stench. Moments later it slid back into the depths, trailing a tail over 2 meters (6 ft) long. The fishermen scurried back to town and told the tale over and over. The story went around and, amplified by time and accounts of half-eaten horse carcasses found floating on the lake, the Monster of Lake Arenal is entrenched in local folklore.

To Arenal via San Ramón

An alternative route to Arenal from San José is via **San Ramón**. It's a good idea to spend the night here as the guest of ex-Costa Rican President Rodrigo Carazo and his wife, Doña Estrella, at **Villa Blanca**, set on 154 hectares (380 acres) of cultivated land, surrounded by the beautiful **Los Angeles Cloud Forest**, also owned by the family. The reserve, which consists of 800 hectares (2,000 acres) of primary forest, has a 2-km (1-mile) trail paved in chicken wire to provide footing on slippery stretches.

From San Ramón continue north through San Lorenzo to La Tigra. On the gravel and dirt road between La Tigra and Chachagua is the Hotel Bosques de Chachagua cattle and horse ranch with 15 guest cabins. Elegant long-necked *Paso Criollo* horses are put through their paces by the Guanacastecan trainer. Guests with riding experience can ride these powerful creatures throughout the ranch's many trails.

North to Caño Negro

Head northeast from San Carlos, crossing the Río Planatar and on to Aguas Zarcas and the luxurious **Hotel El Tucano Resort and Spa**. Here guests enjoy natural hot springs and deluxe accommodations, including an Olympic-size swimming pool, and jacuzzis fed with natural thermal waters. El Tucano has tennis courts, a mini-golf course, and a natural steam sauna made of stone. The pools are also open to non-guests, for a small fee.

North of Aguas Zarcas outside of Pital is **La Laguna del Lagarto**, a remote lodge which offers accommodation, hiking, horseback riding, canoeing and boat trips up the Río San Carlos to the Nicaraguan border. This is an excellent birding destination. A 4-WD vehicle is recommended to reach the lodge.

North of Arenal, toward the Nicaraguan border, is the magnificent and still seldom-visited **Refugio Nacional de Vida Silvestre Caño Negro ㊵** (Caño Negro Wildlife Reserve). It provides excellent birdwatching opportunities, including extremely large flocks of anhinga, roseate spoonbill, white ibis and

Map on pages 178–79

Tourism is booming around the Arenal area and noone wants to be left out: in its own local leaflet, Tilarán proclaims itself as "the city of broad streets, fertile rains, and healthful winds in which friendship and progress is cultivated."

BELOW: having fun on the Sarapiquí.

jabiru stork. The latter is the largest bird of the region, in great danger of extinction. There are also several species of mammals here, including large cats.

In the heart of this vast area is **Lago Caño Negro**. This lake covers around 800 hectares (2,000 acres) during the wet season, but almost dries up completely during the dry season.

Access to Caño Negro is from Los Chiles or Upala, on good roads northwest of Cañas. The best way to see its myriad species of bird and animal life, particularly during the wet season, is by boat, which can be hired in Los Chiles. In the dry season, horse rental is a good idea. The owner of Restaurant El Parque, Doña Julia Pizarro, can help with boating tours. Basic accommodations are available in Los Chiles. There are also several tour agencies in La Fortuna, including Sunset Tours, which offers day trips to Caño Negro.

The Sarapiquí region

The lush, tropical jungles along the **Sarapiquí River** region, on the Atlantic side of the Cordillera Central, are less than 100 km (60 miles) east of San José, yet once you are there it seems as though it is another continent. La Selva Biological Station, Selva Verde Lodge and Rara Avis, private reserves with lodging (*see below*), are all accessible via a paved circuitous highway which begins and ends in San José. The entire circuit, departing via Heredia and returning on the highway through Braulio Carrillo Park, requires approximately 5 hours of driving.

A recommended stop along the route is Rancho Leona in La Virgen. Set right in the jungle, it offers good food, inexpensive lodging and kayaking on the Sarapiquí River.

From San José drive to Heredia, and the highway winds up the slope of Poás Volcano to Varablanca, where the short entry road to Poás intersects the main highway. With an early morning departure, there would be more than adequate time for a visit to the volcano, before crossing the ridge and heading down through heavily-forested mountain slopes, past a spectacular waterfall, to the lowland rain forest of the Atlantic seaboard.

An alternative route to Sarapiquí which is easier and just as scenic is to take the Braulio Carillo Highway east of San José, through Braulio Carillo National Park. Beware of night driving, however, as thick night fog blankets this route.

Puerto Viejo de Sarapiquí and Rara Avis

Puerto Viejo de Sarapiquí ❹, is a small port town from which river boats depart for otherwise inaccessible settlements along these jungle waterways. Motor-driven dugout canoes laden with passengers and cargo depart regularly for the full-day trip up the Sarapiquí to the **San Juan River**, on the Nicaraguan border, and then east to Barra del Colorado and the Atlantic.

Rara Avis is a pristine, 600-hectare (1,500-acre) rainforest reserve in the mountains above Las Horquetas. The main office and departure point for the reserve is in Las Horquetas, about 17 km (11 miles) south of Puerto Viejo de Sarapiquí. From here,

Rara Avis offers accommodations in treehouses, where guests with no fear of heights can spend the night on a platform 33 meters (100 ft) above the ground. The ascent, accompanied by a guide, is made with a rope and harness.

BELOW: the jungle trail to Rara Avis.

whether you are continuing by horseback or tractor-drawn cart, travel to Rara Avis is difficult and can only be recommended for those who are both physically and mentally fit. The grueling four-hour journey, over ruts, bogs and rivers, is all part of the commitment to the adventure. On the road, the transition from cattle ranches to deep jungle illustrates the devastating effects of deforestation more dramatically than any book or film. The tractor and cart lurch along an eroded path, through cattle ranches littered with fallen and unused timber. Even cattle are few and far between. The open land is hot, dry, dusty and inhospitable. Soil is baked crisp by the tropical sun.

Deforested land ends at El Plástico Lodge, the last stop before the final 4 mile trip to Waterfall Lodge, high in the forest. This former prison colony gets its incongruous name from the plastic sheets under which the inmates slept. From El Plástico, the road plunges into a dark, cool cathedral-like forest, which teems with life. The sun-starved earth is a dense tangle of roots, tree trunks and leaves, soaked in water and bathed in mud.

Because it is such a rarified and isolated place, you should always arrange transportation in advance. Access is difficult, but most people feel that the mud and almost non-existent roads into the area are just part of the experience.

To return to San José continue past Las Horquetas for another 30 minutes to the intersection with the Braulio Carrillo Highway, then make a right turn.

La Selva Biological Reserve

Continue for several kilometers past Puerto Viejo and then you will have to ask the help of a local resident for directions to the "OTS" (the Organization for Tropical Studies) in order to locate the unmarked gravel road to La Selva.

Map on pages 178–79

ABOVE: no through road. **BELOW:** beware, African bees are very aggressive.

The diversity and abundance of life in the lowland tropical forest of the Sarapiquí River region attracted tropical biologists, more than 25 years ago. They subsequently founded the Organization for Tropical Studies and established the **Estación Biólogica La Selva** ❷ (La Selva Biological Reserve and Research Station).

In 1986 the Costa Rican government also made a major commitment to rainforest conservation by extending the boundaries of Braulio Carrillo National Park to meet the outer reaches of the 600-hectare (1,500-acre) La Selva Reserve. As a result of this decision, a total of 21,000 hectares (52,000 hectares) of virgin forest now preserves the migratory pathways and large territories required for the survival of several species of Costa Rica's rare and endangered birds and mammals.

Sloths descend to the forest floor once a week to defecate – unusual behaviour which may be in order to leave their scent away from their normal home.

Today, virtually all of the world's tropical biologists have spent time at La Selva as students, teachers or scientists – or at the very least they have been strongly influenced by the vast amount of scientific research which has been accomplished there over the past quarter of a century. Twice a year the Organization for Tropical Studies holds an eight-week course, open to students of ecology. It's not just biologists who are taught at La Selva, either; many Sarapiquí residents who work at ecotourist lodges were also trained as naturalist guides at La Selva.

BELOW: a stream in the lowland rainforest.

The reserve is primarily a research and educational facility, but tours of the facilities and reserve trails can be arranged by calling La Selva (tel: 236-6696). There is a well developed trail system and some of the trails have boardwalks in order to give access during the wet season. The best choice for accommodation is at Selva Verde.

Selva Verde

In 1986, Giovanna and Juan Holbrook, conservationists from Florida, bought **Selva Verde** ❸, which consists of 200 hectares (500 acres) of primary and secondary tropical lowland forest, along the banks of the Sarapiquí River, in order to save the land from deforestation.

Map on pages 178–79

They designed their beautiful river lodge specially to have a minimal impact on the environment. It rests lightly on posts above the forest floor, resembling the jungle spiders which inspired its construction. Guests reside in tropical hardwood rooms at the end of covered corridors, which radiate from a central conference room into the forest. The jungle and its denizens are never more than a few feet away. This immersion in the lowland forest creates an extraordinary feeling of stillness which encourages people to whisper as they speak.

Spectacular birds are commonplace at Selva Verde, keel-billed and chestnut-mandibled toucans are two of the most common species to be seen feeding on the fruit of the nutmeg trees, near the front porch of the lodge. A stroll along the path to the main lodge building is likely to be rewarded with the iridescent colors of several species of hummingbirds. Nearby, Montezuma Oropendulas utter gurgling mating calls, which harmonize with the songs of other birds and countless frogs and insects in a continual symphony. In all, there are nearly 100 species of birds to be seen at Selva Verde. The Lodge's other main attraction is its incredibly slow-moving arboreal sloths, which have a metabolic rate of half of what is normal for an animal of its size.

From Selva Verde you can make a short excursion back through Puerto Viejo to the MUSA, a cooperative of Sarapiquí women. Watch them at work, take a cup of herbal tea, and perhaps buy a supply of medicinal herbs. ❑

ABOVE keel-billed toucans are common at Selva Verde.
BELOW: the canopy viewing system at Rara Avis.

MOUNTAINS OF FIRE

Vulcanologists are always busy in Costa Rica, which has nine active volcanoes and some 200 dormant and extinct ones

▽ **GUANACASTE ERUPTS**
Rincón de la Vieja soars 1,900 meters (5,760 ft) above the forests of Guanacaste. One of its nine craters is active, and fumaroles bubble on the ground.

Costa Rica is a land of earthquakes and volcanoes, where time-strapped tourists, hikers and mountaineering enthusiasts can climb the Central Valley's four active cones in just two days. Visitors should remember, though, that an active volcano demands respect; proper

▽ **THE VIEW FROM IRAZU**
On a clear day, visitors to Irazú can see both the Atlantic and Caribbean. Its rich soils are excellent for growing potatoes, onions and other crops.

equipment (good shoes, and in the case of Rincón de la Vieja, a compass) are essential. Taking a guided tour will ensure greatest safety. Locals are proud of their explosive geology, and have made Poás and Irazú volcanoes the country's most visited parks.

The most dynamic and majestic of Costa Rica's active volcanoes is Arenal, a nearly perfect cone. The 1,633-meter (4,950 ft) high volcano rises above Alajuela's farm lands, adjacent to its own lake, and offers a spectacular show. Loud thunder-like explosions announce an eruption, and colorful clouds of gas and steam spew out of the top. While visitors to the conservation area find the explosions awe-inspiring and/or frightening, locals barely look up when Arenal thunders.

A VIOLENT PAST

Dormant until the late 1960s, Arenal was thought to be an extinct volcano until a series of earth-quakes began on July 28, 1968. Arenal blew the next morning, causing damage that stretched approximately 5 km (3 miles) west and shock waves that were felt as far away as Boulder, Colorado. Seventy-eight people died after being poisoned with volcanic gas and struck by rocks, and many homes were leveled. Since then, the volcano has continued to rumble and erupt on a more reduced scale, sometimes several times per day, spewing forth fiery cascades of lava and rocks the size of small houses.

POAS VOLCANO IS IN ACTIVITY
YOU ENTER UNDER YOUR OWN RISK
SPN – MIRENEM

◁ DEADLY BEAUTY

Arenal is most impressive at night, when incandescent rocks and lava cascade down the north slope, which is bare of vegetation most of the way down. There are explosions every few hours during the volcano's active periods, but it can rest for months without activity. The cone is often covered by clouds.

▽ MOON WALK

While the crater of Poás looks like the moon, the rest of the park is green: There is a dwarf cloud forest near the crater and a high altitude wet forest also shelters the Resplendent Quetzal. The park has a good museum and hiking trails.

BELOW THE VOLCANOES

It's an ill wind that blows nobody any good, and to observe Arenal in true luxury by day or night, pamper yourself at the Spanish colonial-style Tabacón Hot Springs Resort, built on the site of a 1975 hot avalanche deposit which provides the source of heat for the thermal waters.

Although vulcanologists feel there is a risk of future hot avalanches, this hasn't stopped the Ticos and tourists who flock here to exclaim excitedly over the activity of the volcano and soak their aching muscles. A dip in the waters is also supposedly beneficial for anyone suffering from skin problems and arthritis.

Five large pools of varying depths and temperatures (the warmest is a sizzling 38°C/102°F), a jacuzzi, hot waterfall, slides, and an individual tub tucked deep in the beautifully landscaped tropical gardens mean fun for everyone from kids to old-age pensioners.

A professional massage therapist also gives mud facials, and the resort has lockers, towel rental, and showers. Tabacón recently added an elegant hotel across the street.

If you are on a tight budget, there are cheaper springs just opposite.

◁ ACTIVE POAS

Volcán Poás is just coming out of an active phase, and fumaroles are visible from the viewing point above the crater. However, sulfur gas emissions mean visibility is often poor.

▷ SPRINGS OF DELIGHT

One of the best places to view Volcán Arenal is from Tabacón Hot Springs.

THE CARIBBEAN COAST

Map on page 230

Beautiful warm water, glowing blue and bluey-green, radiant sunshine and coconut palms rustling in the gentle breeze welcome you to Costa Rica's Caribbean coastline

The two-hour drive from San José to the Caribbean Coast is on a good highway winding through the canyons, mountains, waterfalls and virgin forests of Braulio Carrillo National Park. Descending from the cool cloudiness of Braulio Carrillo into the tropical lowland forests of the Caribbean, the temperature rises and the air becomes heavy.

Puerto Limón

Puerto Limón ❶ is pure Caribbean – with its rich, ripe jumble of sights and sounds and smells, it is a hot, steamy, laid-back place. Most middle-class Ticos who live in the Central Valley consider it something of a disgrace, while most young European and North American travelers are enamored with the idea of Puerto Limón, if not the place itself.

In the center of Limón, there is not the usual cathedral or soccer field facing a plaza, such as you see in all the towns of the Central Valley. Instead **Vargas Park**, named after a local governor, is filled with huge banyan trees with buttress roots that the townspeople use for bus stop seats. If you notice cab drivers and children from time to time looking up, they are probably watching the family of *perezosos*, three-toed sloths, that live in the trees of the park.

A good starting point for getting to grips with Puerto Limón and its people is the **Museo Etnohistorico de Limón** (Ethnohistorical Museum of Limón). Its displays illustrate the contributions in literature, education, art, sports and politics that the Limónense have made to Costa Rica, as well as the town's fascinating and colourful history (open Mon–Thur afternoons only; entrance fee).

Commerce began in Limón in the 17th century, when cacao plantations were worked by slaves. But pirates from Jamaica continually raided the area until production was finally abandoned in the early 1800s, and the region, which was impossibly hot, humid and swampy, was once again forgotten for several decades.

Coffee, bananas and the railroad

The growth of the coffee market meant that an Atlantic port was required for exporting to England and Europe, and in 1871, this was established on the site of "El Limón" a migrant black fishermen's village consisting of five huts. That same year, the government contracted the construction of the Atlantic Railroad from San José to the Atlantic Coast. Laborers from Jamaica, Italy and China were brought in to work on the railroad and many made permanent homes in the area.

Meanwhile, Minor Keith, the North American res-

PRECEDING PAGES: the road to Cahuita. **LEFT:** tributary in Barra Colorado. **BELOW:** sloth at Aviaros del Caribe.

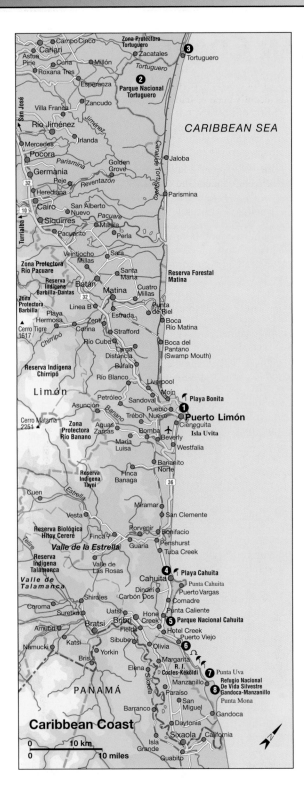

ponsible for building the railroad, had the bright idea of planting and cultivating bananas alongside the track in order to raise additional funds for the ever-increasing costs of construction of the Atlantic railroad.

Limón thus became a railroad and banana town, populated largely by black Afro-Caribbean and Chinese immigrants who had come to Costa Rica looking for work. Since 1872, Limón and the banana industry have experienced great booms and busts: bumper banana crops (even exceeding the value of Costa Rica's coffee exports); labor troubles and violent strikes; and hard times of high unemployment when the United Fruit Company abandoned the Atlantic Coast.

Yet Limón was effectively ignored by the Central Valley government of Costa Rica for all these years. The black workers and their families had no rights of citizenship; they were not permitted to work in the Pacific Zone nor in the Central Valley.

However, since the Civil War of 1948, living conditions have improved somewhat for the black residents of Limón. Today, they are full-fledged citizens of Costa Rica, and can travel and work anywhere they wish.

Problems

There are few decent hotels in Limón. Most travelers stay at the Hotel Acón or in one of the basic hotels near the park. Beware, however, that theft (particularly from cars) and muggings are a problem in the city.

A severe earthquake in 1991 damaged much of Limón's infrastructure, but the roads and bridges have been repaired and the water distribution system is now functioning properly, making the water safe to drink.

Carnaval

For many people, Puerto Limón's annual *Carnaval* (Carnival) is the best reason to visit the place. This week-long jubilant event is held every October*. Carnival first began in 1949,

Map on page 230

under the leadership of a barber called Alfred Henry King, who timed the festivities to coincide with the anniversary of Christopher Columbus's landing near Limón on October 18, 1502. *El Día de la Raza,* "the Day of the People", which falls during Carnival Week and traditionally includes the participation of the indigenous people who live in the region, has recently been re-named the *Día de las Culturas* (Day of the Cultures), in recognition of the fact that not everyone remembers Columbus with equal affection and also as a tribute to the contributions made by people of all cultures to Costa Rica.

The highlight of Carnival Week is the parade, when local people and thousands of visitors take to the street to join in a glorious music and dance spectacle. The drums, the heat, the beat, the shining bodies of dancers and drummers in bright costumes, urge spectators to abandon their inhibitions and to surrender to the Caribbean magic. And so they do, *Limónenses,* and tourists alike, filling the streets, shimmying, shaking, singing and carousing while the irresistible rhythms of steel drums fill the warm, humid air.

Tortuguero

Travel on the **Tortuguero canals**, up through the area north of Limón, has been likened to a trip on the *African Queen,* or to floating dreamily down the Amazon. It is certainly one of the most wonderfully lyrical trips to be taken anywhere. As you float dreamily amidst the fragrance of white ginger blossoms, lavender water hyacinths, and the *Ilan Ilan* flower, there is a tranquility that soothes all your cares away.

Look around and you may catch occasional glimpses of sloths, crocodiles, and basking freshwater turtles. High up in the exuberant vegetation, green macaws

ABOVE: some eating places in Costa Rica also cater for vegetarians.
BELOW: Carnival revellers in Limón.

and multi-colored parrots squawk noisily, while agile howler monkeys shake the branches.

Around 19,000 hectares (47,000 acres) of the coast and hinterland have been designated as the **Parque Nacional Tortuguero ❷** (Tortuguero National Park). There are many ways to navigate its maze of waterways, including hitching a ride on a cargo boat, or by renting a dugout canoe, or speedboat. Or you can simpy take a package tour which will include a lodge room, meals, naturalist guides and the trip through the canals. A personalized tour up the canals is offered by Fran and Modesto Watson on the *Francesca*. They will also provide transport from San José.

Launches going up Tortuguero depart from Moín, just a few miles north of Limón. Travelair and SANSA have short flights from San José to Tortuguero and **Barra del Colorado**, which is north of Tortuguero, near the Nicaraguan border. From there you can hire a boat to travel south through the canals.

Barra del Colorado is a wildlife refuge famous for its sport fishing. Tours are available, but beware high humidity, high temperatures and a voracious mosquito population. Much of the refuge is unexplored with few marked trails.

The green sea turtle

Tortuguero, from *tortuga*, which means turtle, is the main nesting area in the Caribbean for the green sea turtles, which come here to nest and lay their eggs. The turtles have been listed as endangered since the 1950s and the **Caribbean Conservation Corporation** (CCC) has been established at Tortuguero for the purpose of studying and protecting these vulnerable creatures.

The CCC operates a **Natural History Center** located between the village and the John H. Phipps Biological Field Station on the Tortuguero River. The center features large, colorful displays packed with information about the region's plant and animal life, including, of course, the green sea turtle. The area has been

BELOW: Tortuga Lodge, along the Tortuguero canals.

known for its turtle hunting grounds since at least the mid-16th century, and turtles were exploited for their meat, shells and eggs with impunity until as recently as 1970, when the area was established as a national park. Now at least the visiting green sea turtles and their leatherback cousins are afforded some degree of protection.

If possible, go to Tortuguero during the turtle nesting season. And insist on having a knowledgeable naturalist guide to advise you of things to do (and things to avoid), in the spirit of understanding the habits and sensitivities of these magnificent creatures. Between July and October is the best time to view the prehistoric ritual of the nesting of the green turtles, and between February and July is best for the leatherback turtle. The enormous tractor-tread trails, which they leave in the sand as they laboriously make their way up the beaches to dig their nests, are easily visible even at night under a thick stormy sky. And following these freshly-made trails to observe the nesting of one of these turtles is an experience which affects even the most worldly traveler.

At the southern entrance to Tortuguero National Park, at Jalova, the parks service has built a visitors' information center and a well-labeled 1-km (half-mile) nature trail providing information about the park's flora and fauna.

Tortuguero village

Further north, up the canals, the village of **Tortuguero** ❸ sits on a narrow spit of land bordered by the Caribbean Sea and the Tortuguero River. A brief history of Tortuguero is available at the information kiosk near the soccer field. The village is an interesting place to visit. Narrow paths wind through exuberant greenery. Palm trees rustle overhead. Wooden houses sit on stilts. Restaurants, shops and *cabinas* catering to tourists have been constructed, but even so, village life seems to continue in a timeless way.

Antoinete Gutierrez, one of the owners of the Jungle Shop, sells souvenirs and can answer your questions about Tortuguero. And if you're hoping to sample Caribbean rice and beans cooked in coconut milk, you can do so in one of the village's restaurants, but you will need to give advance notice.

ABOVE: a guided tour of Tortuguero is recommended.
BELOW: paddling up a Talamanca tributary.

Talamanca

Most travelers who come to the Caribbean Coast spend only a short time in Puerto Limón, and then quickly head south to the Talamanca coast.

The drive south runs parallel to the Atlantic, with glimpses of rivers off to the right, and the sea to the left. On this highway, some 32 km (20 miles) south of Puerto Limón, is Aviarios del Caribe, a comfortable bed and breakfast located on a bird and wildlife refuge, in the midst of tranquil canals and islands.

Somewhere near Tuba Creek begins the **Talamanca** region of Costa Rica, extending from the Caribbean Coast and reaching into the mountains which run from the Central Valley southeast into Panamá. This area was the refuge of many indigenous people who fled the Spaniards – and the last area of the country to be conquered by them.

Until the 1970s, the Talamanca region was popu-

TIP

A good place to stay betwen Puerto Limón and Cahuita is Aviaros del Caribe, a comfortable bed and breakfast, located on a bird and wildlife refuge in the middle of tranquil canals and islands. The star of the place is Buttercup the sloth.

lated mainly by the Bribri and Cabécar Indians who lived in the mountains, and by the descendents of English-speaking black immigrants from the Caribbean islands, who settled along the coast. The black people were farmers and fisherman, following the old ways brought from Jamaica, most affectionately described in their own words in Paula Palmer's folk history, *What Happen.* (This book is a great read for anyone interested in the history of this region.) The settlers planted the coconut trees which still line the beaches, developed a local cuisine based on the foods they grew, and sold coconut oil, hawksbill turtle shells and cassava starch for the little money they needed.

They spoke a Creole English, played cricket, danced quadrilles, carved dugout canoes from local trees, and recited Shakespeare for amusement. Isolated by the sea and the mountains, there were no roads connecting these people with the rest of Spanish-speaking Costa Rica, and their life continued quite peacefully and independently. All that has changed now, with the opening of a slick new highway and other roads connecting the sleepy coastal towns of Talamanca with San José and the rest of the world.

Most black residents of the coast now speak both English and Spanish, but you'll have to listen carefully to pick up this local Caribbean patois form of English. A few of the more common expressions: "Wh'appen," ("What's happening") is the usual form of greeting, replacing the "Adios," of the Central Valley. "How de morning?" is "Good morning," and "Go good," is "Take care." The courteous form of address, especially towards an older person, is to use his or her first name preceded by Mr or Miss.

The indigenous people of the region now, for the most part, speak Spanish in addition to their own native language (of which there are several), and take

BELOW: black beach at Puerto Viejo.

part in regional political and economic life, although many maintain ancient beliefs and customs. There are three indigenous reserves in Talamanca: the large Talamanca-Bribri Reserve the Talamanca-Cabécar Reserve, and the smaller Kékoldi Reserve. Access to the reserves by non-indigenous people is limited, and usually only by obtaining permission in advance. Mauricio Salazar of Puerto Viejo's Cabinas Chimuri, however, is authorized to take visitors on horseback trips through the Kékoldi Reserve and can provide information about how to gain access to the Talamaca-Bribri Reserve.

Map on page 230

Cahuita

Local legend has it that in 1828, a turtle fisherman, named William Smith, (known as "Old Smith"), rowed and sailed north from his home in Panamá to fish for turtles. Finding a beautiful calm bay protected by a coral reef near Cahuita Point, he decided to settle there with his family. In those early days, green and hawksbill turtles were plentiful and, as they had not yet learned to fear man, made an easy catch. Old Smith is said to be the first English-speaking Afro-Caribbean settler to the area, which at that time was populated with Indians, and frequently visited by pirates.

Cahuita ❹ is the largest and most developed of the Talamanca towns. Faded but dignified-looking wooden houses, once painted bright colors that are now soft pastels, and with a touch of Caribbean whimsy in the gingerbread details, look out over dusty streets. Young travelers from Europe, Canada and the US, oblivious to local sensibilities, amble along the beaches and roadways in scanty, bright beachwear.

ABOVE: a bike is often a handy means of getting about on the coast. **BELOW:** red-eyed tree frog, Cahuita.

Cahuita Tours, on Cahuita's main street, rents out snorkeling equipment, and surfboards. It can also arrange fishing trips, jungle treks and other excursions. A number of guides are usually available to show visitors around the sights.

Beware that Cahuita has drug problems and petty crime against tourists is also rife, even though the authorities crack down every so often in an attempt to keep the lid on the situation.

Cahuita National Park

To the immediate south of Cahuita is **Parque Nacional Cahuita** ❺, famous for its fine, sandy beach and coral reef. The reef extends 500 meters (1500 ft) out to sea from **Cahuita Point** and offers great snorkeling, although the point of the reef was severely displaced during an *earthquake. There are many species of tropical fish, crabs, lobsters, sea fans, anemones, sponges, seaweed and innumerable other marine creatures to observe amidst the coral formations. You can admire it all and keep your feet dry aboard a glass-bottom boat, or you can swim from the Puerto Vargas end of the beach. Diving equipment may be rented in Cahuita town.

Camping is permitted in the park; to get to the **Puerto Vargas** camping area enter from the south side of the park, 5 km (3 miles) from Cahuita. Coatis and raccoons frequent the campgrounds looking for fruit and other edibles, and are not above overturning a tent to get them. Fresh water, outhouses and picnic

tables are available. From Puerto Vargas you can hike along a nature trail into the jungle or explore the wreck of a British slave galleon from which cannons, cannon balls, swords, copper and bronze manacles and arm bands have been retrieved.

North of Cahuita is a black-sand beach where the waters are gentle and good for swimming. Accommodations, some with kitchens, are available throughout town and on the beach. Reservations are essential during Christmas, Easter and during Carnival, the second week in October. The best time to visit Cahuita is from February to April and in October.

Good food is served at Cabinas Algebra, on the north end of town, and at Miss Edith's. Just ask anyone where Miss Edith's is: the place has an enviable reputation for good, down-home Caribbean cooking. The Hotel Jaguar is also known for its innovative French-Caribbean cuisine.

Along the roadside look out for stands selling green drinking coconuts "Hay pipas". The vendor will slice it open for you with a wicked-looking machete.

Coconuts and cacao

Heading south towards Puerto Viejo, along a pretty paved road which runs parallel to the beach, you pass houses of all styles and incomes; but there is something magical about the Caribbean air and even the humblest shack has a picturesque quality, when it is set amidst tall coconut trees. In many yards are low, wooden dryers with tin roofs, used for drying cacao and coconut. The roofs are opened to the bright sun on clear days, and closed in the rain.

Just before the turn-off to Puerto Viejo is **Hone Creek**. Hone is the name of a short palm with large roots. The palm bears a fruit, also called hone, from which the local Indians made cooking oil. When the Jamaicans came to the Talamanca coast to work on the railroad in the 1890s, they began calling it "Home Creek," and today there are official-looking road signs in the area, announcing both "Hone Creek" and "Home Creek."

BELOW: a beach near Punta Uva after a storm.

There is usually a checkpoint with a guard at Hone Creek, seeking to stem the flow of contraband goods from Panamá. To get to Puerto Viejo take the gravel road to the left. Watch for cacao trees in the now-abandoned cacao plantations along the sides of the road. The fruit grows from the trunk of the tree and turns wonderful colors as it ripens: some become a soft turquoise color, others a brilliant coral. The seeds of the ripe fruit are slightly sweet and undeniably chocolatey, even in this raw state.

Puerto Viejo

While Cahuita has a certain shabby dignity, **Puerto Viejo ❻** is a tumbledown community. It is a hodge-podge of small, dilapidated wooden houses amidst tall grass. At the entrance to the town, you pass a rusted-out barge which is permanently anchored just off the black-sand beach.

It wasn't long ago that there were no roads to Puerto Viejo; no cars, no tourists, no money. But things have changed. Puerto Viejo's beautiful undeveloped beaches and easy-going ways have been discovered. New *cabinas*, hotels, and developments throughout the area proclaim the arrival of tourism.

Puerto Viejo is famous in surfing circles for the **Salsa Brava**, a hot, fast, explosive wave which breaks over the reef from December to April and again in

Map
on page
230

June and July. It attracts surfers from all over the world. During the remaining months of the year the sea is quiet, particularly inside the reef, and good for snorkeling.

North of town is the road to Cabinas Chimuri – a collection of *cabinas* constructed of thatch over bamboo in the traditional Bribri Indian style. Chimuri's owner, Mauricio, is wise in the way of the jungle and gives guided horseback tours. El Pizote Surf Lodge, located on the right just before town, offers lovely cabins and rooms, well-groomed grounds with trails, and even California-Tico-style meals. It also rents bikes, diving gear and horses.

Soda Támara offers Caribbean-style fish or chicken served with tasty beans and rice, and a good selection of fruit drinks. Stanford's on the beach is famous for its night-life and fish dinners. The Coral has what is easily the best breakfast in town, maybe in all of Costa Rica, and excellent pizza. And The Garden serves beautiful, exotically-spiced dishes decorated with blossoms and fruit.

To the south of town there are *cabinas* along the road across from beautiful stretches of white-sand beaches edged by palm and beach almond trees. Rivers are bridged by precarious-looking wooden structures, which become slippery in the rain. Signs advertise bicycles for rent, a great way to get around Puerto Viejo and to the nearby beaches.

If you would like to learn a bit more about the Talamanca region, the non-profit **Talamanca Association for Ecotourism and Conservation** (ATEC) provides environmentally and culturally oriented tours led by local guides who speak Spanish and English. Choices for outings include snorkeling, fishing, birdwatching, adventure treks, visits to the Talamanca indigenous reserves and visits to houses of local people for home-cooked meals.

ABOVE: there is no shortage of rest and refreshment in Puerto Viejo.
BELOW: a Mexican hairy porcupine.

Punta Uva and Manzanillo-Gandoca

To the south of Puerto Viejo is heavenly **Punta Uva** ❼, probably the best easily accessible beach along Costa Rica's Caribbean Coast. Crystalline, aquamarine water laps quietly on palm-lined beaches, and both the air and water temperature seem fixed at a constant, perfect 27°C (80°F). You can cycle here from Puerto Viejo and there are plenty of charming and affordable accommodations all the way down the road to Punta Uva.

Further south, still on the beach, is **Manzanillo**, a tiny village which can be reached by walking along the sand for about two hours from Punta Uva, or 20 minutes from Puerto Viejo by car along the dirt and gravel road which terminates here. Surfers enjoy it for its fast beach break.

There are a cluster of houses, a restaurant, a bar, a grocery store, empty beaches and very inexpensive *cabinas*. Local children play in the waves or bathe in the river, young men fish in dugout canoes, elders sit around and talk quietly in the shade, and not much more goes on around here. This is Costa Rica at its most relaxed. Local women will prepare meals for visitors in their homes if asked, and fishermen and farmers are usually happy to chat about their work and the land.

South of the village of Manzanillo is the **Gandoca-Manzanillo Wildlife Refuge** ❽, which protects swamplands, coral reefs, turtle nesting grounds and the only mangrove forest on Costa Rica's Caribbean Coast. The Gandoca River Estuary is a nursery for tarpon. Most of the refuge is flat or has gently rolling hills, covered with forest, grasslands and some farms. Hiking is limited to the coast. Bring along your own supply of water as there are no facilities available in the refuge.

ABOVE: snacking on the street is a way of life in Costa Rica. **BELOW:** United Fruit banana train, *circa* 1916.

Banana country

Map on page 230

Sixaola is a banana town on the Panamá border. To get there continue along the paved road from Hone Creek to the south, instead of turning off to Puerto Viejo and Manzanillo. The road is paved until just outside of Bribri: the rest of the way it is gravel, in fair condition.

In the early 1900s, the United Fruit Company expanded its successful banana plantations from across the Panamá side of the Sixaola River into Costa Rica, and although the company has long gone, the area stretching from just outside the village of Bribri to the border at Sixaola is still very much Banana Land.

The road is lined on both sides with acre after acre of banana trees as far as the eye can see, the ripening fruit wrapped in blue plastic bags which are impregnated with insecticide. Small banana villages and settlements, some consisting of only a few unpainted company houses, a company store and bar, are the only interruptions in a sea of banana leaves.

Banana processing plants occur at intervals along the road: it's interesting to stop for a break at one of the open-air plants to watch the workers handling the large bunches, called *raicimos*, pulling the dried flowers off the ends of individual bananas, cutting bunches of bananas off the stalks, sorting, washing and putting them in boxes which no longer say "United Fruit" but "Chiquita."

Mountains of green bananas which look perfectly acceptable, but don't meet the specifications of Chiquita's North American and European consumers, are formed next to the sorting area. They are used for animal feed, given away or allowed to rot. The smell of fermenting bananas is a familiar one here even though the fruit is used in a number of resourceful ways, from green banana *ceviche* to banana vinegar compresses, a folk remedy for sprained muscles. ❑

ABOVE: six foot, seven foot? Even eight-foot!
BELOW: banana plantations near the Panamanian border.

CARIBBEAN BANANA REPUBLIC

Banana cultivation in Costa Rica began as a by-product of the Atlantic railroad. The crop was only planted by the side of the track in order to help finance its construction. However, the easy success of the banana venture quickly attracted foreign capital and export of the fruit in huge quantities was soon under way.

In 1889 Minor Keith, the Atlantic Railroad pioneer, formed the United Fruit Company and turned Costa Rica into Central America's first banana republic.

United Fruit soon became a symbol of the evils of foreign domination and control over the local economy, making huge profits for the few at the top. The company's ruthless methods and exploitation of labor was widely reviled, but it was also highly successful. By 1913 the plantations were producing 11 million bunches a year and Costa Rica was the world's top exporter.

Unfortunately, banana disease on the Caribbean Coast devastated the crop and in the 1930s United Fruit pulled out of Limón province for good, leaving behind a virtually destitute region which saw little activity until as recently as the 1970s. Today, the area is once again producing bananas on a large scale with more than $500 million worth exported each year.

Sea Turtles

S ea turtles look more like their close but extinct relatives, the dinosaurs, than modern animals. Remarkable adaptations to life in the sea have enabled them to survive, largely unchanged, for more than 150 million years. They "fly" like birds through the water using front flippers as wings. Yet they retain terrestrial traits and must surface to breathe air and crawl ashore to nest and lay their eggs.

Costa Rica is home to five species of sea turtles: Green, Hawksbill, Olive Ridley, Leatherback, and Loggerhead. They are more easily viewed here than anywhere else in the world. They nest at several well-known beaches on both Caribbean and Pacific shores, and during the nesting season, if you happen to be in the right place at the right time, you may see one of the most amazing spectacles in the animal kingdom: *the arribada*, when 100,000 or more Olive Ridley turtles come ashore to nest simultaneously (*see page 202*). Or, equally spectacular, the sight of a 1,500-pound leatherback hauling her massive body out of the water and up the beach to bury her clutch of eggs in the sand.

Tortuguero Beach, a 35-km (22-mile) stretch of beach on the Caribbeanside of Costa Rica, is the most important nesting area for Green Turtles in the Western Caribbean. Here, you can see green turtles, hawksbill turtles and Ridleys.

Green turtles mate and nest several times from September through November. With the sharp hook on his front flippers, the male holds and mounts the female. If the sexually-aggressive male can't locate a mate, he will eagerly clamber on top of anything that floats. Chunks of wood, other male turtles, even skin divers are not safe from a male's misguided passion.

An impregnated female waits offshore until dark before beginning her long struggle up the beach to the nesting site. During her crawl up the beach, disturbances such as noise and light will cause the female to abort the nesting procedure, and to return to the safety of the sea. But once she has begun digging the nest, nothing will distract her. Using her rear flippers, she scoops out a vase-shaped urn, approximately 1 meter (2-3 ft) deep. One hundred or more leathery, golf-ball-sized eggs covered with a mucus "fungicide" drop into the nest one or two at a time until the entire clutch is deposited. She covers the nest, tamps down the sand and begins her crawl back to the sea, leaving her progeny at the mercy of coatimundis, dogs, raccoons, and human scavengers, known as *hueveros,* who steal the eggs and sell them to local bars.

In undisturbed nests, baby green turtles hatch in a couple of months. Using a temporary egg tooth, they tear open their shells. Soon the entire clutch is ready to rise to the surface. A critical mass of about 100 turtles all working together is needed to excavate the 1 meter (3 ft) of sand which is covering them. Usually before dawn, they erupt onto the beach, look for the brightest part of the horizon over the sea, and scramble for the water through a gauntlet of ghost crabs and birds, perhaps then only to be met by sharks and predatory fish once they do reach the water. Hundreds of thousands race for the

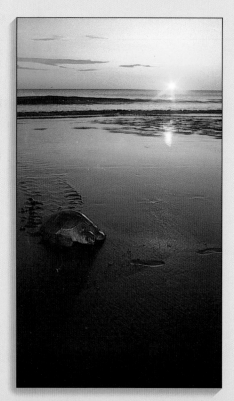

sea and probably less than 3 percent, survive. Those that do make it go offshore to floating rafts of Sargassum weed where they find shelter and food for their first and most difficult months at sea.

For several decades they live nomadic lives, migrating over vast distances of the open ocean to feed on turtle grass in the remote Miskito Keys off Nicaragua or at Cahuita on the Talamanca coast. Some navigate several thousand miles to the Windward Islands, using no apparent landmarks or visual cues. It is thought that crystals of magnetic iron located in the turtles' brains perhaps serve as internal compasses, guiding them across the seas, or more prosaically they may just follow a certain smell or substance.

In 50 years they reach sexual maturity and reconvene on the beaches where they were born to mate, nest and complete their incredible reproduction cycle.

To early explorers fresh turtle meat was a welcome change from salt beef and sea biscuits. Tropical peoples still relish meat from the sea turtle. But sadly, the species is being endangered more from frivolous use than for subsistence purposes, six of seven species of sea turtle are on the brink of extinction. In bars from the Caribbean to Sri Lanka, sea turtle eggs are sucked from the shells as aphrodisiacs. Tortoiseshell has a high value when carved, polished, and made into jewelry, combs and spectacle frames. Turtle skin is even being used as a substitute for alligator skin in shoes and purses.

Sea turtles remain on the endangered species list, although worldwide conservation programs are under way. Importation of turtle products into the US and other countries is illegal, and carries stiff penalties. But adult turtles are accidently caught in shrimp trawls; and fishermen continue to hunt them, sometimes legally – the Costa Rican government grants permits to the people of Limón province to take 1,800 turtles a year. Silt from illegally deforested land near Tortuguero washes onto the beaches, bringing weeds which grow and take valuable nesting space from the turtles. Floodlights from beachside hotels and developments frighten off females ready to nest, and disorient hatchlings trying to find the sea.

The future for many turtles is bleak, though in 1991 a new national park was created at Playa Grande on the Nicoya Peninsula and named Las Baulas, which means leatherback turtle. And the National Park authorities now take a very strict line on poaching. Perhaps this, plus the efforts of the many volunteer programs and the commercial demands of eco-tourism will yet save the turtles.

People tend to like turtles, even though they are not at first glance particularly lovable or even very attractive. In contrast to the modern way of life, the turtle's ponderous pace, non-violent nature, and steady perseverance in getting from here to there seems a more reasonable way to conduct affairs.

Turtles even have a prominent place in the religious and folk histories of many cultures. Some Hindu sects venerate the turtle as a living god, the reincarnation of Shiva, creator and destroyer of all life. Myth states that a turtle brought the Buddhist world from the sea on its back. ❑

LEFT: struggling ashore to lay and bury eggs.
RIGHT: loggerheads are Caribbean dwellers.

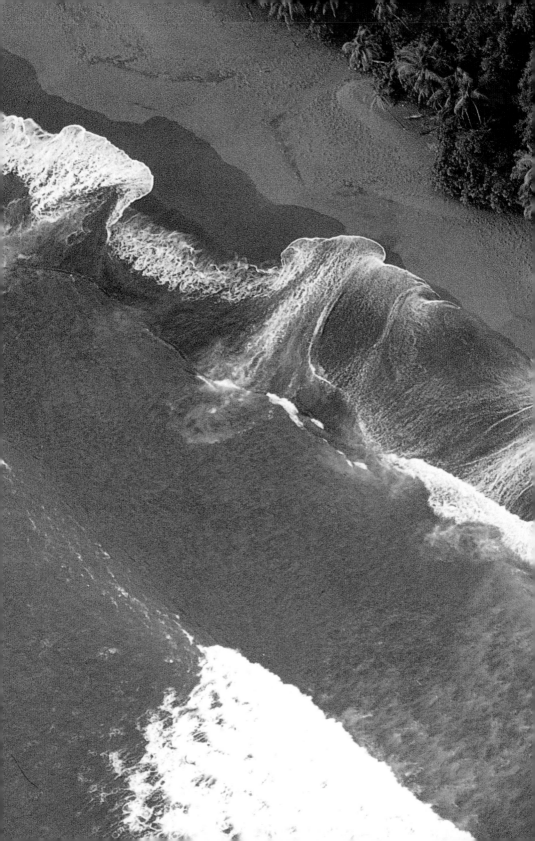

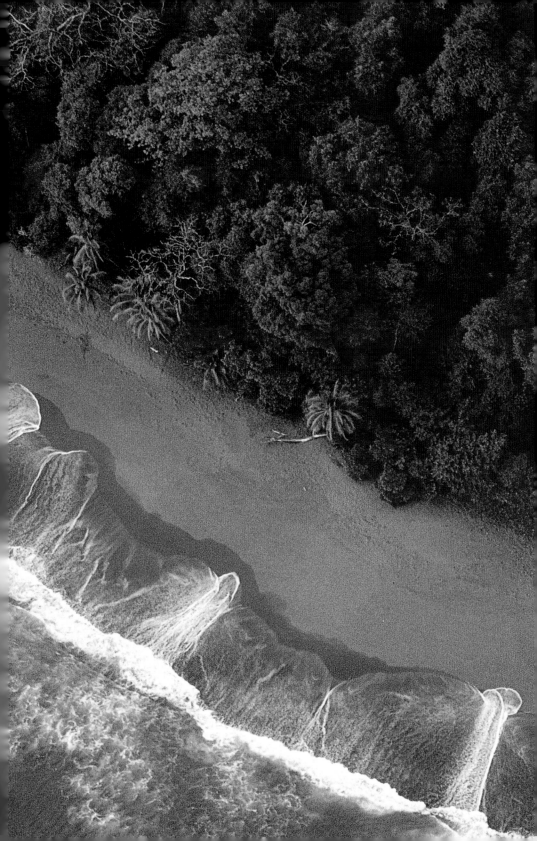

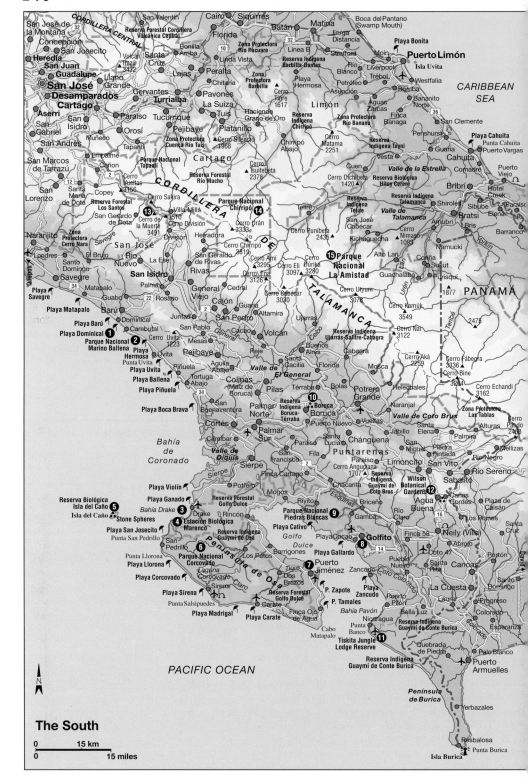

The South

PACIFIC OCEAN

CARIBBEAN SEA

PANAMÁ

0   15 km

0   15 miles

N

THE SOUTH

Map on page 246

Even by local standards, the south is a wild region. It includes the highest peak in Central America, the largest, most inaccessible national park and the most pristine tropical wet forest

The *Zona Sur,* or southern zone, begins in the agricultural lands of the Valle de El General, rises to the highlands around the Cerro de la Muerte, then falls away to the valleys of the far south and the Panamanian border. The Interamericana Highway runs like a spine through the whole length of the region. This is an area for those who like hiking and exploring off the beaten track. One thing is for sure, it rains a lot, so bring your waterproofs.

Playa Dominical

A beautiful drive of 35 km (22 miles) via mostly paved road from San Isidro, through the southern section of the Valle de El General, brings you to **Playa Dominical ❶**. (The trip from San José to Dominical via San Isidro takes about four hours, including rest stops.) Dominical can also be reached by a two-hour drive along the coast from Quepos. The coast road from Quepos, the *Costanera Sur*, has recently been improved and the scenery is wonderful. Stop off for a night at the pretty and well-kept Cabinas Punta Dominical, the simple and secluded Pacific Edge, or the more luxurious Escaleras Inn, high on a hill in the jungle overlooking Playa Dominical. Call ahead to make sure they have space.

The beach is a long stretch of brown, silty sand offering good waves for surfing, though beware dangerous currents when swimming. There are pleasant, shady places on the sand for camping but no facilities. "Town" is a small, somewhat funky settlement, with a few basic vacation homes, *cabinas* and *sodas*. During the dry season Playa Dominical's weather can be impossibly hot, breezeless and the landscape barren.

A horseback trip to **Nauyaca Falls**, also known a Santo Cristo Falls, takes about two hours. The falls consist of two cascades a total of 65 meters (210 ft) high, which tumble into a glorious warm-water swimming hole. The Finca Bella Vista and several tour operators in the area, including Selva Mar Reservations, arrange trips to Nauyaca.

Just south of Dominical is **Playa Domincalito,** where there are good point-break waves for surfers. Swimming is best at low tide when beaches are exposed beyond coral rocks and there are beautiful views of the overlooking hills.

Marino Ballena National Park

Seventeen km (11 miles) to the south of Dominical lies **Parque Nacional Marino Ballena ❷**. It is not an easy place to get to and you will need either a sturdy 4-wheel drive vehicle or come by bus from San Isidro de El General. One of Costa Rica's smallest and most recently dedicated national parks, Marino Ballena offers beautiful beaches, mangroves where you can

PRECEDING PAGES: Pacific breakers at Corcovado National Park; ox-cart on the Pacific coast. **BELOW:** ancient buttress roots.

spot raccoons, lizards and caimans, and the most intact coral reefs on the Pacific Coast. Dolphins are commonly seen and the park's two sandy beaches provide nesting grounds for the Olive Ridley and hawksbill turtle.

The **Islas Ballenas**, also part of the park, provide refuge to humpback whale and their young from December through April. Two sandy beaches within the park sweep to a meeting point at Punta Uvita, and at low tide, produce remarkably calm conditions for underwater exploration. Local boatmen will take visitors out to the reef for snorkeling, fishing or birdwatching, although at the north end of the park good snorkeling spots can be reached on foot at low tide.

In **Bahía Uvita**, the entry point to the park, there are a number of *cabinas* and *sodas*. Boats are available for diving, fishing and sightseeing trips. Ask for Captain Jenkin in Bahía Uvita or contact Jonathan Duron through Selva Mar Reservation Service.

Further south along the **Costanera Sur Highway** are the beaches of **Playa Hermosa** and **Playa Uvita**. With a four-wheel drive vehicle, you can cross the Uvita River, which has no bridge, and continue on to Cortés, where the road connects with the Inter-American Highway once again.

The Osa Peninsula

Jutting out more than 50km (30 miles) into the Pacific, the Osa Peninsula shelters Golfo Dulce from ocean swells and creates a magnificent natural harbor. It is sculpted with picturesque beaches, rocky headlands, and is dissected by streams and rivers that cascade over volcanic cliffs on their way to the sea. The most majestic forests in all Costa Rica cover the hills and line the valleys of the Osa Peninsula and, in many cases, represent the last stronghold of nature and en-

Drake Bay is an unlikely spot for shopping, but the village of Agujitas is one of the few places in Central America which makes molas – handmade reverse-appliqué stitched blouses and fabrics more often associated with Panama.

BELOW: the jungle airstrip at Marenco.

Map on page 246

dangered animals and plants that are endemic to Southern Pacific Costa Rica. It is an imposing, impressive and wild place.

The indians of the Diquis region were the first inhabitants of the peninsula, named Osa after one of their chiefs. They were accomplished goldsmiths and fashioned religious and ceremonial pieces from gold they found in the Tigre and Claro Rivers. Throughout the Conquest, the Spanish made repeated explorations into Osa, killing the indians, plundering their gold and searching for the legendary mines of Veragua.

Sadly, little has changed and gold continues to cause problems for the people of the Osa Peninsula. In the 1980s, the discovery of a 25-pound gold nugget created a gold rush and havoc in the Corcovado National Park. Farmers-turned-prospectors invaded the area, tore up creeks and rivers for flakes of placer gold, hunted wildlife, and burned the forest to plant crops. Gold fever destroyed many thousands of acres of parkland and alcoholism, prostitution, and other socioeconomic ills accompanying a gold-rush boomtown plagued Corcovado.

In response, government officials closed the Corcovado National Park for years while they attempted to evict the trespassers. Then, after a minor civil war, officials reluctantly agreed to pay the miners a stipend to leave the park. The payoff was moderately successful, but 100 or more miners continue to live and mine gold inside Corcovado. Their impact on the El Tigre River continues, yet the government has chosen to ignore them rather than risk more civil strife.

ABOVE: one of region's mysterious giant stone spheres (*see page 251*).
BELOW: small insects often make the most noise.

Drake Bay

On the northern coast of the Osa Peninsula, **Drake Bay** ❸ is said to be the place where Sir Francis Drake, the first English navigator to sail around the world, landed in 1579. Accessible only by water and air, it is a land of crystal blue waters, pristine beaches, and jungle. Your lodge will make your travel arrangements from San José, which usually involve a flight to Palmar, transfer to Sierpe, then a boat ride to the lodge. The flight passes over Manuel Antonio Park and provides aerial perspectives of the south Pacific Coast en route to Corcovado. As you land on the grass airstrip, look for scarlet macaws flying from their roosts in the trees nearby. You can also travel to Palmar overland, by bus or car, a 5½-hour trip through very remote country.

Just south of Drake Bay **Marenco Biological Station** ❹ is situated on its own 500-hectare (1,200-acre) reserve above the beach. Guests reside in rustic, thatched-roof lodgings with views of the Pacific and Caño Island Biological Reserve (*see page 251*). Three-day package tours include naturalist-led hikes through Marenco's rainforest, a day on the fringes of Corcovado hiking the trails to Llorona waterfall and swimming in the freshwater pools of the Río Claro, followed by a day exploring Caño Island. Drake Bay Wilderness Camp, just north of Marenco, is located directly on the beach at Drake Bay and offers similar programs as well as offshore fishing, canoeing, ocean kayaking and whale-watching trips (during January and February). La Paloma Lodge is built into a hillside and offers sweeping views of the ocean. Its rustic

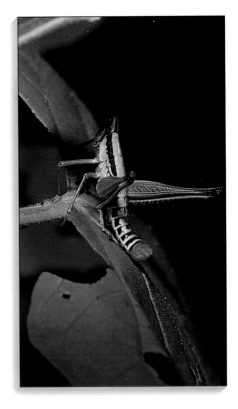

Ants in Your Plants

Should someone point out a "bull's horn acacia" to you, stop and have a close look at this thorny shrub. Measuring from between 1.5 to over 3 meters (4-10 ft) tall, along the branches are pairs of reddish spines that look like miniature replicas of a Texas steer's horns. Hence its name.

Of the many relationships that have evolved between tropical ants and plants, that of the bull's horn acacia and its stinging ants is one of the most curious. It is also one of the most dramatic examples of tropical co-evolution between species.

With some caution, shake the end of a branch. Ants burrow into the end of the spines (notice the tiny hole), excavate the inside of the branch, and set up a colony where they rear their young and go about the business of being ants. When the plant is disturbed, as in the case of your shaking the branch, the pugnacious ants charge aggressively from the spines, stingers armed and ready to defend their acacia host. It would only take one nasty sting to convince you that this unusual defense system works.

In addition to repelling would-be grazers, ranging in size from caterpillars to cattle, the ants manicure the ground around the acacia, keeping it clear of sprouts from other plants which might deprive their host of living space in a tropical forest containing 1,200 species of trees and countless other plants.

And the acacia is appreciative. Not only does it shelter its guardians, it also feeds them. Tiny, sausage-shaped bodies hang from the ends of the leaflets. Loaded with sugar and protein, these are harvested gratefully by the ants.

On the forest floor you're almost sure to spot trails carved by leafcutter ants as they march through the jungle in search of tender leaves to attack. Their trails are veritable highways of activity. Imagine thousands of people walking home on the highway, each rushing along, carrying a 1.5 meter by 2.5 meter (4 ft by 8 ft) sheet of green plywood overhead, and you have the concept of these ants. Leafcutters are amazingly industrious insects. They can completely denude a full-grown mango tree overnight, carving circular slabs of leaf about half an inch in diameter, hoisting them overhead and marching down the tree trunk back to the hive, which may be a kilometer (half a mile) away or more.

Several highways lead to their hive – often around the buttress roots of a large tree. Hives of over 100 square meters, 2 meters deep in the forest floor are not uncommon. In these hives, millions, perhaps billions, of ants chew the leaf fragments, mixing them with nutrient-rich saliva, into a gruel. From this gruel the ants grow and harvest mushrooms which provide their food source.

Large ant colonies can cut and process nearly 45 kg (100 pounds) of leaves a day. During the decades-long lifespan of an ant colony, tons of vegetation decompose and are worked back into the forest floor. Constant rain and heat rapidly degrade tropical soils, and so the vast storehouse of nutrients and compost from the ant mounds create a rich oasis in the soil, without which the busy ants would be nearly sterile. ❑

LEFT: a leafcutter ant, found in the lowland forests of Costa Rica.

cabinas, with thatch roofs and private decks, blend unobtrusively into the jungle environs. From the lodge you can arrange expeditions to fish or dive, take dreamy trips up the river in sea kayaks and visit Corcovado and Isla del Caño.

Map on page 246

Isla del Caño

The biological reserve of **Isla del Caño ❺** sits low on the horizon, 15 km (9 miles) seaward of the Corcovado coastline, and is a pleasant 1-hour boat ride from either Marenco or Drake Bay. According to archaeologists, the island was both a cemetery for indigenous people and a refuge for pirates.

Spotted dolphins riding the boat's bow wave, and flying fish sailing off the top of ocean swells sometimes escort the traveler to the island. Between December and April, 40-ton humpback whales come from their feeding grounds in Alaska. Males sing haunting songs to attract females, and often leap high in impressive breaches during their procreative sojourn through Costa Rican waters.

The island is ringed with turquoise water, tiny beaches, and acres of coral-covered rock reefs. Brilliantly-colored tropical fish are easily seen by skin divers within 15 meters (50 ft) of the shore at the park headquarters.

Well-manicured trails lead through a rich forest drooping with epiphytes and with philodendrons so large that any of them would easily fill a living room.

Parque Nacional Corcovado

Covering 40,000 hectares (100,000 acres), **Corcovado National Park ❻** is an important sanctuary of biological diversity and endangered wildlife, dominating the rugged **Osa Peninsula**. It is the site of many of Costa Rica's most significant environmental conflicts. Wild animals live among tall trees that are draped

The locals of Palmar take great pride in their stone spheres and when, in the 1980s, the San José authorities tried to remove a pair of them for display in the capital, they were prevented from doing so by student demonstrations.

BELOW: a gift from outer space or an ancient headstone?

MYSTERY OF THE SPHERES

At the highest point on Isla del Caño, where the forest thickens and becomes silent, dried leaves crackle underfoot as you approach the pre-Colombian cemetery of the Bruncas indians.

Two stone spheres sit among the trees. Green with moss and highlighted by shafts of sun from the forest canopy, the enigmatic spheres seem impossibly symmetrical in this forest of twisted plants. Thousands of spheres like this have been found in many locations in the south of Costa Rica and a few also in northern Panama. They pose one of the country's great riddles. Though their exact origin and significance have defied explanation, it is speculated that they were made in villages on the Osa Peninsula near Palmar Norte, brought to Caño in canoes, then possibly rolled to the cemetery at the highest point of the island.

The smaller stone spheres, which are the size of oranges, were possibly toys but the huge spheres, over 2 meters (6 ft) in diameter, may have indicated the political or social standing of the deceased. Graves with spheres as headstones, oriented to the east, had secret chambers for precious ornaments and were covered with layers of sand, coral and pebbles. Many spheres found in groups have been placed to reflect the positions of the stars.

with vines and lianas, supported by massive buttress roots, on a forest floor teeming with life.

Because Corcovado Park is innundated with nearly 6 meters (20 ft) of rain a year, it is technically known as a "tropical wet forest." The simplicity of that classification belies the ecological complexity of the park. Thirteen distinct habitats here are each characterized by unique assemblages of plants, animals and topography. Five hundred species of trees – one quarter of all the species in Costa Rica, 10,000 insects, hundreds of species of birds, frogs, lizards and turtles, and many of the world's most endangered and spectacular mammals live in this place.

One of Corcovado's blessings is its inaccessibility. It is a park only for those naturalists and visitors who are prepared to make a considerable commitment in time and energy.

There are several different ways to sample the beauties of Corcovado and the Osa Peninsula, from charter flights into the peninsula and accommodations at luxury ecolodges to days of grueling hikes, fording rivers and battling insects with nights spent in a tent on the beach.

At one end of the scale is **Lapa Ríos**, a renowned luxury resort consisting of thatched-roof bungalows perched on the hillside of a 400-hectare (1,000-acre) reserve, with a calm and tranquil beach nearby. **Bosque del Cabo** is a smaller, friendlier place, and a favorite hangout for scarlet macaws; the owner claims to have seen 60 of them on the beach in one day. **Corcovado Lodge Tent Camp**, located within earshot of the crashing surf near La Leona, is another good place to stay. Guests are driven or flown from Puerto Jiménez to Carate, and make the rest of the journey in horsedrawn carts.

TIP

In Corcovado Park, you are largely on your own among such dangerous wildlife as coral snakes and fer de lance vipers. Although it is rare to come across these creatures, serious explorers may wish to carry an anti-venom kit on their travels.

BELOW:
a lonely beach on Isla del Caño

Corcovado National Park – an itinerary

The ideal time to go hiking and camping in Corcovado is in the dry season, December through April, and might include two nights at each of the three park stations, with days spent hiking from one station to the next. (Stations are joined by trails, each of which requires from three to ten hours of hiking time.) It is important to come well-equipped in the insect-battling department. A tent, mosquito net, insect repellent, and long socks are essential, and in addition to the usual camping gear, a machete is also a good idea. Make arrangements for visiting the park by contacting the park's administration office, next to the Banco Nacional in Puerto Jiménez (*see page 254*). The park stations will provide room and meals, but require at least one week's notice. The stations can be reached by charter plane, by hiking or by vehicle during the dry season.

The **Sirena Station**, near the beach, is a pleasant place to spend at least a couple of days. There are trails into the forest and along the beach. Swimming in the nearby Río Claro is refreshing, but sharks are said to frequent the ocean near the river mouth.

Los Patos Station is an 11-km (7-mile) hike from Sirena on a wide trail which runs parallel to the El Tigre River. The heavy siltation in the river is the result of illegal gold panning activity, which continues in this area. The wide trail allows relatively easy wildlife viewing. Even though it passes through thick forest, you stand a reasonably good chance of seeing at least tracks of jaguar, ocelot and tapir, if not the animals themselves. At Los Patos, there are simple accommodations available. A road to the station, accessible by 4-wheel drive vehicle, is open during the dry season.

The trek to or from **San Pedrillo Station** and nearby **Llorona Waterfall** requires careful advance planning. Two rivers must be crossed at low tide during the seven- to ten-hour hike. Rangers at Sirena can provide estimates of transit times and tidal heights. Plan to take a tide-table, food, water, and camping gear, as you may need to use them en route. San Pedrillo is also accessible by a two-hour trail from the Marenco-Drake Bay airstrip.

Corcovado fauna and flora

Of the estimated 250 jaguars remaining in the country, most are found in the forests of Corcovado, Tortuguero, and the Talamanca Cordillera. An adult jaguar needs an enormous amount of land with abundant prey animals such as peccaries, deer and agouti to meet its food requirements. Since Corcovado Park was established, its jaguar population has more than tripled. Tracks are commonly seen on many of the trails, and are relatively easy to identify. The prints are wider than they are long, have three rear pads, and four unequal toes showing no claw marks. A large male jaguar has been seen regularly in the forest just behind the Marenco-Drake Bay airstrip.

Herds of white-lipped peccaries (wild pigs) roam the forest and root in the leaf litter for food. Evidence of their passing is easily seen. It will look like a bulldozer has gone through the forest.

Nearly 300 species of birds live in Corcovado, of which scarlet macaws are the most spectacular. They

Map on page 246

ABOVE: strelitzia.
BELOW: Pacific brown pelican.

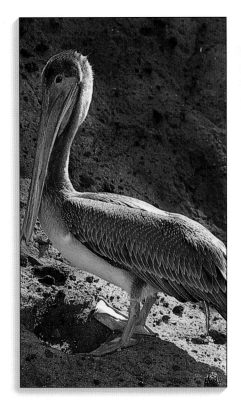

Peccaries (wild pigs) have an exaggerated reputation as the forest's most ferocious animal. Nonetheless, if a group of them approaches, or worse, surrounds you, then you would do well to climb the nearest tree.

loudly announce their arrival with gravelly shrieks. If you hear a cry like a puppy, look for a toucan, with its outlandish yellow bill, hopping through the trees. Seeds or husks dropping through the forest will often reveal the presence of a flock of yellow-cheeked parrots, or possibly troops of squirrel monkeys or spider monkeys foraging in the canopy overhead. To improve your chances of seeing these animals, be on the trail very early, preferably before dawn.

Orchids, bromeliads, philodendrons and ferns grow attached to trees high in the forest where they find abundant light, airborne nutrients and water. Rich compost created by the epiphyte gardens is often exploited by the host tree which sprouts roots from its branches, and taps into the aerial soil.

The dense growth of epiphytes in the trees creates a fantastic home for tiny red and blue poison-arrow frogs, who live in pools of water caught by bromeliad leaves. Females lay their eggs on land, and later carry the developing tadpoles on their backs over a distance of 30 meters (100 ft) or more up the trees to these pools, where they lay unfertilized eggs to feed their offspring.

Mushrooms and bracket fungi with strange shapes and astounding colors stud the rotting trunks of fallen trees. Fingernail-sized frogs, and tiny salamanders live in the damp hollows of logs or under moist leaf litter. They are difficult to see, but the sudden movement of a leaf might reveal their whereabouts.

Puerto Jiménez

BELOW: a naturalist gathers butterflies at the Golfito reserve.

Just outside the Corcovado National Park to the east is **Puerto Jiménez ❼**, the main town of the Osa Peninsula and a gateway to the park. It's a friendly place with a burgeoning tourist infrastructure and its own Ecotourism Chamber, which will recommend guides and assist you in planning your visit around the

peninsula. Inexpensive meals and lodging are available in Puerto Jiménez, and a number of lodges and ecotourism projects in all price ranges are to be found in the surrounding area. Puerto Jiménez is accessible by car or bus. It's about a seven-hour trip from San José and most lodges will arrange transportation.

Map on page 246

Inland to Sierpe

An adventurous way to leave the Osa Peninsula is to charter a boat from Marenco Station or Drake Bay Wilderness Camp, or hire a local dugout canoe, and travel up the wide muddy Sierpe River towards the little town of **Sierpe**. Beware, however, that the mouth (the *boca*) of the river is often very choppy. Make sure your boat is equppied with lifejackets and, as a precaution, put yours on when you near the *boca*.

The shores of the river are lined with mangrove trees. The maze of roots of these trees is inhabited by many species of small fish. Blue herons and flocks of snowy egrets may fly from the trees as the boat passes.

Even these maritime mangrove forests are not immune to deforestation. They are cut and used to make charcoal or the bark is stripped and tannin, used to cure leather, is extracted. Fortunately, damage has been minimal so far, and the Sierpe mangroves continue to provide refuge for many animals living on the boundary between land and sea.

A wide variety of boats ply their trade on the Sierpe. Weatherbeaten dugout canoes loaded down with bananas, and smoking cargo boats share the river with vacationers' speedboats and naturalist tour vessels from nearby lodges. About two hours upriver at the Las Vegas Bar in the dusty town of Sierpe you can catch a bus to travel south to Golfito.

ABOVE: raccoons are often eager for a human hand-out. **BELOW:** "Little mirror" butterflies in the act of mating.

Wild Cats of Costa Rica

Costa Rica is home to half a dozen kinds of wild cat. Secretive and nocturnal, they include some of the most endangered and elusive of the country's animals.

Costa Rica's wild cats – both big and small – are extremely wary of humans, and few visitors to the country are lucky enough to see them. Although they are now fully protected, their fear of people is understandable: over the years, hunting and deforestation have reduced their numbers to a fraction of their former level.

Like all cats, these animals are elegant and efficient predators. Most hunt on their own, and most hide away by day, camouflaged by beautiful spotted coats that, ironically, have made them such valuable quarry. They range in size from the jaguar – commonly known as "el tigre" – which can tip the scales at over 100kg (220lb) to the little spotted cat, which is smaller than

many of the cats that people keep as pets.

For a cat the jaguar shows an unusual liking for water. Its preferred habitats include mangrove swamps and the forested banks of rivers, and it seems to enjoy swimming. One of its favourite foods is peccary (a kind of wild pig), but it also catches fish and even turtles, breaking open their shells with its powerful teeth. Unfortunately, it also attacks cattle, particularly where new pasture has been created out of the former forest. As a result, many Costa Rican farmers view el tigre not as a national asset, but as a dangerous marauder. At one time, it was found throughout the entire country, but today its strongholds are in the national parks, particularly Santa Rosa, Tortuguero and Corcovado. You may not actually see a jaguar in the flesh, but you stand a chance of at least being shown its tracks.

Almost as large as the jaguar is the puma or mountain lion, one of the two Costa Rican cats that do not have spotted coats. It is a truly Pan-American animal, ranging from Canada as far south as Patagonia. The other unspotted cat, the jaguarundi, is much smaller, and has short legs and a curiously flattened forehead. Jaguarundis live in a range of habitats, but unlike pumas, they are most common in low-lying parts of the country.

The last three species have all paid a heavy price for the beauty of their coats, but with changing fashions, and a ban on the trade in pelts, their future prospects look brighter than they once did. The ocelot – perhaps the most beautiful of them all – hunts mainly on the ground, although it climbs and swims well. The margay, which looks like a miniature long-tailed ocelot, is an extremely agile climber, and catches most of its food off the ground. It is the only cat that can climb head-first down a tree, instead of having to back down while holding on with its claws.

The little spotted cat is also a forest animal, sometimes living at altitudes of over 3,000 meters (9,850ft). Although it was once widely hunted, relatively little is known about its habits in the wild. What is certain is that, despite its small size, it packs a punch: in encounters with domestic cats, the little spotted cat often comes out on top. ❑

LEFT: a young watchful puma (cougar), near La Pacifica reserve.

Golfito

Situated on the eastern shore of the Golfo Dulce, **Golfito** ❽ is sheltered from the open sea by islands and peninsulas which form a perfect harbor within the gulf. In 1938, United Fruit Company (*see page 239*) realized Golfito's potential, and built a major shipping port here. By 1955 over 90 percent of the bananas shipped from Costa Rica departed on the Great White Fleet of banana boats from Golfito. Boatloads of crewmen and 15,000 *Guanacasteco* immigrants came to work the plantations. They turned Golfito into a boomtown of brothels, smugglers and drunks. United Fruit or "Mamita Yunai," was seen to be funneling profits out of Costa Rica and into the pockets of rich North American stockholders and became the symbol for hated Yankee imperialism.

Following crippling strikes and conflicts with labor, United Fruit decided to close down and leave Golfito in 1985. Economic depression set in and former employees of the company found themselves leaving town or searching for work as fishermen or farmers. Recently Golfito has begun to make a slow comeback and the old town, referred to as the **Pueblo Civil**, is regaining a touch of its boomtown atmosphere. Bars and prostitutes do business on the side streets; lively outdoor cafes overlooking the pier have taken over the main street. And in the recently classified "duty free zone" on the waterfront, known as El Depósito, TVs, refrigerators, stereo sets and other consumer durables sell at about 40 percent off the San José price. If you're searching for bargains, try the huge outdoor mall with air-conditioned shops.

The **American Zone** of Golfito has a sleepy, suburban atmosphere. This former United Fruit Company neighborhood comprises large wooden plantation-style homes on stilts, with screened porches and hip roofs.

Before leaving Golfito, drive to the top of **Golfito Forest Reserve**. A sign marks the road in Barrio Invu across from the Plaza Deportes soccer stadium. During the drive, watch for toucans and sloths in the trees beside the steep, winding gravel road. At the top, the panoramic views of the beautiful bay of **Golfo Dulce** are spectacular.

There are regular flights to Golfito; check with the airline offices for their current schedules. For the more patient traveler, the very scenic seven-hour bus ride from San José to Golfito is a memorable experience.

North of Golfito

North of Golfito are beautiful rocky beaches and dense jungle, now made accessible to visitors by a number of lodges. **Rainbow Adventures Lodge,** on Playa Cativo, is an adventure in itself. A 45-minute boat ride from Golfito, this beautifully-designed lodge is furnished with antiques and silk rugs. Hike the trails of the 500-hectare (1,200-acre) reserve with a naturalist guide or enjoy kayaking, snorkeling, fishing and dolphin watching. Nearby is **Casa Orquidea**, a beautiful landscaped garden cultivated by long-time local residents the McAllisters. They grow ginger, cacao, papaya, orchids and tropical plants. Tours last one hour (open daily; entrance fee).

In 1991, 1,200 hectares (3,000 acres) of rainforest on the west side of Golfo Dulce was declared the

Map on page 246

TIP

If you would like to learn more about the harsh conditions of the banana plantations, read the exuberant *Mamita Yunai*, written by pioneer labor organiser Carlos Luis Fallas and set in the 1930s and 1940s in Limón province.

BELOW: giant philodendrums.

Parque Nacional Piedras Blancas . However, as the government didn't have the funds to compensate the landowners, the possibility remained that title could revert to the former owners and that the logging operations which had been under way could resume. Michael Schnitzler, an Austrian violinist and Golfito homeowner, solicited contributions from his countrymen and women, and with additional funds contributed by national and international groups, the money was raised to pay the landowners and ensure the continuation of Piedras Blancas as a national park. It is incorporated into Corcovado National Park, and appears under this name on some maps. Even more confusingly, it is also known as Esquinas National Park, for the river which flows through it, and it has also been given the nickname of the "Rainforest of the Austrians."

A biological station owned and operated by the University of Vienna offers basic accommodations for a minimal fee, and students and scientists from around the world are invited to stay and contribute to research into the new park's biodiversity. More luxurious accommodation is available at Esquinas Lodge. Trails in the park are rough and undeveloped. Guides for park exploration are available and are strongly recommended.

If you continue on the Inter-American Highway past Palmar Norte, and just past Puerto Nuevo, a rough track leads to **Boruca** ⑩. This is a small indigenous village located in a valley near Buenos Aires, where life moves at a leisurely pace. Local people make carved balsawood masks, woven belts, purses and tablecloths. On December 30 each year, the Boruca indians celebrate the *Fiesta de los Diablitos* (Celebration of the Devils), a re-enactment of the war between the Spanish and Indians – only this time the indians win.

South of Golfito

Between the mouth of the Río Coto (which lies just south of Golfito), to Punta Banco the last major point of land before the Panamanian border, lie some of Costa Rica's most inaccessible and remote beaches.

Take the ferry across the river then, in Pueblo Nuevo, turn right for **Playa Zancudo**, an 8-km (5-mile) long, sandy crescent with excellent swimming and surfing, and several nice places to stay. Cabinas Sol y Mar is friendly and serves good food, including homemade bread. Continue on the road parallel to the coast to **Pavones**, just before Río Claro. The beach is not suitable for casual swimming, but this is a renowned surfing spot. Basic lodging is available. After the seemingly endless potholes, bogs and washboard bumps in the road, continue on for another 30 minutes to **Punta Banco**. Wide intertidal flats of volcanic and sedimentary rock, riddled with tidepools full of marine life and battered by continual surf characterize Punta Banco.

At the end of the point, a pasture and gate on the left mark the entrance to **Tiskita Jungle Lodge** ⑪, Peter Aspinall's private rainforest reserve, experimental tropical fruit farm, and eco-lodge.

The tortuous drive (a four-wheel drive vehicle is essential) can be avoided by using a package tour, which includes a private airplane charter that sets down on a grass airstrip near the lodge. Isolated

BELOW:
capuchin monkey.

cabins with ocean views are a short walk from the main lodge. Well-designed, manicured trails lead to waterfalls, idyllic swimming holes, and various points of natural history interest in Tiskita's 162-hectare (400-acre) forest. Over 100 species of fruit trees from around the tropical world are under cultivation here.

Map on page 246

Wilson Botanical Gardens

For a more academic experience in tropical botany visit **Wilson Botanical Gardens** ⑫ in Las Cruces, some 6 km (4 miles) from San Vito on Highway 16. The gardens, adored by botanists and non-botanists alike, are operated by the Organization for Tropical Studies (OTS) as a center for research, scientific training and public education (open Tues-Sun, 8am–4pm; entrance fee). Designed by an Italian landscape architect, trails wind through extensive collections of "lobster claw" heliconias, bromeliads, tree ferns, orchids and palms, and ultimately lead into the wild forest reserve behind the gardens. This offers splendid mountain vistas and hiking to rocky pools around the Rio Java.

The gardens also offer simple, dormitory-style accommodations and the opportunity to talk with visiting scientists in residence, or attend seminars by horticultural societies from around the world.

The **Villa Neilly-San Vito Road** was built in 1945 by the USA as a strategic protection point, being situated due west of the Panamá Canal. The gravel road rises sharply into the cool mountains that lead to **San Vito** at 960 meters (3,150 ft) above sea level. San Vito was founded by immigrants from post-war Italy, who were encouraged by the Costa Rican government to settle there. It's a clean, modern town of 10,000 inhabitants, located high in a mountain valley, where you can get a good Italian meal and hear Italian spoken on the streets.

ABOVE: giant bromeliad at Wilson Botanical Gardens. **BELOW:** a moment of jungle quietude.

Valle de El General

The finca of former president Don Pepe (José) Figueres lies just off the highway as you start to climb Cerro de la Muerte. The house is called La Lucha Sin Fin *(the Endless Struggle) since it was here that he formulated many of the political views that led to the Civil War.*

Several people had attempted to find a pass through the Talamanca Mountains to join the Central Valley with the unknown lands on the other side of the Dota Mountains since Colonial times, but it was not until the end of the 1860s that Don Pedro Calderón, responding to a prize offered by the government, found a way through the mountains. The opening of the road led to the colonization of the **Valle de El General**, and later, to the building of the Inter-American Highway, which connects San José and the Central Valley with the southern Pacific section of Costa Rica.

If you are travelling south to the Valle de El General, try to make an early start, and hopefully you will avoid the fog and rain which often appear later in the day. From San José take the Inter-American Highway through Cartago. Once on the other side of Cartago, take the road to San Isidro.

The route to the Valle de El General passes over the spectacular **Cerro de la Muerte ⑬** (Mountain of Death), which rises to 3,350 meters (11,000 ft). Named for early foot travelers who died from exposure to hunger, cold and storms while crossing the mountain, Cerro de la Muerte today is not as inhospitable as its name suggests. Still, it is not difficult to imagine the hardships the early - pioneers endured on the week-long journey. Rain, cold and fog can make the first half of the drive miserable, but the road is quickly above the clouds in cool, crisp sunshine, surrounded by fields of flowers and hillside farms. Purple foxglove, azaleas and white cala lilies grow wild. Clouds swirl through the valleys and over peaks. Views are unsurpassable.

There are a number of small hotels just off the highway. One of the first, just as you start climbing the mountain, is Genesis II, a private cloud forest reserve,

BELOW: Mount Chirripó, the tallest peak in southern-Central America.

which is recommended for birdwatchers. Over 150 species have been spotted at Genesis II, including the elusive quetzal.

Map on page 246

Villages of the Valley

Down the road to the right from Empalme is **Santa María de Dota**, a small town with a beautiful little park and a monument commemorating those who lost their lives in the Civil War. The road which continues towards San Marcos de Tarrazú, San Pablo de Léon Cortes and San Cristóbal Sur is called **La Ruta de Los Santos** (The Route of the Saints), and is best tackled in a 4-wheel drive vehicle.

In **Copey**, a village in the mountains above Santa Maria, you can rest at a waterfall and lake, visit rose nurseries, Don Fernando Elizando's trout farm, rent horses and have a trout lunch at William Rodríquez's *soda*.

Continuing on the Inter-American Highway, about half an hour from Empalme, is a sign which says "San Gerardo." This is the turn-off for **San Gerardo de Dota**, 9 km (6 miles) down a good but unpaved road which runs parallel to the Río Savegre. In the midst of the valley, Don Efráin Chacón and his family offer simple *cabinas*, delicious homemade meals and a taste of Costa Rican hospitality at its best. Look for a bridge and some clean white buildings painted with bright red apples on the left just above the river.

San Gerardo de Dota and **Cabinas Chacón** are known for their cloud forests and offer one of the best opportunities in the world to see the Resplendent Quetzal. The quetzals feed in trees almost in Don Efráin's backyard, and the guest book is full of enthusiastic comments such as: "8 quetzals today!" Bring plenty of warm clothing and dress in layers. It becomes surprisingly chilly and the three heavy blankets on the bed are welcome at the end of the day.

BELOW: downtown San Isidro.

Map on page 246

The drive to **San Isidro de El General** is beautiful once the fog clears from Cerro de la Muerte. San Isidro is the commercial center for this agricultural area, a busy town with a large central park and lots of noisy traffic.

Parque Nacional Chirripó

Situated 150 km (94 miles) south of San José, **Chirripó National Park**  covers 43,700 hectares (108,000 acres). Its main attraction is its diversity of landscapes, including páramos: Andean-like flatlands with stunted growth; oak forests; fern groves; cloud forests; swamps; crystal-clear glacial lakes; and the highest peak (3,800 meters/12,500 ft) in southern Central America.

Only steadfast hikers willing to brave long days of hiking, in the cold and quite possibly rain, make the ascent to the very top of **Mount Chirripó**. A modern, rustic-style lodge and several trails, which are regularly maintained make the ascent, if not easy, at least possible. Maximum daytime temperatures reach over 27°C (80°F) but at night time they can drop to almost freezing point. The best months to attempt Chirripó are February and March, the driest time of year, but hikers who have gone during the rainy months say the flora is splendid. Visits to Chirripó require advance reservations, which you can make by going to the Ministry of Natural Resources (MIRENEM) office in San José on Calle 25, Avenida 8 and 10, and paying the admission fee. The hike to the top of Chirripó, including a day on the summit, takes at least five days.

You can spend the first night in Chirripó in San Gerardo at any number of inexpensive *cabinas*. The owner of **Posada del Descanso** is very knowledgeable about the area. Before entering the park, check in at park headquarters in **San Gerardo**. Park maps are available there, but they are basic and abbreviated, and rangers often do not have the information hikers request. Good, large-scale topographical maps are available in San José, however. Rangers can put you in touch with local *campesinos* with horses who will haul your pack to the hut ahead of you.

The area around San Gerardo is well worth visiting, even if you do not attempt to climb Chirripó. Bird-watching is good, with frequent sightings of quetzals, and hiking is very satisfying, with beautiful scenery, natural hot springs and waterfalls.

Parque Nacional La Amistad

La Amistad National Park  is an enormous protected area that covers approximately 12 percent of Costa Rica's total territory. Adjacent to Chirripó, and on the interior of La Amistad Biosphere Reserve, the park is for the most part inaccessible.

La Amistad (which means "Friendship") has been declared a Biosphere Reserve and a World Patrimony site because of the diversity of its flora and fauna, and because of its great scientific value. Over half of La Amistad has yet to be explored. Hiking near the **Las Tablas Forest Reserve** is safe and rewarding, but only experienced tropical trekkers should venture into the interior. There are no park visitor facilities as such, though you can contact the Parks Service and ask about the availability of guides and horse rental. Day trips are possible from San Isidro or San Vito. ❏

ABOVE: close to nature, but with creature comforts.
BELOW: mist-clad foliage in Cerro de la Muerte.

Isla del Coco

Isla del Coco, or Cocos Island, is the most remote of Costa Rica's territories, adrift in the Pacific Ocean nearly 600 km (over 360 miles) southwest of the mainland, on the same latitude as Colombia. Because of this isolation it only counts its visitors in the hundreds, yet millions have seen it on film, in the opening moments of *Jurassic Park*. In all senses, this is a place of high drama.

At its crown is a thick coniferous forest, full of springs and rivers. The cliffs which tower over 100 meters (300 ft) around the entire island are covered with incredibly thick tropical vegetation, with magnificent waterfalls plummeting straight down to the sea. In all, there are 200 waterfalls on the island. Lionel Wafer, a pirate physician who visited over 300 years ago wrote "what most contributes to the loveliness of the place is the number of clear, freshwater springs that fill the entire lower part of the island." And there are rocky crags and wondrously-formed islets that have been shaped by the wind and water. No wonder then that it inspired Stephen Spielberg, to whom it was "Isla Nebular".

Measuring roughly 12 km by 5 km (8 miles by 3 miles), Isla del Coco is the largest uninhabited island in the world. It is now a National Park and the richest in endemic species belonging to Costa Rica.

As if these facts were not sufficiently alluring, the island's history is also full of pirate stories. Many insist that there is treasure hidden here still, yet in over 500 expeditions none has ever been found.

Two bays, Wafer Bay and Chatham Bay, offer a way to tie up and gain entry to explore the island. Chatham Bay is small, with a rocky beach. Here, the ghosts of past explorers, and of pirates, are almost tangible. Today's visitors are mostly treasure hunters, divers and environmentalists.

Most visitors consider Wafer Bay to be the best access route to the island. After anchoring and reaching the shoreline, steep cliffs follow ancient natural paths, leaping from rocks across rivers all the way to the highest part of the humid forest. Here there are bountiful bromeliads, giant ferns, orchids, unnamed flowering plants, mosses and ferns covering almost everything. And from a high peak there are views of an unbelievably blue sea above an impossibly green landscape, with white, angel-like doves moving gently, hovering and fluttering in the air. Every natural path, every river, every waterfall, every beach has some rare treasure. The peace is astounding and deafening. And the views of the coral reef, the crisp clarity of the water, the lushness of the landscape, all somehow contribute to an atmosphere where the mysterious legends of the past come alive.

Camping is not permitted on the island: you must sleep on your boat. There is potable water, however; and hiking, although the trails are not marked. Contact the National Parks Service for information and permission to enter. Specialist tour companies operate out of Puntarenas but, be warned, the price of a trip is very high. For the majority of people the Isla del Coco remains just a dream – and perhaps that is no bad thing. ❑

RIGHT: the dense deep little-known jungle interior of Isla del Coco.

INSIGHT GUIDES

TRAVEL TIPS

New Insight Maps

Maps in Insight Guides are tailored to complement the text. But when you're on the road you sometimes need the big picture that only a large-scale map can provide. This new range of durable Insight Fleximaps has been designed to meet just that need.

Detailed, clear cartography
makes the comprehensive route and city maps easy to follow, highlights all the major tourist sites and provides valuable motoring information plus a full index.

Informative and easy to use
with additional text and photographs covering a destination's top 10 essential sites, plus useful addresses, facts about the destination and handy tips on getting around.

Laminated finish
allows you to mark your route on the map using a non-permanent marker pen, and wipe it off. It makes the maps more durable and easier to fold than traditional maps.

The first titles
cover many popular destinations. They include Algarve, Amsterdam, Bangkok, California, Cyprus, Dominican Republic, Florence, Hong Kong, Ireland, London, Mallorca, Paris, Prague, Rome, San Francisco, Sydney, Thailand, Tuscany, USA Southwest, Venice, and Vienna.

☀ INSIGHT GUIDES
The world's largest collection of visual travel guides

CONTENTS

Getting Acquainted

The Place

Area: 51,000 sq. km (19,700 sq. miles).
Capital: San José.
Highest mountain: Mount Chirripó, 3,820 m (12,500 ft).
Coastline: More than 1,200 km (750 miles) of Caribbean and Pacific coastline.
Population: 3.6 million.
Language: Spanish. English (Creole) is spoken by Costa Ricans of Caribbean descent, most of whom live near the Caribbean Coast.
Religion: Catholic (81 percent); most others are Protestant and there is a small Jewish community.
National flower: *Guaria Morada* (orchid).
Time zone: GMT less 7 hours. Central Time in the US.
Currency: *colón*.
Weights and measures: metric.
Electricity: 120 volts, 60 cycle current. Two-prong flat and round plugs.
International dialing code: 506.

Climate

Costa Rica has two seasons; the rainy or green season, which Costa Ricans call winter (*invierno*) and the dry season or summer (*verano*). In the Central Valley, the rainy season lasts from May to November and the dry season from December through April. Even during the rainy season, most mornings are bright and sunny. Many people visit during the rainy season and take advantage of green season discounts in hotels and less crowds everywhere.

Rain can fall at any time on the Caribbean coast. It is generally more humid on the Caribbean side than the Pacific. The average temperature in San José is 75°F (24°C). In the highlands, temperatures drop 10°F for each 150 m (500 ft) of elevation. The temperature on the coast varies from the high 70s°F (25+°C) to the low 90s°F (30+°C).

The Economy

Tourism, coffee and bananas, in that order. Costa Ricans enjoy one of the highest standards of living in the Americas. They have free health care and public education, and one of the highest literacy rates (93 percent) in Central, South or North America.

Government

Costa Rica is a democracy governed by a president who is elected every four years. An incumbent president may not be re-elected (although this is under discussion and could change). There are two vice presidents and a cabinet of 12 ministers. Members of the Legislative Assembly are elected every four years. The Constitution, adopted in 1949 after a civil war, abolished the military. There is no capital punishment.

Courtesies & Customs

Greeting: People in Latin America shake hands with each other when first introduced. In Costa Rica this may be an even more friendly wrist or forearm shake, where the hand is purposely missed and the wrist or forearm is lightly held instead. It is considered somewhat discourteous to look someone directly in the eye when shaking hands in greeting.

Women usually greet each other with a kiss on the cheek and say goodbye in the same fashion; this also applies when a friendly relationship exists, and men and women often greet in the same way. Children are very affectionate and greet their elders with a kiss. However, among adults, excessive demonstrations of affection in public are not well received. As an indication of the formality of the country, note that in Spanish the "*Usted,*" or formal pronoun for "you" is used even between parents and their children.

Nude bathing on beaches is not acceptable to Costa Ricans; nor is wearing bathing suits on the streets.

Prostitution is legal in Costa Rica and prostitutes are supposed to be certified by the health department. Some beautiful women are in fact transvestites. Aids is a formidable reality in Costa Rica and safe sex is encouraged. Sex with a minor is illegal and punishable by imprisonment.

Planning the Trip

US, Canadian and UK citizens

To enter Costa Rica you need a valid passport. US citizens can enter with any ID or with a tourist card available from the Costa Rican consulate, port of entry, some travel agencies or the ticket office of your airline. Travelers may remain for 90 days without a visa extension.

A US citizen who is traveling from other countries may be required to have a valid passport and a visa.

Other requirements: You must have $300 and a departure ticket (a ticket to another country) to enter Costa Rica.

Visa extensions: If you plan to stay longer than 90 days, any local travel agent can solicit a visa extension for you at a small charge (or you can do it yourself at Immigration, but it is a huge hassle). Give your passport to the travel agent several days before you need it back: the fee is around US$40 plus US$1.50 for each month or partial month

Further Information

Embassies of Costa Rica:
in US: 2112/S Street, NW, Washington DC 20008.
Tel: 202-234-2945.
in Canada: 135 York Street Suite 208, Ottawa, Ontario, K1N 5TA.
Tel: 1 613-562-2855.
in UK: 14 Lancaster Gate, London, W2 3LH.
Tel: 020-7706-8844.
Website: www.costarica.com

you have overstayed; the travel agent's own fee should not exceed around US$20.

Identification: Always carry identification (or at least a photocopy of it) in case of immigration authorities' spot checks. Report lost identification immediately.

Travelers from other nations

Contact the nearest Costa Rican consulate or embassy, or try the website: www.rree.go.cr.

Customs Regulations

Personal effects may be taken into the country and up to six rolls of film, 500 g (18 ounces) of tobacco, 2 kg (4 lbs) of candy, and 3 liters (106 fl.oz.) of wine or liquor (if over 21). Carry prescription drugs in original containers. Anyone caught with illegal drugs can face 8–20 years in jail and no bail.

Exit Regulations

Anyone who resides in Costa Rica as a resident, retiree, or a tourist with a stay of longer than 90 days might be required to obtain a document in order to leave the country. This document states that the traveler is not leaving behind any family members who might become destitute during the traveler's absence; it may be obtained from the Alcaldía de Pensiones Alimenticias at the Supreme Court building.

Costa Rica, like many other Latin American countries, does not permit minors (up to and including 17 years of age) to leave the country unaccompanied by both parents without the permission of the child welfare organization, *Patronato Nacional de la Infancia* (tel: 223-8355). If one parent wishes to take the child out of the country, or the parents wish to send the child with a designated guardian, both parents must go to the

Pets

To bring in pets, an import permit is required, and obtaining this permit can take from three days to three or four months. Contact: **Jefe del Dept. de Zoonosis,** Ministerio de Salud, Apdo 10123, San José, Costa Rica. Tel: 223-0333 ext. 331.

Patronato offices, calle 19, ave 6, with the child's passport and request permission. Because of the above restrictions, a child visiting Costa Rica may fall under the jurisdiction of the *Patronato*. Should the child be traveling in the company of a guardian or of only one parent, written permission to travel (notarized by the Costa Rican consul abroad) must be presented to the *Patronato* to permit the child to leave the country. Travel agents will handle some of the steps involved for a fee.

Health

Costa Rica ranks near the United States, Canada and other Western nations in health care standards.

Inoculations: No inoculations required for visiting Costa Rica.

Water: in San José and Central Valley, water is treated. It is, with some exceptions, potable throughout the country. If you have persistent intestinal problems, take a stool sample to the American Clinic (tel: 222-1010) or the Clínica Bíblica (tel: 221-3922) to be analyzed (about $4, results in 24 hours).

Illness: Malaria is not generally a problem in Costa Rica, except in the remote regions of Talamanca. Cholera is not usually a problem, either, due to Costa Rica's strong public health efforts. There have been incidences of dengue fever, however. Dengue symptoms

Public Holidays & Festivals

January 1–2 New Year's Day, culmination of week-long festivities in San José and other locations (*Fiestas del Fin del Año*): parade of horses (*tope*); carnival; *Feria de Zapote* with bullfights. Celebrations continue on the following day.

Mid-January Fiestas in Santa Cruz (Nicoya Peninsula), and rodeos, bullfights, music and dancing in Palmares (Alajuela).

February/March Annual Orchid Show; also the best time to see orchids in bloom at Lankester Gardens, Cartago. San José National Theater Symphony season begins in March. Rodeos in San José.

Mid-March National Handicraft Fair, downtown San José. Feast of San José (St Joseph), Patron Saint of San José. *Día del Boyero* (Day of the Ox-cart Driver) parade and blessing of the ox-carts (*carretas*), San Antonio de Escazú.

March/April *Semana Santa*, Holy Week: Thursday and Friday banks, post offices, and government offices are closed,

as well as most shops and restaurants; *Jueves Santo*, Holy Thursday: start of Holy Week ceremonies. *Viernes Santo*, Good Friday: religious processions at 1am and 4pm. "Roman soldiers," biblical personages and black-clad mourners, in San José, Cartago, Heredia, Escazú and especially San Joaquín de Flores.

April 11 Juan Santamaría Day; hero of Costa Rica, died in the Battle of Rivas in action against William Walker in 1856; celebrated in Alajuela.

May 1 Labor Day, Worker's March in San José. Election of the President of the Parliament.

May/June Feast of Corpus Christi on the Thursday after Trinity Sunday.

June 29 Feast of Saints Peter and Paul.

July 25 "Anexión de Guanacaste".The President and his Cabinet commemorate the "Partido de Nicoya". Horseback parades and concerts.

August 2 *Nuestra Señora de los Angeles*, Feast of Patroness of Costa Rica, at the Basilica in Cartago, site of a miraculous appearance in 1635.

August 15 Feast of the Assumption and Mother's Day.

September 15 Independence Day. Independence from Spain since 1821 is celebrated nation-wide. All traffic in San José stops at 6pm on the 14th, and every-one sings the national anthem.

October 12 Columbus Day. *El Día de la Raza* (also called *El Día de las Culturas*). Week-long Carnival in Puerto Limón with floats, dance contests, ending with an elaborate parade.

October 31 Halloween.

December 8 Feast of the Immaculate Conception. Holy Communion Day. Fireworks the night before to honor the Virgin.

December 25/last week of year Christmas Day. Opening of the "Festejos Populares" with fireworks and bullfights at the Rendondel de Zapote.

include the sudden onset of fever, headache, severe joint and muscle pains followed in most cases by a rash which starts on the trunk of the body and spreads to the limbs and face. The fever subsides in a few days and recovery begins, usually with no serious side effects. Dengue is spread by a mosquito with striped legs, *Aedes aegypti,* which bites principally at dusk. There is presently no prophylactic treatment available for dengue.

Money Matters

The currency unit is the *colón*. The current rate of exchange

can be found in the English language *Tico Times* business pages or the same section of the daily *La Nación.* Or call a private bank for the current rate. **Private banks:** The main ones are Banco Banex (tel: 257-0522) and Banco San José (256-9911). Other private banks are Bancrecen, Interfin, Scotiabank and Citibank. **Cash and traveler's checks:** Cash machines are available in the biggest shopping centers and petrol stations of the Central Valley. If you travel to the beach or the mountains, you will probably need cash or travelers' checks for expenses, other than at large hotels. It is

advisable to have some travelers' checks, notes and change in small denominations. You may not be able to break 5,000 *colón* notes when paying for taxis and such. **Credit cards:** American Express, Visa and MasterCard are widely accepted in the Central Valley area. Hotels and other establishments usually add a surcharge of 7–8 percent to credit card purchases, so be prepared and check before you book. **Changing money:** Money can be changed on arrival at the airport until 5pm. Banking hours are weekdays 9am–3pm. Private banks are a much better option for changing dollars and dollar travelers' checks than state banks, which are terribly slow in exchanging currency (having to wait in line for two or more hours is not uncommon). You could also consider using the *Casas de Cambio*, or money exchange houses, which provide a more rapid service. Ask at your hotel about their availability. Your hotel may change money for you.

It is common to change money on the streets. Be careful if you do, as tourists changing money are sometimes cheated and/or robbed.

It may be advisable to exchange *colones* back into dollars before departing Costa Rica. The airport bank may cash only US$50 worth back into dollars for departing travelers.

What to Bring

Clothing and footwear: Plan to dress in layers. Sweaters and jackets are needed for activities in the mountains and cool evenings. Shorts are worn for athletic activities or at the beaches, not normally in the cities. Bring rain gear and boots if you plan to do much hiking. Have a comfortable pair of walking shoes that are already broken in. Sidewalks are non-existent in many areas, and uneven at best.

Costa Ricans dress formally, and the women especially are always well groomed, even the poor majority who can be seen emerging perfectly made-up from one-room shacks. Bring dressy clothes for upmarket San José restaurants and nightlife. **Personal items**: A folding umbrella will often be welcome. Bring what medications and film you need. It is a good idea to bring insect repellent, sunscreen, tampons, and contraceptives with you. They are often expensive and difficult to find outside San José. Avon bath oil, Skin So Soft, rubbed on the skin, is reputedly

effective at keeping the "no-see-'ems" at the beach from biting; also check out the Avon Skin So Soft sunscreen.

Getting There

By Air
International flights arrive in Costa Rica at Juan Santamaría Airport, located in the Central Valley about 16 km (10 miles) from San José, the capital city. Some international flights (mostly charter flights for beach-bound tourists) now arrive at Daniel Oduber Airport in Liberia, Guanacaste Province (also called Tomas Guardia). Condor, LTU and other companies fly directly there. Make reservations as far ahead as possible, especially during December–February, as these flights are usually booked well in advance. Confirm 72 hours before departure. For the budget traveler, or those making last-minute reservations, a number of discount "bucket shops" should be considered. Check the Sunday editions of the *New York Times* and *Los Angeles Times*. To lessen the chance of getting "bumped" by overbooking, arrive two hours before your flight.

Weight limits are usually 30 kg (66 lbs). If necessary, determine how the airline is equipped to handle surf boards, bicycles, etc. Have your luggage well tagged and identified. Be prepared in case your luggage is lost. There is a US$17 airport exit tax for tourists when departing Costa Rica.

It is a 20-minute ride (about US$12–20 by taxi) to San José from the airport. If there is no meter in the cab agree on the fare before committing yourself. A bus into town is also available for under US$1.00.

By Bus
Bus services to Costa Rica are available from Panamá or Nicaragua.

Tica Bus, Calle 9, Ave 4, tel: 221-8954 or 221 9229 provides a comfortable, reliable service throughout Central America. Daily buses to Nicaragua and Panamá.
Trans Nica, Calle 14, Ave 3, tel: 221-0953.
Nicaragua, tel: (505) 278 2090. El Salvador, tel: (503) 240 1212.
Panaline, Calle 14 y 16, Ave 13, tel: 255 1205/258 0022.

By Car
The Inter-American Highway allows fairly rapid transit into Costa Rica by way of Panamá or Nicaragua. Avoid traveling at night. Bringing a vehicle into the country must be noted in your passport. Leaving the country without a vehicle that has been registered in your passport will be difficult.

By Sea
Cruise ships come into Puerto Limón on the Caribbean coast and Puerto Caldera on the Pacific. Check with a travel agent about which companies currently sail to Costa Rica.

Airlines

Aero Costa Sol, (domestic flights only), tel: 440 1444.
American, tel: 257 1266.
Continental Airlines, tel: 296-4911, fax 296 4920.
Delta, tel: 257 4141.
Grupo Taca, US and Canada: tel: 1 800 535 8780; UK: 0870 241 0340.
Iberia, tel: 257 8226, fax: 223 1055.
LACSA, tel: 296 0909.
Lufthansa, 256 6116, fax: 233 9485.
LTU, tel: 234 9292.
Martinair, tel: 220 4111, fax 220 3092.
MEXICANA, tel: 257 6334, fax: 257 6338.
SANSA (domestic flights only), tel: 257 9444
United Airlines, tel: 220 4844, fax: 220 4895.

Private yachts are popular as a means to visit. Check into a port of entry with four copies of the crew list, ship's papers and a notarized statement from the owner (if not on board). Fly a yellow quarantine flag upon arrival and wait until boarded and cleared before going ashore.

By River

The truly adventurous can travel through Nicaragua down the Río San Juan, which is the border between Nicaragua and Costa Rica. To do this, take a bus from Managua to Granada on Lake Nicaragua. The boat to the village of San Carlos, where the Río San Juan begins, leaves from the pier. Use a hammock for the overnight trip, which arrives at dawn.

Buying a canoe: Negotiate in San Carlos for a dugout canoe that will be large enough to be comfortable, but not so heavy as to be unmanageable; or purchase passage on the river boat to El Castillo and buy a dugout there. Ensure that the paddles are well seasoned, otherwise they will be heavy and tiring to handle. If the river is raging because of recent rains, wait until it is manageable.

Food and drink: Small amounts of cash can be exchanged for food and a covered place for your hammock at many of the small farms along the river. Be prepared to camp. Do not drink any untreated water or eat uncooked food or unpeeled fruit.

Crossing the border: About halfway through this trip you will enter Costa Rica. Have your passport stamped (or signed if the official cannot find his inkpad) at the *aduana* shack. It is less than a two-week trip from Lake Nicaragua to the Caribbean Coast where you can take the protected and fairly well traveled coastal canal. Alternatively, descend on a coconut barge or other river traffic to Limón.

Specialist Tours

Aventuras Naturales
Tel: 225-3939
Fax 253-6934.
E-mail: avenat@sol.racsa.co.cr
Specialist in adventure tours within a natural setting. Offers rafting, kayaking, cycling and hiking.

Costa Rica Expeditions
Tel: 257-0766
Fax: 257-1665.
The original whitewater rafting company. Offers nature tours to Tortuguero, Corcovado, with knowledgeable, bilingual guides.

Costa Rica Sun Tours
Tel: 255-3418
Fax: 255-4410.
Off-the-beaten-track tours with a naturalist focus. Volcanoes, national parks, cloud forests, rainforests, beaches. Turtle-watching tours. Whitewater rafting, hiking, biking and horseback tours.

Discovery Costa Rica
Tel: 394-3257/228-9261.
E-mail: discovcr@racsa.co.cr
Design your own package from a large range of tours.

Horizontes
Tel: 222-2022
Fax: 255-4513.
Customized nature tours of all types throughout Costa Rica, including tours for families. Day trips in the Central Valley.

Intertur
Tel: 253-7503
Fax: 234-6308.
www.interturcostarica.com
Natural history tours including fishing, birding, diving, ballooning. Tours to volcanoes and rafting trips.

Kapi Tours
Tel: 223-5822/255-3659
Fax 256-5368,
www.kapitours.com
Special rates for groups and students. Scuba diving, eco-tourism, adventure tours and local flights.

Pachira Lodge
Tel: 256-7080/257-2242
Fax 223-1119,
E-mail: paccira@sol.racsa.co.cr
Special package of three days/two nights from San José to Tortuguero National Park. Bilingual guides.

Savic Tours
Tel: 233-4748
Fax: 222-1097
www.savi.co.cr
Caters for all tastes, with city tours, Pacific island cruises, volcano treks, white water rafting.

Serendipity Adventures
Tel: 289-9043
Fax: 450-0328.
Offers exceptional, personalized tours and adventure trips. Specialists in hot air ballooning.

Insurance

It is essential to have comprehensive insurance when traveling to Costa Rica. Some bank and credit cards may include insurance, but this may not provide adequate medical cover. In Costa Rica, you need a minimum of $2 million of cover for medical expenses and repatriation.

Insure yourself against theft of personal items and loss of passport and money.

Certain sporting activities may necessitate paying an insurance premium – always read the small print to make sure that you are covered for any accidents.

Practical Tips

Business Hours

Business hours are generally 9am to 5pm, with a lunch-break between noon and 1pm. Banks are usually open from 8.30am until 5.30pm.

Taxes & Tipping

Hotels and restaurants add 10 percent service charge and 13 percent tax to the bill. Hotels also charge a 3 percent tourism tax on room charges.

Hotel bellboys should be tipped. In restaurants tipping is not expected.

Media

Radio

Radio stations in English include 107.5, which plays classic rock and has news and other information in English, and Radio Dos (99.5), a Spanish-language station that plays English pop and rock classics, and has news in English every other hour.

Television

There are 45 TV channels received, via cable. Programming includes approximately 25 channels in English, two in German, one in French, and one in Italian. There are also programs in Hindi, Japanese, and Tagalog. There are TV programs received from many Latin American countries as well.

Two English-language FM stations are transmitted, including that of the University for Peace in Cuidad Colón.

Newspapers & Magazines

Available in English, Spanish and other languages, at bookstores, supermarkets, newsstands and hotel outlets.

Weekly English-language publications include: *Tico Times* (tel: 258-2558), published on Friday. Widely available. For the week's news in Costa Rica, up-to-date listings of what's happening, and where. An annual Tourist Edition gives an overview of the country.

Costa Rica Today (tel: 296-3911), published on Thursday. Tourist magazine/newspaper with features on places of interest, wildlife, calendar of events, etc. Widely available.

Daily Spanish-language newspapers include: *La Nación*, *La Prensa Libre*, *La República* and *Al Dia*.

Telecommunications

Costa Rica has one of the best telecommunications systems in Central America. Fax machines are popular, with public access from most post offices around the country. E-mail is easily sent and received.

For written telecommunications contact:
Radiográfica Costarricense, S.A. (RACSA), ave 5, calle I, tel: 287-0087. Services include telegraph, telex, facsimiles and e-mail.

Making Telephone Calls

Use a 10 or 20 *colón* coin. Set the coin(s) in the slot on top of the phone, then dial the number; the coin will drop down when the connection has been made. Extra coins set in the slot will fall automatically, only as needed. Most telephones work with telephone cards now.

International Calls

See the telephone directory under *Lista Alfabética de Códigos* MIDA for the codes for various countries. If you do not

Tourist Offices

Costa Rican Tourism Institute (ICT), open 8am–5pm, staffed by bilingual operators, tel: 1-800 343-6332 (from the US) or 506-223 1733 (from the UK), fax: 223 5452.
www.tourism.costarica.com
National Parks Information, (SINAC), tel: 257-2239, fax: 283-7118.
Corcovado Park Administration, office in Puerto Jiménez, tel: 735-5036.
Santa Rosa National Park Headquarters, tel: 666-5051, fax: 660 5020.
Palo Verde National Park, tel: 284 6105.
Ostional Wildlife Refuge, for accommodation information or to find out if the turtles are active, call the village grocery store, tel: 680-0476.
Tapantí National Park, to make arrangements to hire a guide or to ask about staying in a house rented by park personnel, call SINAC (listed above), which has radio contact with Tapantí.
Curú Wildlife Reserve, call ahead for information about staying in a rustic beach cabin on the privately owned reserve. Contact the Schultz family, tel/fax: 661-2392.

have access to a telephone, international calls can be made from Radiográfica (Calle 1, Ave 5) or Telecomunicaciones Internacionales (Ave 2, Calles 1 & 3).

Credit Card Calls

Visa, MasterCard and American Express are handled by local credit card firm **Credomatic**, tel: 257 0155.

Access numbers for international credit card calls are:
AT&T: 0 8000 114 114
MCI: 0 8000 122 222
Sprint: 0 8000 130123

Medical Services

Costa Rica has an excellent health care system, much less expensive than in the US. Many doctors, trained in the US or Europe, speak English, especially at private clinics.

Public Medical Centers
San Juan de Díos Hospital
Tel: 257 6282.
México Hospital
Tel: 232 6122.
Dr Calderón Guardia Hospital
Tel: 257 7922.
National Children's Hospital
Tel: 222 0122.

Private Medical Centers
American Clinic
Tel: 222 1010.
Clínica Bíblica
Tel: 257 5252.
Catholic Clinic
Tel: 283 6616.

Hospital San José Cima
Tel: 208 1000
Fax: 208 1001
Hospital Cristiano Jerusalem
Tel: 216 9191.
Santa Rita Clinic
Tel: 221 6433
Fax: 225 1248.
Specializes in maternity and gynecology.

Plastic Surgery
Plastic surgery is a big business in Costa Rica, with people coming from North America and Europe for reconstructive and cosmetic procedures, which often cost less than half of US prices. Consult the *Tico Times* for adverts placed by English-speaking plastic surgeons.
Health Tourism
Apartado 1518–2100,

Guadalupe.
Tel: 253 2308
Fax: 225 8860.
Contact Dr Giovanni Montoya;
E-mail: caravana@sol.rasca.co.cr

Dentists
Costa Rican dentists also provide competent and inexpensive cosmetic as well as general dentistry.
Dr Arturo Acosta
Tel: 228 9904.
Specializes in "dental vacations."
Center for Dental Implants of Costa Rica
Tel: 253 2308
Fax: 225 8660.
Contact Dr Mario E. Garita.
The *Tico Times* contains adverts placed by English-speaking dentists.

Canadian cards: 0 8000 151161
British cards: 0 800 0441044

Postal Services

Air mail between the US or Europe and Costa Rica should take about five days, but a wait of two or more weeks is not uncommon. The Central Post Office is located at Calle 2, Ave 1–3, tel: 223-9766. Mail can be received there in the general delivery section (*Lista de Correos*). Outgoing mail should be posted at either a hotel desk

Useful Numbers

Local collect calls: 110
Information: 113
International calls: 124
Operator assistance (inter-national calls): 116
Airport information: 443-2622
Tourist information: 222-1090
Rate of exchange: 243-4143
Time: 112
Fire, police, ambulance: 911

or a post office. It is usually difficult, time-consuming, and expensive to receive packages in the mail. Outrageous duties are sometimes applied and you can spend days trying to deal with numerous officials. A receipt showing a low value may help if included with the package. There are agents (*agencias de aduana*), listed in the phone book, who will handle the hassles of customs clearances for a fee.
Couriers: There are many international courier services. Some of the most popular include: FedEx, DHL, UPS, TNT Skypack, and Lacsa Flash.
Aero Casillas
Tel: 255-4567
Located at Centro Comercial Yaohan across from Hotel Corobicí and above Yaohan supermarket, is a mailing service that uses a Miami address to send and receive mail for a monthly fee. You are billed for US postage, and have the benefit of reliable and timely service.

Emergencies

Security & Crime
Theft is a growing problem in Costa Rica. Pickpocketing, chain and watch snatching, backpack grabbing and other kinds of theft are becoming more common, especially in downtown San José. It is, for the most part, non-violent, snatch-and-run thievery. Do not become paranoid and frightened, but do be vigilant.
• Do not take valuables with you when you walk on the streets of San José. Carry only as much cash as you will need. Leave your backpack, passport, jewelry, cameras, watches and even sunglasses at your hotel. Be aware of wallets and shoulder bags. If you buy valuable items, make your return trip by taxi.

Emergency Number

For emergencies requiring police, fire and ambulance (bilingual operator), tel: **911**

- While walking on the street, be aware of who is around you, especially who is behind you.
- When driving through the city by car, keep your windows rolled up high enough that no-one can reach inside.
- Avoid the streets at night.
- Avoid walking in isolated areas.
- Be especially watchful in the following areas: from Plaza de la Democracia to the San Juan de Díos Hospital; near the Coca Cola bus terminal; the Plaza de la Cultura; Parque Central and areas where dollars are changed on the streets, such as Ave 4 and Ave Central, and Calle 12 from Ave 10 to Ave 5.
- Thefts from rental cars, which bear license plates identifying them as such, are common in all parts of the country. Do not leave anything unattended in your car. Do not assume items in a locked trunk are safe: they are not. Whenever possible, park in a guarded area.
- Do not leave things unattended on the beach. This includes towels, clothing, tents and camping gear.

Consulates

Canada
Tel: 255-3522
UK,
Tel: 258-2025
Fax: 233-9938
US
Tel: 220-3939 or 220-3050
Fax: 220-2405

Getting Around

Finding Your Way

San José uses a grid system for its streets. North–south-running streets are *calles*, east–west-running streets are *avenidas*. Avenida Central (ave ctl) divides the city north and south; it becomes Paseo Colón west of Hospital San Juan de Dios. Calle Central (calle ctl) divides San José east and west. The southern and eastern streets are numbered evenly. The northern and western streets have odd numbers.

Abbreviations used for addresses: ave = avenida, ctl = central, apto or apdo = apartado (post office box, for mailing addresses). When an address is given using the street and avenues, the first part is the street or avenue on which the building is located, and the second part of the address indicates the streets or avenues the building is between. For example: the location of the Metropolitan Cathedral is: calle ctl, ave 2–4. That is, the Cathedral is on Calle Central between Avenidas 2 and 4. (*See* San José city map, page 130.)

For the most part, there are no addresses nor are there street names in Costa Rica. Although downtown San José has numbered avenues and streets, Costa Ricans do not refer to them. Homes and buildings are not numbered. Usually an address is given as the distance in meters (*metros*) north, east, south, or west from a known landmark.

By Air

Domestic flights (*vuelos locales*) are fairly inexpensive and can provide a comfortable alternative to many hours on bad roads.

SANSA
Tel: 257 9444
Fax: 255 2176.
Offers service to Coto, Golfito, Puerto Jimenéz, Palmar Sur, Barra del Colorado, Nosara, Sámara, Tamarindo, and La Fortuna, Quepos, Tambor, Liberia. No reservations accepted by phone. You will have to go to their Paseo Colón (San José) office and pay for the tickets in advance. If you have not paid for your flight, or have paid for it on their website (www.groupotaca.com), even if you have a confirmed reservation your seat will be sold as the flight fills up. Extra charge for surf boards.
Travelair
Tel: 220 3054
Fax: 220 0413.
Flies to Liberia, Tamarindo, Nosara, Carrillo, Tambor, Quepos, Palmar Sur, Golfito, Puerto Jiménez, Barra del Colorado and Tortuguero. Surf boards accepted if there is space available, with an extra charge. Slightly more expensive than SANSA but worth it.
Helisa
Tel: 231 6867
Fax: 231 5885.
Helicopter tours to most parts of the country, including the Orosi Valley, Arenal,

Airports

Juan Santamaría (international flights), tel: 441 4781.
Daniel Oduber (Liberia) (international flights), tel: 668 1010.
Tobias Bolaños (or **Pavas**) (domestic flights), tel: 232-2820.
Limón (international and domestic), tel: 753 1379.

Taxi Companies

CGT, tel: 254 6667.
Coopetaxi, tel: 235 9966.
Coopetico, tel: 224 7979.
Coopeirazu, tel: 254 3211.
Coopeguaria, tel: 226 1366.
San José Taxis, tel: 221 3434
Taxis Aeropuerto, tel: 441 0333.
Taxis Unidos, tel: 221 6865.

Monteverde, the national parks, and Río Chirripó.
Aero Costa Sol
Tel: 440 1444
Fax: 441 2671.
Charter flights throughout Costa Rica, Nicaragua and Panamá.
Alas Anfibias
Tel: 232 9567
Fax: 233 6884.
Pavas Airport. Seaplanes capable of landing on almost any lake, river or ocean site.
Pitts Aviation Skytours
Tel: 296 3600

Fax: 296 1429.
Pavas Airport. Each flight is attended by music, high quality binoculars and a detailed description of the itinerary. Also runs a services to elsewhere in Central America.
www.pitts-aviation.com
Flying Crocodile
Tel: 656 0483
Fax: 656 0196
E-mail: flycroc@sol.racsa.co.cr
Operates from Crocodile Lodge in Samara. Scenic flights in an ultralight plane over sea, beaches and tropical forests. Lessons on how to fly ultralights.

By Bus

You can go virtually anywhere by bus in Costa Rica; it is the way most Ticos travel. Drivers take great pride in their vehicles. The main bus stop in the center of San José is the "Coca Cola" terminal, located near a former

bottling plant at calle 16, ave 1–3. Departure places and times may change. The Costa Rican Tourist Institute (ICT) office located below the Plaza de la Cultura has a list of bus companies' names and telephone numbers, tel: 222-1090. The weekly English language magazine/newspaper *Costa Rica Today* often carries a page of bus information. Or call INFOtour, tel: 223-4481.

By Taxi

Taxis are widely used and inexpensive. All should have operational meters (*marias*); be sure the drivers use them. If not, negotiate before getting in. If you are greatly overcharged, write down the driver's name and license number, and call the taxi company number marked on the outside of the cab, or tell the driver to find a policeman. Overcharges can be taken to the

Driving: A Survival Guide

Four-wheel drive (*doble tracción*) is recommended for many areas as the roads outside the Central Valley, especially during the rainy season, are muddy and rutted. Chains work well in the mud; try letting some air out of your tires, to increase traction, if the car is stuck.
Licenses: Operating a motor vehicle without a license is a serious violation of Costa Rican law and invalidates any insurance carried on the vehicle. A valid driver's license from another country can be used for three months. Always carry your passport or tourist card (photocopies will suffice).
Import: Foreign vehicles brought into Costa Rica for a period over 90 days must pay a large import tax. If you enter with a vehicle, you will have to leave with it or show papers proving you have sold it.

Driving habits: Drivers weave all over the road to avoid the many ruts and holes, called *huecos*. Two headlight blinks usually indicate the other driver is giving you the right of way (especially when you are making a left turn); on the highway two headlight blinks may mean that the police are ahead. Radar is often used. If waved over by the police, don't try to get away. They will radio ahead to have you stopped.
Accidents: Costa Rica has a high accident and death rate. Always drive defensively. Don't drive an uninsured vehicle. The law requires motorists to carry a set of reflecting triangles. If you are in an accident, do not move your car until the police arrive. Give no statements, but take witnesses' names.
Parking: Be careful not to park illegally. The yellow curb means no stopping. Even if you are in

the car, police may prevent you from leaving and call a tow truck (*grúa*). You can ride in the car to the yard, where you will be required to pay the towing charges. It is better to park in one of the inexpensive parking lots (*parqueos*). This will reduce the chance of theft.
Corruption: Unfortunately, there are corrupt police who target foreign drivers for the purpose of extracting some *colones*. You may be stopped for no apparent reason. Have all necessary automobile documents in the car and be polite. It is illegal for the police to demand payment on the spot. If you are badly treated, or if the policeman solicits a bribe or asks that you pay the fine immediately, ask for the ticket, then ask for the officer's identification. Write it down, and report to the *Dirección de Tránsito* as soon as possible.

Transportation Department.

Arrangements can be made to take trips by taxi to places outside San José. Beware, taxi drivers who are parked in front of major hotels will always charge more. Taxis are red and have a Taxi sign on the roof of the car. If they are not red, then they are pirate taxis, or *piratas,* and are unlicensed.

By Ferry

Peninsula de Nicoya.
de Coonatramar R.L.
Tel: 661-1069, fax: 661-2197.
Puntarenas to Playa Naranjo.
Departs 3.15am, 7am,
10.50am, 2.50pm, and 7pm.
Playa Naranjo to Puntarenas.
Departs 5.10am, 8.50am,
12.50am, 5pm and 9pm.
Puntarenas to Paquera.
Departs 6am and 3pm daily.
During high season, there is also an 11am ferry.
Paquera to Puntarenas.
Departs 8.15am and 5pm daily.
During high season, there is also a 12.30pm ferry.
Tempisque Río.
On the hour, 7am–6pm.

By Bicycle

Mountain bikes are a good way to see Costa Rica's back country, especially on the lightly traveled dirt roads which crisscross the rural areas. Bicycle riding can be dangerous on the roads as they have no shoulders. Check with the consulate about import taxes. Consider installing KEVLAR inner tube protectors (such as Mr Tuffy). Bring a good lock. Check with your airline about shipping.

By Car

Car rental

Renting a car makes sense for trips outside San José. Reserve a car well in advance and get written confirmation. Pre-payment is advised, especially during high season. Rates are generally around US$50 per day, including insurance. Four-wheel drive vehicles are usually around US$65 per day. Renting without a credit card usually involves a large deposit. When reserving four-wheel drive, find out what kind of vehicle you are getting. Elegante is one of the few companies that provide non-deductible insurance, as an option. All other insurance is deductible for the first US$750–$1,000. The following agencies all accept American Express, MasterCard and Visa. Prego is recommended. Most agencies insist that the driver is over 21 years of age, they hold a valid tourist card or passport and driver's license, and have a valid credit card for a deposit (not cash).

Ada and Alamo, calle 11–13, ave 18, tel: 233 7733; US toll free: 1 800 5700671; Costa Rica toll free: 800 232 7368. www.adarentacar.com
Budget, tel: 223 3284. www.budget.co.cr
Discovery, tel: 293 2865/293 2866; fax: 293 2932.
Dollar, Paseo Colón, calle 32, tel: 222-8920.
Elegante, calle 10, ave 13–15, tel: 257 0026; toll free from US: 1 800 582 7432; toll free from Canada 1 800 283 1324. www.centralamerica.com/cr/tran/elegante.htm
National, tel: 290 8787; fax: 290 0431; reservations: 800 CAR RENT. e-mail: reservations@natcar.com Bilingual chauffeurs available.
Prego, tel: 257-1158.
Toyota, calle 30–32, Paseo Colón, tel: 223-2250.

Private Tour Drivers

An alternative is to hire a knowledgeable bilingual driver, experienced with Costa Rican roads. Ask at your hotel or consult the *Tico Times*. Two excellent drivers are **Carlos Mora**, tel: 232-9870 or 284-4576, and **Joaquín (Quincho) Herrera**, tel: 288-1418.

Where to Stay

The airport ICT desk can help if you arrive without advance hotel reservations. Downtown San José is very noisy and polluted so you may well prefer to stay out of the center. Escazú, Santa Ana, Alajuela, Heredia, and other Central Valley towns are less expensive, more enjoyable, and still give a good taste of Costa Rican life.

Reservations made, but not paid for, especially during high season, may not be held, especially near the beaches and Monteverde. Discounts may be given for stays of more than one night. Ask at your hotel about green (wet) season discounts.

The Tourist Institute has a system of classifications for lodging based on size and facility; however, there is a wide range of popular names used unofficially:
Apartotel Apartments with cooking facilities and living area in a hotel-style complex. Weekly and monthly rates.
Cabina Usually a one-room cabin with a shower and bath, often close to the beach in coastal resorts. *Cabinas* vary widely in quality and price.
Bed & Breakfast Price and quality vary widely, from a modest room in someone's own house to elegant guest houses all to yourself with pools and tennis courts.
Lodge Popular in more remote areas, usually near parks or natural attractions. Price usually includes meals.
Villa or Chalet Often indistinguishable from a hotel.
Inn Often a B&B, but with more extensive amenities.

Resort Usually a luxurious, self-contained hotel complex.
Hotel Anything with more than 10 rooms.
Hostel In Costa Rica there is a small youth hostel system. Prices vary.
Albergue/Pensión Modest, small hotels.

Hotels

CENTRAL VALLEY

Expensive
Casa Turire
Turrialba
Tel: 531 1111
Fax: 531 1075
E-mail: casaturire@ticonet.co.cr
Luxurious plantation-style hotel on the grounds of a sugar cane, coffee and macadamia nut plantation. Spring-fed swimming pool. Six-hole golf course. No children.
Finca Rosa Blanca Inn
Near Heredía
Tel: 269 9392
Fax: 269 9555
www.fincarblanco.co.cr
A lovely, small hotel in the foothills of Heredia.
Hotel Chalet Tirol
Tel: 267 6222
Fax: 267 6229
E-mail: info@chalet.tirol.com
Tyrolean-style A-frame cottages in the cloud forest above Heredia, bordering a National Park.
Tara
Tel: 228 6992
Fax: 228 9651
E-mail: taraspa@sol.racsa.co.cr
San Antonio de Escazú. Straight out of *Gone with the Wind*. Wonderful views. Pool. Health and beauty spa.
Hotel Grano de Oro
San José
Tel: 255 3322
Fax: 221 2782
Elegant, restored mansion in a quiet area. Good restaurant.
Puesta del Sol Country Inn
Escazú, 7 minutes from San José
Tel: 289 8775

Fax: 289 8766
Former residence of a European ambassador. Beautiful tropical grounds. Pool. Friendly, helpful staff. Facilities include a tour consultation desk.

Moderate
El Pórtico Hotel
Tel: 237 6022
Fax: 260 6002
In the hills above Heredía. Pool, jacuzzi, sauna and acres of green hills with hiking trails.
Hostel II Milenium
Tel: 441 2365/441 5192
E-mail: bbmilenium@hotmail.com
Bed and breakfast in Alajuela, half a mile from Juan Santamaría International Airport and close to the bus stop. English-speaking owner, well-run and friendly atmosphere. Monthly rates on request.
Hotel Bougainvillea
Tel: 239 0033
Fax: 239 2292
E-mail: bougain@sol.racsa.co.cr
In the picturesque city of Santo Domingo de Heredia this is a perfect setting for nature lovers who like tranquillity. Twelve acres of tropical gardens with reading area, heated pool, sauna and lit tennis courts. 80 tastefully decorated rooms with fresh cut flowers from the gardens.
Guayabo Lodge
Tel/fax: 556 0133
Guayabo area. Pleasant lodge located on a dairy farm. Four-day package includes horseback ride to Turrialba Volcano and a visit to Guayabo National Monument.
La Providencia Ecological Reserve
Poás
Tel/fax: 231 4734
Pleasant, rustic *cabinas* on a former dairy farm located near the top of Poás Volcano. Rates include breakfast.

Budget
Albergue El Marañon
Apartado 6100,
Ciudad Colón,

San José
Tel: 249 1271
Fax: 249 1761
E-mail: cultourica@expreso.co.cr
A typical country house in the small town of La Trinidad. There is a tropical garden with fruit trees and butterflies. The restaurant serves local and vegetarian dishes.
Hotel Wagelia
Turrialba
Tel: 556 1566
Fax: 556 1596
Near central park. Private baths, hot water, TV, refrigerators. Restaurant.
Pochotel
Turrialba
Tel: 556 0111
Fax: 556 6222
Cabinas with private baths and heated water, on a hilltop. Wonderful views. Camping. Restaurant.
Casa Ridgeway
Ave 6 bis,
Calle 15,
San José
Tel: 233 6168
Small *pensión* managed by the Society of Friends (Quakers). A pleasant place to stay. Use of kitchen and laundry.
Hotel Interamericano
Turrialba
Tel: 556 0142
Basic inn near the railroad station. Cold water. Use of kitchen.
Toruma
Ave Central,
Calles 31/33,
San José
Tel/fax: 224 4085
E-mail: recajhi@sol.racsa.co.cr
Costa Rica Youth Hostel Network headquarters in a mansion near downtown. Shared/private baths, hot water. Includes breakfast. Laundry service. Use of kitchen.
Turrialtico
Turrialba
Tel: 556 1111
Charming. Rooms above the restaurant have private baths and heated water. Hilltop location. Beautiful views.

CENTRAL PACIFIC

Expensive
Hotel Amapola
Tel/fax: 643 3668
Downtown Jacó, close to the
beach. 44 rooms, sauna, jacuzzi
and pool.
Hotel Eclipse
Manuel Antonio
Tel/fax: 777 0408
E-mail: eclipse@sol.racsa.co.cr
Lovely, Mediterranean villas and
pools. Kitchens and restaurant.
Hotel Karahe
Apartado 100–6535,
Quepos
Tel: 777 0170
Fax: 777 1075
E-mail: karahe@ns.goldnet.co.cr
Nine airconditioned bungalows
surrounded by 1500 acres of
grounds. Swimming pool and
jacuzzi. Outdoor pursuits.
Hotel Marriott Los Sueños
Tel: 298 0000
Fax: 298 0033
E-mail: costaric@marriott.co.cr
Beach and golf resort on the
Central Pacific Coast, near Playa
Jacó. 201 rooms. Tours
arranged.
Hotel Punta Leona
Punta Leona
Tel: 231 3131
Toll free: 800-231 3131
Fax: 232 0791
Resort with access to good
beaches. Kitchens available.
Sapo Dorado
Monteverde
Tel/fax: 645 5010
E-mail: elsapo@sol.racsa.co.cr
Nice *cabinas* with fireplaces.
**Tango Mar Surf and Saddle
Club**
Tel: 288 1257
Resort on Bahia Ballena with
thatched-roof cabins. Kitchens
available. Tennis. Diving.
Seaside golf course.
Villa Caletas
Near Jacó
Tel: 257 3653
Fax: 222 2059
A luxurious French colonial
fantasy retreat on a
mountaintop overlooking the
Pacific. Lovely pool.

Villas Nicolás
Manuel Antonio
Tel: 777 0481
Fax: 777 0451
Terraces with beautiful views.

Price Categories

Price categories are for
double occupancy per night
without breakfast:
Expensive: US$70 and up
Moderate: US$40–70
Budget: US$40 and under

Moderate
Arco Iris Lodge
Apartado 03–5655, Puntarenas
Tel: 645 5067
Fax: 645 5022
Small lodge near to Monteverde
Cloud Forest. Rooms with hot
water and private bathrooms.
Laundry. Tours offered.
Belmar
Monteverde
Tel: 645 5201
Fax: 645 5135
E-mail: belmar@sol.racsa.co.cr
Chalet-style and homey. Views.
El Establo
Monteverde
Tel: 645 5110
Fax: 645 5041
Comfortable. Horseback riding.
Heliconia Hotel
Monteverde
Tel: 645 5109
E-mail: heliconi@sol.racsa.co.cr
Southern European atmosphere.
Hotel Amor del Mar
Jacó
Tel/fax: 642 0262
On the beach, peaceful and
pleasant.
Portobello
Puntarenas
Tel: 661 1322
Fax: 661 0036
Air-conditioning. Gardens.

Budget
Cabinas Las Olas
Playa Hermosa (near Jacó)
Tel: 233 4455
Fax: 222 8586
Rooms have private baths,
heated water, ceiling fans,

kitchens. Pool. Friendly surfer's
hang-out.
El Bosque
Monteverde
Tel: 645 5158
Fax: 645 5129
Cabinas and campsites with
toilets and hot water.
El Coquito del Pacífico
Matapalo
Tel: 233 1731
Fax: 228 8849
Pleasant, light *cabinas* with
screens and reading lamps.
Cabinas Iacona
Montezuma
Tel/fax: 642 0272
Well-designed cabins just off a
beautiful, white sand beach,
kitchens, fans, cold water.
Hotel Ancia de Oro
Tel/fax: 642 0369
In Cabuya de Cobano, close to
the National Reserve. Seven
rooms with bathroom and hot
water. No credit cards.
Hotel Bahía Gigante
Bahía Gigante
Tel/fax: 661 2442
Friendly sportfishing hotel. Tours
arranged.
Hotel Ceciliano
Quepos
Tel: 777 0192
Well kept and pleasant. Rooms
with shared/private bathrooms,
cold water, ceiling fans.
Hotel La Aurora
Tel: 642 0051
Fax: 642 0025
Near Montezuma Beach. Nine
rooms with bathroom and
kitchen. Room service and
laundry.
La Felicidad Country Inn
Apartado 73–6300, Parrita
Nice cabinas and rooms near
Esterillos Beach. Tours offered.
No credit cards.
Naturist Beachfront Aparthotel
Manuel Antonio
Tel: 777 1473
Tel/fax: 777 1475
Studio apartments with
kitchens, on the beach.
Cabinas Doña Alicia
Quepos
Tel: 777 0419
Clean and friendly. Private

Price Categories

Price categories are for double occupancy per night without breakfast:
Expensive: US$70 and up
Moderate: US$40–70
Budget: US$40 and under

bathrooms, cold water and ceiling fans.
Hotel Moctezuma
Montezuma
Message/fax: 642 0058
Overlooks the beach. Shared bathrooms, cold water, ceiling fans. Restaurant downstairs.

GUANACASTE

Expensive
Capitán Suizo
Tamarindo
Tel: 653 0075
Fax: 653 0292
E-mail: capsuizo@racsa.co.cr
Elegant, well-designed rooms and bungalows. Pool.
El Ocotal Hotel
Playa Ocotal
Tel: 670 0321
Fax: 670 0083
E-mail: elocotal@pop.racsa.co.cr
Elegant and secluded hotel overlooking the beach. Tennis. Pool. Sportfishing.
Guanamar
Playa Carrillo
Tel: 239 2000
Fax: 293 4839
Exclusive fishing resort. Lush grounds. Terraces overlooking the bay.
Hacienda Los Inocentes
La Cruz
Tel: 279 9198
Lovely old hacienda, remodeled with care. Well-trained horses with guides, to explore the countryside.
Hotel Playa Nosara
Nosara
Tel: 680-0495
On a hill overlooking the beach, with magnificent views. Pool.
La Ensenada Lodge
Palo Verde
Tel: 289 6655

Breezy *cabinas* overlooking the Gulf of Nicoya. Meals, horseback and boat tours included.
Punta Islita Hotel
Punta Islita
Tel: 231 6122
Fax: 231 0715
www.puntaislita.co.cr
Wonderful ocean views; swimming pool; private porches with hammocks.
Villas Playa Sámara
Playa Sámara
Tel: 256 8288
Fax: 220 3354
E-mail: htlvilla@sol.racsa.co.cr
Rambling complex of villas on the beach. Many activities.
Villa Serena
Playa Junquillal
Tel/fax: 680 0573
Nice small hotel facing the beach. Meals included.
Hotel Las Tortugas
Playa Grande
Tel/fax: 653 0458
Turtle-friendly hotel on a wide, long, beautiful beach. Conservationist management. Good restaurant. Pool. Excellent surfing directly in front of hotel.
Hotel Sugar Beach
Sugar Beach
Tel: 654 4242
Fax: 654 4239
E-mail: sugarb@sol.racsa.co.cr
Great views. Nice beach. Charter boat for fishing and snorkeling trips.
El Jardín del Edén
Tamarindo
Tel: 653 0111
Fax: 653 0111
Red tile roofs and Mediterranean touches in the hills above the beach. French and Italian cuisine.
Nosara Retreat
Nosara
Tel: 233 8057
Fax: 680 0749
Beautiful beach hotel with friendly, personalized service. Offers yoga retreats. Pool.
La Pacífica Ecological Center
Near Cañas
Tel: 669 0050
Fax: 669 0555

E-mail: pacifica@sol.racsa.co.cr
Nice *cabinas* with a beautiful pool and grounds. Hiking trails. Good bird watching.
Rancho Humo
Palo Verde
Tel: 255 2463
Fax: 255 3573
Lodge located on a large cattle ranch. Views.

Moderate
Albergue Zapandí
Palo Verde
Tel: 255 2463
Fax: 255-3573
Comfortable thatched-roof *cabinas* on the Río Tempisque. Shared baths, cold water, fans.
Condominiums Los Flores
Nosara
Tel: 680 0696
Comprehensively equipped two-bedroom/two-bathroom apartments. Discounts for longer-term rentals.
Diría
Santa Cruz
Tel: 680 0080
Fax: 680 0442
E-mail: barrene@sol.racsa.co.cr
Air conditioning and pool.
Hotel El Velero
Playa Hermosa
Tel/fax: 672 0036
Graceful, breezy, white beachfront house. Sailboat.
Hotel Hibiscus
Playa Junquillal
Tel: 653 0487
Very nice bungalows. Rate includes breakfast.
Hotel Las Brisas del Pacífico
Playa Sámara
Tel: 255 2380
Pleasant and well designed. Pool fronts the beach. Good restaurant.
Villa Casa Blanca
Playa Ocotal
Tel/fax: 670 0448
E-mail: vcblanca@sol.racsa.co.cr
Pleasant B&B. Sumptuous breakfasts.

Budget
Albergue Buena Vista
Rincón de la Vieja
Tel/fax: 661 8158

E-mail: rincon@sol.racsa.co.cr
Nice rooms and grounds. Indoor garden. Waterfalls with pools deep enough for swimming. Located 17 km (11 miles) down a rough road.

Albergue de la Montana Rincón de la Vieja
Rincón de la Vieja
Tel: 256 8206
Fax: 256 5410
Rustic and comfortable. Meals available. Tours to the park.

Cabinas Playa Hermosa
Playa Hermosa (Guanacaste)
Tel: 672 0046
On the beach, with a good Italian restaurant. Cabinas have private bathrooms, heated water and ceiling fans.

Cabinas Chorotega
Nosara
Tel: 680 0836
Friendly and clean.

Cabinas Zully Mar
Tamarindo
Tel: 226 4732
E-mail: ysumar@sol.racsa.co.uk
Clean rooms, friendly management. Rooms with hot water, refrigerator or air conditioning are more expensive.

THE CARIBBEAN

Expensive
Villas del Caribe
Puerto Viejo
Tel: 233 2200
Fax: 221 2801
Delightful two-story condo-minium-style units on a lovely white sand beach. Kitchens.

Hotel Maribú Caribe
Limón area
Tel: 758 4010
Fax: 758 3541
Circular, thatched-roof *cabinas* on a cliff, with beautiful views. Restaurant. Tours.

Hotel Matama
Limón area
Tel: 758 1123
Fax: 758 4499.
Friendly and pleasant with shady gardens. Rooms have no cross-ventilation, so air conditioning is a must. Restaurant.

Mawamba Lodge
Tortuguero
Tel: 223 2421
Fax: 222 5463
www.crica.com/mawamba
Pleasant *cabinas* and good meals. Offers package deal including meals and transportation from San José.

Tortuga Lodge
Tortuguero
Tel: 257 0766
Pleasant lodge 2 km (1 mile) from the village. Offers package deal including meals and transportation from San José. Fishing trips.

Moderate
Avarios del Caribe
Off coastal highway to Cahuita
Tel: 382 1335
Fax: 798 0374
Comfortable bed and breakfast and wildlife sanctuary on the Río Estrella. Canoe trips through miles of freshwater canals and lagoons. Good for watching birds and butterflies.

El Pizote Surf Lodge
Puerto Viejo
Tel: 221 0986
Fax: 750 0088
Nice wooden cabins and rooms with pleasant grounds across the road from a black-sand beach. Trails. No children.

Magellan Inn
Cahuita
Tel/fax: 755 0035
Cahuita's most elegant option. Pool and luxuriant landscaping.

Tatané
Tortuguero area
No phone
Remote *cabinas* on the canal to Barra del Colorado. The owner is an authorized turtle guide. Ask for Marcos Zamora in Tortuguero village.

Budget
Apartotel Cocorí
Limón area
Tel: 758 2930
Fax: 798 1670
Two-bedroom apartments accommodate up to five people. Kitchens. Pool.

Homestays

If you would like a better understanding of the people and culture of Costa Rica, try the **Home Stay Service**. It is designed to offer a cross-cultural experience to both visitors and Costa Ricans. Visitors are lodged in the guest room of a host family and participate in as much (or as little) of the family activities as they wish. Families have been chosen on the basis of the quality of their homes and their hospitality, and most speak English. Often long-lasting friendships are formed. Most are in the San José area, close to public transportation, and are quite inexpensive.

Visitors receive an information pack with their reservation, including data on Costa Rica, a map with directions to the host residence and an introduction to the host family. Airport and hotel pick-up service is available.

The best homestay agency is **Bells' Home Hospitality**, PO Box 185–1000, San José, Costa Rica, tel: 225-4752, fax: 224-5884. Or, in the US, Department 1432, PO Box 25216, Miami, Florida 33102-5216.

Local families sometimes rent rooms at a price including meals and laundry. Check around the university and the bulletin board at the Costa Rican/North American Cultural Center, *see* the *Tico Times* or the local papers, or call the language schools.

Cabinas Bello Horizonte
Cahuita
Tel: 785 1515 ext. 206
Clean, cheery, Caribbean-style *cabinas* with private baths, heated water and ceiling fans.

Cabinas Chimurri
Puerto Viejo
Tel: 750 0119

National Parks

Name	Distance from San José	Highlights	Accommodation	Topography	Facilities
Volcán Arenal	170 km NW	Active volcano	None	Rainforest	Toilets
Ballena	189 km SW	Diving and snorkeling	None	White sand, mangroves	None
Barra Honda	335 km NW	Deep caves	Lodge, meals	Mixed forest	Toilets
Guanacaste	264 km NW	Howler monkeys	Lodge	Mixed forest	Biological station
Palo Verde	240 km NW	Waterbirds, monkeys	Lodge, meals	Dry forest, wetlands	Toilets
Santa Rosa	264 km NW	Turtles, sandy beaches	Lodge, meals	Dry forest	Historical museum
Rincón de la Vieja	264 km NW	Volcano, waterfalls	Camping area	Mixed forest, savanna	Toilets
Las Baulas	300 km NW	Turtles, surfing beach	None	Sandy beach, mangrove	None
Corcovado	235 km SW	Macaws, monkeys	Lodge, meals	Rainforest	Toilets
Manuel Antonio	132 km S	Sandy beaches	None	Transitional forest	Visitor center, showers
Braulio Carrillo	20 km NE	Good hiking	Camping	Mixed forest	Museum, toilets
Cahuita	211 km SE	Coral reef, sloths	Camping area	Rainforest, coral reef	Toilets, showers
Volcán Irazú	54 km E	Active volcano	Camping	Páramo	Museum
Volcán Poás	37 km NW	Volcano crater	Camping	Páramo	Museum, cafe
Tapantí	35 km SE	Good hiking, birding	Lodge	Rainforest	Toilets
Tortuguero	254 km NE	Turtles, canals	Camping	Rainforest	Exhibition, toilets
Guayabo	85 km E	Archaeological site	Camping area	Rainforest	Museum
Chirripó	151 km SE	Highest peak, good hiking	Lodge	Cloud forest, páramo	Toilets, museum
Isla del Coco	550 km SW of Cabo Blanco	Diving, hiking	Anchorage	Rainforest	None
La Amistad	410 km SE	Experienced hikers only	Camping	Rainforest	None

Shaded *cabinas* constructed of thatch over bamboo, in the traditional Bribri Indian style. Common cooking area. Guided horseback tours.
Cabinas Iguana
Cahuita
No phone. Nice *cabinas* with kitchens. Ceiling fans. Porches. Hammocks.
Colibrí Paradise
Cahuita
Tel: 755 0263
Pleasantly designed and furnished, with private baths, heated water and ceiling fans. Kitchens and hammocks.
Escape Caribeño
Puerto Viejo area
Tel/fax: 750 0113
Cabinas near Punta Uva. Porches. Communal cooking area. Private bath, cold water, table fans, refrigerators.
Cabinas Tamara
Puerto Viejo
Tel: 750 0148
Rooms with shady, furnished porches a few blocks from the beach. Private bathrooms, cold water, fans. Some cabins have kitchens.
The Kiskadee
Puerto Viejo
No phone
Pleasant dormitory-style accommodation. Shared bathroom, cold water, no fans. Communal kitchen. Many birds.

THE NORTH

Expensive
El Plástico Lodge
Rara Avis
Tel/fax: 253 0844
Rustic but comfortable dormitory-style lodging. Meals and guided tours are included.
Selva Verde Lodge
Near Puerto Viejo de Sarapiquí
Tel: 766 6800
Fax: 766 6011
Beautiful river lodge. Great birdwatching. Nature walks. Horseback riding. Meals are included.
Villa Blanca
Near San Ramón

Tel: 228 4603
Fax: 228 4004
Well-appointed *casitas* modeled after colonial-era workers' homes. Fireplaces, generous bath tubs, refrigerators. Located adjacent to Los Angeles Cloud Forest Reserve.
Waterfall Lodge
Rara Avis
Tel: 253 0844
Comfortable rooms with private baths. Near a 55-m (180-ft) waterfall and swimming hole. Meals and guided tours included.
Arenal Volcano Observatory Lodge
La Fortuna area
Tel: 257 9489
Fax: 257 4220
E-mail: arenalob@sol.racsa.co.cr
Best site for volcano viewing. The more expensive rooms have views of the volcano. Lots of observation decks. Trails. Includes meals.
Hotel Bosques de Chachagua
La Tigra
Tel: 239 1049
Fax: 293 4206
Cabinas on a 150-hectare (380-acre) cattle and horse ranch. Guests with riding experience can ride elegant *Paso Criollo* horses on the ranch's trails.
Las Cabiñitas
Tel: 479 9400
Fax: 479 9408
E-mail: cabinita@sol.racsa.co.cr
One of La Fortuna's nicest places to stay. Comfortable, traditional tile-roofed *cabinas*. Includes breakfast.
La Garza
Platanar (overlooking the Platanar River)
Tel: 475 5222
Fax: 475 5015
Riverside *cabinas* on a large working cattle and horse ranch. Beautiful gardens. Horseback riding. Fishing.
La Laguna del Largarto
San Carlos area
Tel: 289 8163
Fax: 289 5295
Remote lodge on a hill with views, with comfortable rooms.

Hiking. Horseback riding. Boat trips on the Río San Carlos.
Hotel El Tucan Resort and Spa
San Carlos area
Tel: 460 3152
Fax: 460 1692
Resort built around natural hot springs. Olympic-sized swimming pool, jacuzzis. Tennis, mini-golf.
Hotel Tilajari Resort Hotel
Near Muelle
Tel: 469 9091
Fax: 469 9095
Spacious rooms and acres of rolling lawn on the San Carlos River. Tennis, swimming, racquetball, horses. Pool.
Tilawa Viento Surf
Nuevo Arenal/Tilarán
Tel: 695 5050
Fax: 695 5766
Comfortable hotel with pool and tennis court.

Moderate
Club Marina Arenal
La Fortuna area
Tel: 479 9178
Pleasant modern cabins with lake and volcano views.
La Ceiba
La Fortuna area
Fax: 695 5387
Lovely bed and breakfast on a hilltop with goats and an organic garden. Trails. Sailboat.
Xiloe Lodge
Nuevo Arenal/Tilarán
Tel: 259 9806
Fax: 259 9882
Cabinas with private bathrooms. Hot water, refrigerators, some kitchens.

Budget
Burio Inn
La Fortuna
Tel/fax: 479 9076
Small, pleasant rooms. Private baths, heated water, table fans.

Price Categories

Price categories are for double occupancy per night without breakfast:
Expensive: US$70 and up
Moderate: US$40–70
Budget: US$40 and under

Includes breakfast. Discounts for hostel card holders.

Eco Center La Finca Lodge
Tel: 476 0279/284 5904
Fax: 476 0279
E-mail: lafinca@sol.racsa.co.cr
Two wooden country homes, each with five rooms. The owners are currently trying to breed macaws. Daily tours with bilingual guides avaiable.

Hotel Don Goyo
San Carlos
Tel: 460 1780
Pleasant, newer hotel in town.

Hotel Mi Lindo Sarapiquí
Tel: 766 6074/766 6281
Fax: 766 6074
E-mail: lindo@sarapiquiranforest.com
Small hotel close to the rain forest. Clean rooms, TV and hot water. Student discount.

La Riviera
Fortuna
No phone
Clean and quiet rooms on a small family farm, on the bank of a creek.

Rancho Leona
Puerto Viejo de Sarapiquí area
Tel/fax: 761 1019
Basic lodging with shared bath, solar hot water, pool and sauna. Kayaking. Hiking. Friendly ambience. Good food.

THE SOUTH

Expensive

Albergue de Montaña Río Savegre
San Gerardo de Dota
Tel: 771 1732
Simple *cabinas*, excellent food and exceptional hospitality offered by the Chacón family, in the cool mountains near Cerro de la Muerte. Spot quetzals and enjoy fresh trout. Meals included.

Bosque del Cabo
Puerto Jiménez/Corcovado
Tel: 735 5062
Fax: 735 5043
Small, friendly inn where you can watch macaws. Meals included.

La Paloma Lodge
Drake Bay
Tel: 239 2801
Fax: 239 0954
E-mail: lapaloma@lapalomalodge.com
On a hillside, with sweeping views. Rustic thatched-roof *cabinas* with private decks. Pool. Tours to Isla del Caño. Fishing trips. Meals included.

Lapa Ríos
Puerto Jiménez/ Corcovado
Tel/fax: 735 5130
E-mail: laparios@sol.racsa.co.cr
Luxurious thatched-roof bungalows built on the hillside of a large reserve. Meals included.

Marenco Biological Station
Drake Bay
Tel: 221 1594
Fax: 255 1346
Rustic, thatched-roof lodgings with views of the Pacific. Naturalist-led hikes through Marenco's rainforest and local attractions, including Isla del Caño, the Río Claro and Llorona Waterfalls. Meals included.

Punta Encantado
North of Golfito
Tel: 735 5062
Fax: 735 5043
Comfy lodge in the jungle.

Tiskita Jungle Lodge
Near Pavones
Tel: 233 1511
Fax: 233 6890
E-mail: tiskita@sol.racsa.co.cr
Rustic and comfortable *cabinas* with great ocean views and sea breezes. Over 100 varieties of tropical fruit trees attract many birds and monkeys. Trails. Waterfalls. Meals included.

Wilson Botanical Gardens
San Vito
Reservations: OTS
Tel: 773 3278/240 6696
Fax: 240 6783
Bunk rooms and cabins in botanical gardens and reserve. Trails. Meals included. Discounts for Costa Rican residents, children, students, and researchers.

Drake Bay Wilderness Camp
Drake Bay
Tel/fax: 770 8012
Tent/cabins and cabins on the beach. Guided explorations of the area. Meals included.

Escaleras Inn
Dominical
Tel/fax: 771 5247
High on a hill overlooking Dominical. Includes breakfast. Good restaurant.

Rainbow Adventures Lodge
Playa Cativo
Tel: 775 0220
A 45-minute boat ride from Golfito, on a large reserve. Beautifully designed lodge with antiques and silk rugs.

Moderate

Albergue de Montaña Tapantí
Cerro de la Muerte area
Tel: 290 7641
Tel/fax: 232 0436
Cozy *cabinas* and good restaurant.

Albergue Jinetes de Osa
Bahía Drake Bay
Tel: 385 9541
E-mail: crventur@costaricadiving.com
On the beach. Bunk beds. Includes meals.

Cabinas Punta Dominical
Dominical
Tel/fax: 787 0016
Pretty, well-kept *cabinas* overlooking the ocean. Ocean breezes and tranquility.

Corcovado Lodge and Tent Camp
Corcovado
Tel: 257 0766
Fax: 257 1665
Large tents on wooden platforms. Beautiful location on the beach. Meals included.

Hotel Sierra
Golfito
Tel: 775 0666
Fax: 775 0087
Best accommodation in Golfito. Pool. Air conditioning.

Las Esquinas Rainforest Lodge
Golfito area
Tel: 293 0780
Fax: 293 2632
www.regenwald.at
Rainforest jungle lodge with *cabinas*, pool, and large, comfortable common areas. Excursions and activities. Profits are used to finance projects in the nearby village of La Gamba.
Pacific Edge
Dominical
Tel: 787 0031
Simple and secluded.

Budget

Cabinas Sol y Mar
Playa Zancudo
Tel: 776 0014
www.zancudo.com
Tranquil *cabinas*, private bathrooms, cold water and fans. Friendly atmosphere.
Hotel del Sur
San Isidro del General
Tel: 771 3033
Fax: 771 0527
Pool, tennis. Bike and horse rental.
Cabinas Las Mirlas
San Vito
Tel: 773 3714
Clean and pleasant *cabinas* with private baths and cold water. Overlooking a creek.
Hotel Amaneli
San Isidro del General
Tel: 771 0352
Basic and clean, with private baths and heated water.
Hotel Chirripó
San Isidro de el General
Tel: 771 0529
Clean and inexpensive. Shared bathrooms, cold water.
Hotel El Ciebo
San Vito
Tel/fax: 773 3025
Pleasant accommodation with private bathrooms and heated water. Good restaurant. Attractive views.
Posada del Descanso
San Gerardo de Rivas
No phone.
Simple, clean lodging with shared baths and heated water. Owner is knowledgeable about Chirripó.

Where to Eat

Eating Out

While Costa Rican cuisine may not rank among the world's greats, there are lots of very good things to eat all around the country. Refer to chapters on *Tico Cooking* (*see page 108*) and *Fruits of Costa Rica* (*see page 112*).

Restaurants

SAN JOSÉ AND ENVIRONS

Expensive

Angus Steak House
250m/yds north of Suburu in Los Yoses
Tel: 225 0415
Great steaks, meats and salads.
Bijahua (Nouvelle Costa Rican)
La Granja, San Pedro, 50m/yds west, 300m/yds south of Mas por Menos
Tel: 225 0613
Remarkable food as art and entertainment, elegant atmosphere, good service.
Le Barbizon (French)
Heredia. Above Monte de La Cruz
Tel: 267 7449
Large elegant restaurant, lovely mountain views.
Fuji (Japanese/Sushi)
Meliá Confort Corobici Hotel, San José
Tel: 231 5834, ext. 191
E-mail: corobici@sol.racsa.co.cr
Tatami-covered private dining rooms.
Le Monastère (French)
Escaz mountains
Tel: 289 4404
www.lemonastere.com
View of the Central Valley and,

with a bit of luck, the Golfo de Nicoya. Elegant atmosphere with cheerful bar in the basement with live show on Friday.
Las Orquídeas (International)
On the road to Guápiles
Tel: 268 8686
Fax: 268 8989
Large restaurant with views over the exotic garden, surrounded by the mists of the rainforest.
Ram Luna (International and Costa Rican)
On the way to Tarbaca
Tel: 230 3060
Fax: 228 2958
Exceptional mountain views in clear weather. Folkloric performances and buffet during the week.
Sakura (Japanese)
Hotel Herradura. Autopista General Cañas, on the way to the Airport
Tel: 239 0033
Fax: 239 2292
One of the best Japanese restaurants in the country. A bar with a variety of Sushi.

Moderate

Ave Fenix (Chinese)
San Pedro, 175m/yds west of the church
Tel: 225 3362
Delicious soups and sauces, delicate Chinese vegetables.
Café Mundo (Fusion)
Barrio Amon
New fusion cuisine in an attractive old house in this historic district.
Capriccio (Italian)
300m/yds south of Periféricos, Los Anonos, 150 m east, San Rafael de Escazú
Tel: 228 9332
Real Italian food. Exceptional pastas. Vegetarians will enjoy the extensive antipasto buffet.
Casa Quitirrisí (Costa Rican)
In Santa Ana, not far from San José
Tel: 282 5441
Fax: 282 7772
Traditional Costa Rican dishes served in the corridor of a typical house. Live music at the weekend.

El Exótico Oriente (Indonesian and Thai)
From Canal 7, 50m/yds north and 25 m west, Sabana West
Tel: 228 5980
Indonesian and Thai classics such as *satay, gado gado* and *phad thai.*

Machu Picchu (Peruvian)
Calle 32 Ave 1–3, 150m/yds north of Kentucky Fried Chicken, Paseo Colón
Tel: 222 7384
Casual, sometimes boisterous ambience. Good food. Try a Pisco Sour and book a driver to get you home.

Grano de Oro (International)
Calle 30, Ave 2–4, Paseo Colón
Tel: 255 3322
Excellent, friendly service and good food served in the covered garden of an elegant, restored mansion.

Los Adobes (Costa Rican)
San Antonio de Belén
Tel: 239 0957
Classic Costa Rican home-cooked food served in a 100-year-old adobe, and its pleasant, covered garden. Music on weekends. Casual.

Lubnán (Lebanese)
Paseo Colón (in front of Mercedes-Benz)
Tel: 257 6071
Sparse decor with a Middle Eastern flavor. Good food.

Nimbé (Pakistani and International)
Escazú
Tel: 228 1173
Sit indoors or outdoors on the covered verandah of an elegant older home. A number of very tasty vegetarian dishes. Friendly service.

Ponte Vecchio (Italian)
San Pedro
Tel: 283 1810
Award-winning food ("one of Central America's top 100") from a New York-Italian chef.

Refranes (Steak House)
San Rafael de Heredia
Tel: 267 6076
E-mail: refranes@usa.net
The focus is on red meat accompanied by a few Costa

Rican dishes. Cozy house in a mountain setting.

Inexpensive

Cafe Ruiseñor (International)
Los Yoses, San Pedro
Tel: 225-2562
A casual place for lunch, dessert or a snack. Espresso and cappuccino. Tablecloths over marble tables. Walls hung with contemporary art.

Il Pomodoro (Italian)
Two blocks north of San Pedro church, also in Escatú
Tel: 224 0966; delivery: 283 1010
Good pizzas (try the panzanella which has cubes of mozzarella cheese and fresh tomato).

La Mazorca (Vegetarian)
From Banco Anglo building, 100m/yds north and 25m/yds west, San Pedro
Tel: 224 8069
San José's original vegetarian restaurant. Casual, university-community ambience. Freshly baked natural fare.

Princesa Marina (Seafood)
On the north side of the Catholic church in Barrio San José de Alajuela (and in Curridabat, Moravia y La Sabana).
Tel: 443 7117
Fresh fish and mixed rice served in a casual atmosphere. Eat in or take away.

Rancho Macho (Costa Rican)
In the hills above Santa Ana. Easy-going atmosphere. Eat on the large covered porch, overlooking city lights, serenaded by strolling musicians. Barbecued chicken and beef, grilled Santa Ana onions, cold beer.

Rosti Pollo (Nicaraguan-style chicken roasted over coffee wood)
San Rafael de Escazú & San Pedro, Centro Comercial de la Calle Real
Casual, good and fast. Take out or eat in.

Sal y Pepe (Italian)
San Rafael de Escazú, El Cruce
Tel: 289 5750
Great pizza.

Soda La Tapia (Costa Rican)
La Sabana across from the Gimnasio, also in Curridabat
Tel: 222 6734
Gallo pinto, sandwiches, and good fruit drinks, served indoors or outdoors.

For good, inexpensive food, also try the neighborhoods around the University of Costa Rica in San Pedro or the National University in Heredia, and the sodas in the Central Market downtown San José and Heredia. Best to go after mealtime rush hours.

THE PACIFIC

Expensive

The Rico Tico (Costa Rican and Mexican)
Si Como No Hotel,
Manuel Antonio Beach
Tel: 777 0777
Fax: 777 1093
E-mail: sicmono@sol.racsa.co.cr
Casual outdoor dining surrounded by jungle gardens and with ocean view. Buffet breakfast, Costa Rican-Mexican Grill. Fresh fish and lobster.

Moderate

Los Faroles
In the town of Jacó Beach
Tel: 643 3167
Mexican-style restaurant with bar area. Various *tacos* feature among other dishes.

Budget

El Pochote (Seafood)
Puntarenas
Tel: 663 0086
This is a tiny, very informal restaurant where fresh seafood is guaranteed. Try the famous *chucheca* soup.

Vela (Vegetarian)
Manuel Antonio, Quepos
Tel: 777 0413
Fax: 777 1071
E-mail: velabar@maqbeach.com
Wooden bungalow with palm roof. Seafood, vegetarian and Costa Rican dishes. Great fresh fruit juices.

GUANACASTE

Moderate

Café de Paris (International)
Guiones Beach, Nosara
E-mail: info@cafedeparis.net
Fresh bread baked daily. French
and American breakfasts. Lunch
and dinner choices include
pizza, paella, beef filet and
fresh fish.

El Ancla (International)
Near Sámara Beach
Tel/fax: 656 02 54
E-mail: elancla@samarabeach.
com
Enjoyable open restaurant in
front of the beach. Spectacular
sunsets. Try the tropical juices.

Budget

La Frontera
Peñas Blancas on the North
Border
Tel: 679 9156
Fax: 679 9271
Country house atmosphere.
Unusual and tasty Tico-style rice
dishes.

THE CARIBBEAN

Moderate

Centro Turístico Pacuare
(International)
600 meters (yds) east of
Siquirres Intersection
Tel: 768 8070
Large rustic restaurant.

Budget

The Red Stripe Café
In front of the bus stop of
Puerto Viejo
Open daily from 6am for a
breakfast of *gallo pinto* and
coffe. Lunch and dinner menu of
soup and fish.

Soda Tamara (Caribbean)
Talamanca, downtown Puerto
Viejo
E-mail: atecmail@sol.racsa.co.cr
Delicious Caribbean dishes and
seafood. Small, friendly
restaurant which plays reggae.

Elenas (Caribbean)
Chiquita Beach, Limón
Tel: 750 0265
Dance, live music and satellite

TV. One of the most popular
places on the way to Puerto
Veijo.

THE NORTH

Expensive

Tonjibe (Steak House)
South side of the central park in
Ciudad Quesada
Tel: 460 1585
Fax: 460 0391
Remarkable meat from the
North Zone. Pizza and fast food
also available.

Moderate

El Mirador (Costa Rican)
On the road to Zarcero, Alajuela
Tel: 451 1959
E-mail: taf@arweb.com
Great wood-roasted cuisine.
Delicious cheese *tortilla* with
sour cream. Try the potato dish
picadillo de papa.

Drinking Notes

There are several beers made in
Costa Rica: Imperial, Pilsen,
Rock Ice and Tropical. All are
good, but none is exceptional.
  Try Cafe Britt's extraordinary
coffee liqueur. You'll never again
even consider the likes of Kahlua.

Bars

In San José try the following:
Café Urbano, El Cruce, Escazú.
Spanish *tapas* bar and café with
outside tables. Good *tortilla
Española*.
La Esmeralda, Downtown. Ave
2, calle 5–7. Mariachi bands.
Open after 4am.
La Puerta de Alcala, Heredia.
Lively. *Nueva Trova* (protest)
music performed by local
groups.
Shakspeare Bar, next to Sala
Garbo, Paseo Colón area. Inter-
national crowd. Darts. Live music.
Salon Musical de Lety, Centro
Comerical El Pueblo, tel: 234
4236. Sophisticated.
Taos, Trejos Montealegre
shopping centre, Escazú. Two-
level pub with dancing area and
balconies. Mostly over 30s.

Tragaldabas, Mall Real Cariari,
tel: 293 5000. Tables in garden
with view. Pop and rock music.
  The **El Pueblo** shopping
center, full of restaurants, bars
and discos, is a good place for
bar-hopping.

Opening Times

From Monday to Saturday, most
bars open any time from 8.30am
to 11am, and stay open until
around midnight or 2am. On
Sunday, some may close earlier,
and others do not bother to
open at all. Friday and Saturday
nights are very busy, but earlier
in the week you may find happy
hours and other attractive offers.

Legalities

You must be 18 years of age to
drink alcohol in Costa Rica.
Some bars may require you to
show some identification before
admitting you.

Boca Bars

Bocas (literally "mouths") are
Costa Rica's equivalent of
Spanish *tapas*. Boca bars are
now found mainly in San
José. They can get very busy,
so you will have to get there
early to find a table.
  The menu may have no
prices, *bocas* traditionally
being free, but the drinks
often cost much more than
they would anywhere else!
The more you drink, the more
you will get to eat.
  Some of the best-known
boca bars are:
Bar Mexico
Opposite corner from the
Barrio Mexico Church,
tel: 222-7000. Live mariachi
bands.
Bar Los Parales
Curridabat, tel: 272 2241.
Famous for its variety of *bocas*
Bar Los Balcones
El Pueblo shopping centre,
tel: 256 9494. Live Andean
and other Latin American
musics.

Culture

This is a continually changing scene. Check the *Tico Times* for a listing of shows and exhibitions in the Central Valley.

Dance

Costa Rica's modern dance scene is one of the best in Central America. The **National Dance Company** performs both classical and modern works, some by Central American choreographers. The **Teatro Melico Salazar** in San José stages productions several times a month; another regular venue for this company is the **Teatro Nacional**. Tickets can be purchased at very reasonable prices.

Traditional dancing and singing can be experienced at the **Fantasía Folklórica** in the Melico Salazar every Tuesday.

Theater

San José has a lively theater scene, with productions in both English and Spanish. *See* the *Tico Times* for information.

Movies

Most cinemas show major US movies with Spanish subtitles.
San Pedro Mall, San Pedro.
Plaza Colonial, San Rafael de Escazú.
Magaly, on Calle 23, Ave Central.
Bella Vista on Ave Central, Calles 17–19.
Multiplaza Mall, Guachipelín, Escazú.
Plaza Mayor Mall, Rohrmoser

Real Mall Cariari, General Cañas Highway.
Two specialist theaters, next door to one another, screen art films from different countries. Check the *Tico Times* as to what language the dialogue/subtitles are in.
Sala Garbo
Ave 2, Calle 28, tel: 222 1034
Teatro Laurence Olivier
Ave 2, Calle 28, tel: 222 1034.

Libraries & Bookstores

The Bookshop & Cafe Casa Amón, Barrio Amón, Ave 11, Calles 3&3 bis. Rooms full of English-language books, arts and crafts. The coffee shop serves soups, salads, sandwiches, desserts and coffee.
Book Traders, Calles 3&5, Ave 1, tel: 255 0508. Used books in English and other languages.
Gambit, Calle 37, Ave 3, tel: 224 5170 (by Centro Cultural), Los Yoses. New and used books in English.
Mark Twain Library, Centro Cultural Costarricense/Norteamericano, Los Yoses, tel: 207 7500; fax: 224 1480 (online at: www.cccncr.com). 200m/yds north of Centro La Mufla near Los Yoses Auto Mercado. English-language reference books, magazines, fiction and non-fiction.
Staufer, Plaza Del Sol, Curridabat, tel: 283 0822. English-language bookstore.
Librería Internacional, Multiplaza and San Pedro Mall Internacional, Aláguela. Home delivery, tel: 800 542 7374. English and Spanish books.

Latin Dance Classes

Centro Merecumbé, tel: 224 3531 or 234 1548. Has studios in San Pedro, Guadalupe, Rohrmoser, Heredia and Alajuela.
Costa Rican Latin Dance Academy and Language School, tel: 233 8914; fax: 233 8670.

Nightlife

Centro Commercial El Pueblo
Near Villa Turnon on the highway to Heredia.
A complex full of boutiques, galleries, restaurants, nightclubs, bars, discos, even a skating rink. Musical offerings range from jazz and Latin Fusion to Argentine Tango and Andean music.
El Cuartel de la Boca del Monte
Ave 1, Calle 21–23
Tel: 221 0327.
Situated downtown, close to Cine California, this is a popular singles bar.
Estrategia Caracol
Escazú.
Techno and rave music, with visiting DJs.
La Caribeña
Zapote.
Caribbean music and food.
Planet Mall
Mall San Pedro.
One of the biggest clubs in town playing a variety of Latin and pop musics.

La Avispa
Calle 1,
Ave 8–10.
Lesbian venue, but men are made welcome, too.
Salsa/Merengue. Three dance floors, pool tables.
Dejá Vu
Calle 2,
Ave 14–16.
Mostly for men, but also welcoming to women. Cabaret.
Pop music.

Casinos

Herradura
Next to the Hotel Cariari on the highway to the airport
Tel: 239 0033
Fax: 239 2292.
Hotel Costa Rica
Downtown San José
Tel: 221 4000
Fax: 221 3501.
Website: www.granhoteler.com
24-hour casino.
Hotel Fiesta
Puntarenos
Tel: 293 4266
Fax: 239 0217.
Hotel Irazú
General Cañas Highway
Tel: 1 800 272 6654.
Hotel San José Palacio
Tel: 220 2034
Fax: 231 1990.
Hotel El Camino Real
Tel: 289 7000
Fax: 289 8998.
Hotel Corobicí
Sabana Norte
Tel: 232 8122
Fax: 231 5834.

Shopping

What to Buy

Coffee
Costa Rican coffee is excellent and relatively inexpensive. Café Britt is recognized as one of the best in the world. It is available in supermarkets and gift shops. Café Britt also makes a delicious coffee liqueur.

Woodwork
Wooden items, including bowls, plates, cutting boards and boxes, are widely available. Most gift shops carry them. The mountain town of Sarchí is known for its woodwork. The finest quality wooden boxes and bowls are made by Barry Biesanz of Biesanz Woodworks. He welcomes visitors to his beautiful, light-filled studio in Bello Horizonte, near Escazú, tel: 228 1811.

Leatherwork
Leather bags, wallets, and briefcases are also a good choice. They are available in many stores throughout the Central Valley.

Woven bags
Look out for interesting woven bags made with natural dyes by the Bribri Indians; these are available at many locations.

Jewelry
Inexpensive handmade earrings and jewelry are sold at street artisans' stalls in San José.

Paper
Beautiful handmade papers, made from recycled plant materials and dyed with natural materials, are sold in many gift stores.

Other Items
Of course there is the usual array of tourist souvenir goods: T-shirts, painted feathers, watercolors of country life, ceramics, and so on.

San José

Atmósfera, Calle 5, Ave 1–3, has rooms full of well displayed Costa Rican folk art and fine crafts.
National Association of Independent Artisans, Calle 5, Ave 4, 200m/yds south of the Teatro Nacional. There are rows of outdoor stalls where independent artisans offer their work for sale.

San Rafael de Escazú

Sabor Tico, behind Plaza Colonial. Well selected crafts of Central America.

Moravia

100m/yds south of the Red Cross (Cruz Roja). Souvenir shops, arts and crafts galleries, line two city blocks in the center of town.
El Caballo Blanco, overlooking the central plaza in Moravia, has a variety of leather goods.

What to Avoid

Travelers **should not** purchase any of the following:
● Coral
● Tortoiseshell items
● Furs (such as ocelot or jaguar)
● Items made from tropical hardwoods (such as mahogany, laurel and purple heart – if in doubt, ask the seller what kind of wood has been used)
● Anything made from alligator or lizard skins

Sport

Bungee Jumping

Tropical Bungee, tel: 233 6455.
Saragundi Specialty Tours, tel: 255 0011.

Cycling

You can rent a bicycle from bike rental shops around the country; mountain biking is only feasible in certain areas.
Aventuras Naturales, tel: 225 3939. Single and multi-day tours.
Frontiers. In the US tel: 612 645 0077, fax: 612 603 1989; in Costa Rica tel/fax: 230 2454. Outdoor adventures including multi-day bike trips.

Diving

Underwater visibility is best during the dry season (November–April). Costa Rican waters are still largely uncharted.
Buceo Aquatour. Located on main road through Punta Uva, 20 minutes south of Puerto Viejo. Reservations through the Pizote Lodge, Hotel Punta Cocles and Villas del Caribe.
Diving Safaris at Hotel el Ocotal, tel: 670 0321, fax: 670 0083. Costa Rica's largest and longest-running operation. Diving expeditions, equipment rental, and diver certification classes.
Ecotreks Adventure Co., Escazú, tel/fax: 228 4029. Diving trips, diver certification classes, equipment rental and a variety of underwater excursions.
Naui Padi, tel: 224 9729, fax: 234 2982. San Pedro. Sales and rental of scuba equipment. Spare parts and repairs. Tank refills. Classes.

Fishing

Fishing permits are required and are usually taken care of by fishing guides. They can be obtained at the Banco Crédito Agricola, on Avenida 4, between Calle Central and Calle 1, in San José. Freshwater permits are cheap. Deep sea fishing permits are much more expensive. If you encounter rangers while fishing, they will ask you to present your permit and your passport (a copy of which may suffice).

Good sources of information on fishing in Costa Rica are:
Carlos Barrantes, La Casa del Pescador, a tackle shop at Calle 2, Ave 18–20.
Deportes Keko, Calle 20, Ave 4–6. There are also the weekly fishing columns in the *Tico Times* and *Costa Rica Today*.

Golf

Cariari Country Club. 18-hole course. Use can occasionaly be arranged by the Hotel Cariari.
Costa Rica Country Club, Escazú. Private; members only.
Los Reyes Country Club, Guácima, Alajuela.
Marriott Los Sueños Golf Resort, 18-hole Ted Robinson-designed golf course. Private.
Hotel Meliá Conchal, Playa Conchal. 18-hole course.
Monte del Barco Resort, north of Liberia. 18-hole course, members and public.
Tango Mar Surf & Saddle Club, Nicoya Peninsula near Tambor.
Rancho Las Colinas Golf and Country Club, Playa Grande, near Tamarindo in Guanacaste.
La Roca Beach Resort, north of Puerto Caldera. 18-hole, par 72 championship course.

Horseback Riding

Horseback riding is widely available in Costa Rica, from hour-long rides on the beach to a riding break on a working cattle ranch. The following offer interesting options:

Finca Los Caballos, Montezuma, tel/fax: 642 0262. Single and multi-day trail rides through beautiful scenery.
Hacienda Los Inocentes, La Cruz, Guanacaste, tel: 679 9190; fax: 265 6431. Lodge with guides. Well-trained horses.
Hotel Bosques de Chachaqua, La Tigra, tel: 239 1049, fax: 293 4206. Cattle and horse ranch. Guests with riding experience can ride the ranch's elegant *Paso Criollo* horses.
La Cabriola, Cuidad Colón, tel: 249 1013. Stables and trails.
La Garza, Planatar, tel: 475 5222, fax: 475 5015. Large working ranch with *cabinas*.

Hot Air Ballooning

Available through **Serendipity Adventures**, tel: 289 9043, fax 450-0328. Balloon trips originate from Naranjo and near Laguna de Arenal.
Intertur, tel: 253 7503; fax: 234 6308. Also online at: www.interturcostarica.com

Mountaineering

Club de Montañismo, tel: 221 4050. Rockclimbing and mountaineering club.
Ríos Tropicales, tel: 233 6455.

Rafting & Kayaking

Costa Rica Expeditions, tel: 257 0766, fax: 257 1665.
Costa Sol Rafting, tel: 293 2150, fax: 293 2155.
Rancho Leona, tel/fax: 761 1019. Kayaking on the Sarapiquí River,
Ríos Tropicales, tel: 233 6455. Rafting and sea kayaking.
Safaris Corobicí, tel/fax: 679 1091. River "floats" on the Corobicí river.

Sailing

Costa Rica Yacht Club, Puntarenas, tel: 661 0784, fax: 661 2885.

Hotel El Velero, Playa Hermosa, tel/fax: 670-0310. Beachfront house/hotel with sailboat.

Island cruises

Calypso Tours, tel: 256 2727; fax: 256 6767; also call toll free: 800 5666 6716. Online at: www.calypsotours.com Catamaran cruises from Puntarenas to Isla Tortuga, or the private reserve of Punta Coral.

Bay Island Cruises, tel: 258 3536; fax: 258 1189; e-mail: bayisland@sol.racsa.co.cr One day tour to Isla Tortuga, passing by another Pacific island. Departs from San José by bus.

Swimming & Surfing

There is good swimming and surfing on both the Caribbean and Pacific coasts, although some beaches may not be suitable all year round. Dangers include rip tides (see page 290) and large waves, caused by heavy swells, that may hit you when leaving the water. There may also be sharks. Always ask the locals before entering the sea.

The following are good surfing beaches:

Pacific coast: Boca de Barranca, Naranjo, Tamarindo, Jacó, Hermosa, Quepos, Dominical, and Pavones.

Caribbean coast: Puerto Viejo and Punta Uva.

For up-to-date information on surfing conditions, call the 24-hour **Costa Rican Surf Report Hotline**, tel: 233 7386.

Tennis

Cariari Country Club, tel: 239 2248.

Costa Rica Tennis Club, Sabana Sur, tel: 232 1266.

Parque Valle del Sol, Near Santa Ana. The 12 exceptionally good courts are open to the general public.

Parque La Sabana, 4 courts open to the public.

Hiking & Camping

Campsites

There are few established campsites with facilities in Costa Rica, and those that do exist are not generally very well advertised. Property owners in rural areas are often willing to permit visitors to use their land for camping.

Sometimes rural hotels, for a small fee, will permit campers to stay on the grounds. Camping on beaches is legal. Some parks and reserves permit camping. Call the National Parks Information Service (tel: 257 0922).

Los Lagos. Campground and park on the lower slopes of Volcán Arenal just a few kilometers northwest of La Fortuna. Feel the volcano rumble as you drop off to sleep. Crowded on weekends.

Tuetal Lodge, Alajuela, tel: 442 1804 (10 minutes north of airport). Camping site and tent rentals. Tree houses and cabins.

Camping Equipment

Alumicamping, Moravia, tel: 225 1532; fax: 225 3732. Purchase, rental and repair of tents and other equipment.

Army & Navy Surplus Store del Ranchos, Moravia, on the same street as the craft stores. Sells clothing, ponchos, boots and camping equipment brought in from the United States.

Centro de Aventura, Paseo Colón between Calles 22 and 24. One of the best equipped stores. Buys, sells and rents camping gear. Helpful staff speak English.

Camping World, San Rafael de Escazú. Sales of camping gear only. Best supply of quality tents in the country.

Taller La Casita, Pavas, tel: 231

Snake Bites

Although snake bites are rare, to avoid being bitten follow these suggestions:

● When walking in the countryside, wear closed, preferably high top shoes or boots.

● Walk with a stick in hand. Use it where visibility of the ground is blocked to probe before you step.

● Try to choose paths clear of high grass and debris.

● Never reach into areas you can't see into.

● If you encounter a snake, remain calm and retreat immediately. Never tease a snake or chase a retreating one. Snakes attack people only when they perceive a threat.

If, despite taking all these precautions, you are bitten:

● Remain calm and try to immobilize the area of the bite.

● If ice is available, apply ice to the affected area. It slows the spread of the poison.

● Do not cut the wound or attempt to suck the venom out with your mouth. This is old Western movie mythology.

● Go immediately to the nearest clinic or hospital or Red Cross agency for an injection of anti-venom. It is not necessary to know what kind of snake bit you. Doctors can tell by the type of wound which kind of anti-venom to administer.

7426. Manufacturers of camping equipment.

Outdoor Safety

Rip Tides

Several beaches throughout Costa Rica are known for their strong rip tides. Rip tides or rip currents are forceful ocean currents that travel 5–10 km (3–6 miles) an hour, faster than even very strong swimmers.

If you are unfortunate enough to get caught in a strong ocean current, relax and don't fight it. Let it carry you. Its strength will eventually diminish. Once it does, swim parallel to the beach, towards the incoming waves, and let them carry you ashore.

The following beaches are famous for their rip tides:

On the **Pacific** coast: Jacó, Esterillos, Junquillal, Dominical, Manuel Antonio's North Espadilla. On the **Caribbean** coast: Cahuita, Playa Bonita.

Plants

On the beach, you should avoid the **manzanillo** tree, a small evergreen with many branches. The leaves, bark and small, yellowish fruit produce a white latex which stings and causes blisters. Sometimes fatal if ingested, one antidote is large quantities of bitter lemon juice. About one in ten persons is allergic to the skin of the **mango**. Reactions are similar to those described above.

Snakes

There are around 135 varieties of snake in Costa Rica. Of those, 18 are poisonous. Snake bites are uncommon in Costa Rica, but the following may be helpful. The only poisonous snake in the San José area is the coral snake (*coralito*), with distinctive red, yellow and black stripes. All other snakes found in this area are harmless.

Outside San José and its environs, the fer-de-lance or *terciopelo* is responsible for more human bites than any species in the country. Few of these bites result in fatalities, however, and many of the strikes from the *terciopelo* are "dry bites," meaning that the skin is punctured but no venom is injected. Anti-venom exists for all of Costa Rica's land snakes. (Currently there is no antidote for the venom of the sea snake, distinguished by its prominent oar-shaped tail. The only reported case of a sea snake bite on record entailed severe pain and swelling, but resulted in a complete recovery.)

Bee Attacks

If attacked by bees, call 911 for assistance. Remember:
- You can outrun them (run in a zigzag pattern)
- They hate water (jump into a river)
- They can't see light colors well (get under a sheet)
- They can't see at night
- They are excited by noise
- They can and will follow you into a house

Africanized Bees

Africanized bees are quite indistinguishable from classic European honeybees and their venom is no more poisonous, but they are easily excited, extremely aggressive, and will attack *en masse*. All of Costa Rica's bees should now be considered to be Africanized. There have been human fatalities in Costa Rica due to Africanized bee attacks. Attacks on tourists are as yet unknown, but it might be helpful to know the following things about them.

They nest in hollow trees, gutters or holes in walls or in the ground. They are not dangerous when swarming in search of a new home, but become very defensive when they are protecting a hive. Attacks are more frequent during the dry season.

Conservation

Costa Rica tries very hard to do a great deal with few resources. The following are some of the more popular environmental organizations which are actively involved in saving and protecting Costa Rica's natural resources.

ASCONA (Asociación Costarícense para la Censervaçión de la Naturaleza): this organization's main goal is to eradicate industrial pollution in Costa Rica. It works through research and lobbying. US contributions are tax-deductible if sent through the WWF. In the US contact: ASCONA, c/o WWF, 1250 24th Street N.W., Washington DC 20037. In Costa Rica contact: Apartado Postal, 8 3790 1000, San José, Costa Rica. Tel: 297 1711/256 3185.

Caribbean Conservation Corporation: This group runs the green turtle tagging project at Tortuguero Beach on the Caribbean Coast, which is the largest nesting colony of this endangered species in the Western Caribbean. For an annual membership fee members receive a quarterly newsletter. Further information from: Caribbean Conservation Corp., PO Box 2866, Gainesville, FL 32602, tel: (904) 373 6441. Or from: Caribbean Conservation Corp., Apartado 448–2120 San Francisco de Guadalupe, San José, Costa Rica, tel: 224 9215; fax: 225 7516; e-mail: baulas@sol.racsa.co.cr

CEDARENA (Centro del Derecho Ambiental y de los Recursos Naturales): this centre operates an environmental "model country", with laws and regulations. Another of its activities is to educate the public and government officials on the use of the law to protect the environment. Contributions are tax-deductible. Contact: CEDARENA, Apartado 134–2050, San Pedro, San José de Costa Rica. Tel: 283 3708.

Conservation International: The goal of this US-based organization is to integrate people as part of the worldwide ecosystem. It works closely with government agencies throughout the world. In Costa Rica, it gives technical and financial support to the 81,000-hectare (200,000-acre) La Amistad International Biosphere Reserve, which makes up 14 percent of Costa Rica's territory. Membership entitles you to a quarterly newsletter. More information from: Conservation International, 1015 18th St N.W., Washington DC, 20036, tel: (202) 429 5660, or Conservation International, Apartado 8–3870, San José, Costa Rica, tel: 225 2649.

Fundación Neotrópica (Neotropic Foundation): This group works to foster "sustainable development" in communities near Costa Rica's wildlife preserves, parks, forest reserves and other protected areas. The annual membership fee brings a quarterly newsletter and gives members a 10 percent discount on gift items from its Nature Stores and on its Heliconia Press publications. More information from: The Nature Conservancy, 1815 North Lynn St, Arlington VA 22209. In Costa Rica: Neotropica, Apartado 236–1002, Paseo de los Estudiantes, San José, Costa Rica, tel: 253 2130, fax: 253 4210.

INBio: (National Biodiversity Institute) This private non-profit making organization promotes awareness of the value of biodiversity. In recognition of its research it has received two important awards: The Prince of Asturias Award for Scientific and Technical Research and the San Francis of Assisi Award for environmental studies. It runs the 20-acre INBioparque in Santo Domingo de Heredia. Experienced guides take visitors on an interactive tour, providing them with information of use on future visits to Costa Rican National Parks. Since 1989 the institute has catalogued many insects, plants, mushrooms and mollusks. Tel: 244 4730; fax: 244 4790. Also online at: www.inbio.ac.cr/inbioparque

Monteverde Conservation League: This group, a community conservation organization in Monteverde, Costa Rica, works on reforestation, environmental education and sustainable development projects. It purchases or leases land to preserve forests. It also co-ordinates the International Children's Rainforest Project (Bosque Eterno de los Niños). The long-range plan is to buy 17,500 ha (43,000 acres) for a preserve. The children of Sweden have donated over $1 million dollars for the preserve and 7,300 ha (18,000 acres) have already been purchased. Each $100 contribution buys 0.4 ha (1 acre) of land. A contribution of $25 entitles the donor to receive the quarterly *Tapir Tracks* magazine. For more information contact: **The Nature Conservancy International**, Children's Rainforest, 1815 North Lynn St, Arlington, VA 22209. Address in Costa Rica: Apdo 10581–1000, San José, Costa Rica, tel: 645 5003.

National Parks Foundation (Fundación de Parques Naçionales): the leading organization devoted to protecting and expanding Costa Rica's reserves. The foundation is in charge of arranging debt-for-nature swaps. They accept contributions to help maintain Costa Rica's world-famous national park system. Contact: Apartado 1108–1002, Paseo de los Estudiantes, San José, Costa Rica. Tel: 257 2239/257 8563/222 4732.

Rainforest Alliance: This New York-based alliance helps the Monteverde Conservation League buy land for its preserve and helps the indigenous tribes of Costa Rica with their agro-forestry projects. For any contribution of over $15 the donor will receive *The Canopy* magazine, devoted to rainforest issues, and notice of Alliance legislative activities in a publication called *Hot Topics from the Tropics.* For more information contact: Rainforest Alliance, 65 Bleeker St, New York, NY 10012-2420, or Apartado 138–2150, Moravia, Costa Rica.

Rainforest Concern: an organization that buys and protects virgin forest, and also works with local people developing responsible ecotourism. It manages the Pacuare Reserve, just north of Limón, including a stretch of coastline that is the breeding ground for turtles. A small lodge can hold up to 24 people. Contact: 27 Lansdowne Crescent, London W11 2NS, UK. Tel: (020) 7229 2093; fax: (020) 7221 4094; e-mail: rainforest@gn.apc.org Online at: www.rainforest.org.uk

Selva Bananito: part of a tourist project to protect a fragile green belt located in Bananito, near Puerto Limón. The Selva Bananito private reserve protects 800 ha (2000 acres) of primary forest. Part of the project is devoted to low-impact farming. The public can enjoy this little-explored area at Selva Bananito Lodge, seven bungalows in Caribbean style with solar-heated water. Contact: Conselvatur S.A., Apartado Postal 801–1007, San José, Costa Rica. Tel: 253 8118; fax: 224 2640; e-mail: conselva @sol.racsa.co.cr mail

World Society for the Protection of Animals: The Costa Rican branch of this society operates the only animal shelter and wildlife rehabilitation center in Central America, the Chompipe Biological Reserve (tel: 506 39 7158) near Braulio Carrillo National Park. It has lobbied the Costa Rican government to adopt strict regulations on tuna fishing to stop the slaughter of nearly 100,000 dolphins per year. For more information contact: WSPA, 29 Perkins St, Box 190, Boston, MA 02130, tel: (617) 522 7000. Or WSPA, Apartado 516–3000, San José, Costa Rica, tel: 239 7178.

Eco-Tourism Guides

Bahía Uvita, Ballena Marine National Park: Captain Jenkin, tel: 771 2311, or Johnathan Duron, tel/fax: 771 1903 (Selva Mar Reservation Service).
Caño Negro Wildlife Reserve: Henry Pérez, tel: 460 2058.
Tortuguero Canals: Fran and Modesto Watson offer transport from San José, meals and lodging, tel: 226 0986.
Barra Honda: Luis Alberto Días, tel: 685 5406.
Cahuita: José McCloud, tel: 785 1515 ext. 256

Birdwatching

Costa Rica has over 800 species of birds, including macaws, hummingbirds, king-fishers, toucans, trogons, and the rather shy, but resplendent quetzal. The following offer birdwatching trips:
Costa Rica Expeditions, tel: 257 0766, fax: 257 1665.
Horizontes, tel: 222 2022.
Bosque de Paz, tel: 234 6676; fax: 225 0203; e-mail: bosque@sol.racsa.co.cr
Private reserve with 250 different species of birds.

Language

Survival Spanish

Learn a bit of Spanish before you arrive, if only the simple courtesies: "Good morning." "How are you?" "I'm well, thanks." These seemingly inconsequential phrases are an important part of daily life in Costa Rica. English is spoken by many people in San José and in the larger hotels, and one can always get by without it; but, if your idea of a good trip includes some contact with local people, then speaking a bit of Spanish is the ticket.

If you are going on an extended trip, consider spending the first week of your trip enrolled in one of the many language schools. Tailored programs and schedules of all kinds, many with excursions and cultural programs, are available.

A pocket-sized English-Spanish dictionary is a good idea, and small electronic dictionaries are also available.

Numbers

1	*uno*
2	*dos*
3	*tres*
4	*cuatro*
5	*cinco*
6	*seis*
7	*siete*
8	*ocho*
9	*nueve*
10	*diez*
11	*once*
12	*doce*
13	*trece*
14	*catorce*
15	*quince*
16	*diez y sies*
17	*diez y siete*
18	*diez y ocho*
19	*diez y nueve*
20	*viente*
21	*viente y uno*
30	*treinta*
40	*cuarenta*
50	*cincuenta*
60	*sesenta*
70	*setenta*
80	*ochenta*
90	*noventa*
100	*cien*
101	*ciento uno*
200	*doscientos*
300	*trescientos*
400	*cuatrocientos*
500	*quinientos*
600	*seiscientos*
700	*setecientos*
800	*ochocientos*
900	*novecientos*
1,000	*mil*
2,000	*dos mil*
10,000	*diez mil*
100,000	*cien mil*
1,000,000	*un millón*

Common Expressions

Good morning *Buenos días*
Good afternoon *Buenas tardes*
Good evening *Buenas noches*
Goodbye *Hasta luego*
How are you? *Cómo está Usted?*
I'm well, thanks *Muy bien, gracias*
And you? *Y Usted?*
Please *Por favor*
Thank you *Gracias*
No, thank you *No, gracias*
You're welcome *Con mucho gusto*
How kind of you *Usted es muy amable*
I am sorry *Lo siento*
Excuse me *Disculpe*
Con permiso (when leaving the table or passing in front of someone)
Yes *Si*
No *No*
Do you speak English? *Habla Usted Inglés?*
Do you understand me? *Me entiende?*
Does anyone here speak

English? *Hay alguien aquí que habla inglés?*
Just a moment, please *Momentito, por favor*
This is good *Está bueno*
This is bad *Está malo*

Shopping & Eating

What is the price? *Cuánto cuesta?* or *Cuánto es?*
It's too expensive *Es muy caro*
Can you give me a discount? *Puede dar me un descuento?*
Do you have ____? *Tiene Usted ____?*
I will buy this *Voy a comprar esto*
Please show me another *Muéstreme otro, por favor*
Please bring me ____ *Tráigame por favor ____*
coffee with milk *café con leche*
black coffee *café negro*
tea *té*
a beer *una cerveza*
cold water *agua fria*
hot water *agua caliente*
a soft drink *un gaseoso*
a menu *un menú*
the daily special *el plato del día*
May I have another beer? *Puede dar me una cerveza más, por favor*
May I have the bill? *La cuenta, por favor*
[To get the attention of the waiter/waitress] *Oiga! Señor/Señora/Señorita*
Where is the dining room? *Dónde está el comedor?*
The pharmacy *la farmacía*
the gas station *la bomba* (the pump)
key *la llave*
manager *el gerente* (male) *la gerente* (female)
owner, proprietor *el dueño* (male) *la dueña* (female)
Can you cash a traveler's check? *Se puede cambiar un cheque de viajero?*
money *dinero* or *plata*
credit card *tarjeta de crédito*
tax *impuesto*
letter *carta*
postcard *tarjeta postal*
envelope *sobre*
stamp *estampilla*

Getting Around

Please call a taxi for me *Pídame un taxi, por favor*
How many kilometers is ____ from here? *Cuántos kilómetros hay de aquí a ____?*
How long does it take to go there? *Cuánto se tarda en llegar?*
What will you charge to take me to ___? *Cuánto cobra para llevarme a ____?*
How much is a ticket to ____? *Cuánto cuesta un billete a ____?*
I want a ticket to ____ *Quiero un billete a ____, por favor*
Where does this bus go? *A dónde va este bus?*
Stop (on a bus) *Parada!*
Please stop here *Pare aquí, por favor*
Please go straight ahead *Vaya recto, por favor*
right *a la derecha*
left *a la izquerda*
What is this place called? *Como se llama este lugar?*
I'm going to ___ *Me voy a ___*
bus stop *parada del bus*
reserved seat *asiento reservado*
reservation *reservacíon*
airplane *avíon*
train *tren*
bus *bus*
Where is there an inexpensive hotel? *Dónde hay un hotel económico?*
Do you have a room with... *Hay un cuarto con ____?*
bath *baño*
fan *abanico*
air conditioning *aire*
Where is ___? *Dónde está ___?*
the exit *la salida*
the entrance *la entrada*
the airport *el aeropuerto*
a taxi *un taxi*
the police station *la delegacíon de policía*
the embassy *la embajada*
the post office *la oficina de correos*
the telegraph office *la oficina de telégrafos*
a public telephone *un teléfono público*
a bank *un banco*

a hotel *un hotel*
a restaurant *un restaurante*
a restroom *un servicio*
a private bathroom *el baño*
the ticket office *la oficina de billetes*
a department store *una tienda*
the marketplace *el mercado*

Driving

Fill it up, please *Lleno, por favor*
Please check the oil *Vea el aceite, por favor*
Please fill the radiator *Favor de llenar el radiador*
the battery *la batería*
I need ____ *Yo necesito ___*
a jack *una gata*
a towtruck *una grúa*
a mechanic *un mecánico*
a tire *una llanta*
Help me, please *Ayúdeme, por favor*
Call a doctor quickly! *Llame un médico y prisa!*

Speaking Tico: Tiquismos

If you already speak some Spanish, learn a few *Tiquismos*, uniquely Costa Rican expressions. Tico (Costa Rican) Spanish is rich with them.

The familiar "*tú*" (you) is not used in Costa Rica, even with children. They often use an archaic form, "*vos*." The rules regarding the use of "*vos*" are tricky and elude even advanced students of Spanish: best to stick with "*Usted*," which is always correct.

When walking in areas outside of San José, people passing on the street greet one another with "*Adios*," or "*'dios*." "*Hasta luego*" is used to say "goodbye."

Costa Ricans love to use *sobrenombres*, nicknames. More often than not, the nicknames used have to do with a person's physical appearance: *Macho/Macha* if he or she is ever-so-slightly fair-skinned or fair-haired (not to be confused with *machismo*, an attribute of Latin males, used in Mexico); *China* if she has a slight slant to the eyes, or is actually Oriental; *Negro* if his skin is dark; *Gordito* for someone even slightly overweight; *Moreno* if the person is slightly dark-complexioned, and so on.

If someone asks, *"Cómo está Usted?"* it's always correct to reply, *"Muy bien, gracias a Díos"* ("Very well, thanks to God") or *"Muy bien, por dicho"* (Very well, fortunately") but you might want to try something a little more zippy and informal, such as: *"Pura vida"* ("Great") or *"Con toda la pata"* ("Terrific" – literally, "with all the paw") or *"Tranquilo"* ("Relaxed, or cool").

Spanish Language Schools

Whatever a student's language needs, whether merely conversational, for business, or to master the structure of Spanish, an appropriate language school exists in Costa Rica. Listed below are some of the better-known schools. Consult The *Tico Times* or *Costa Rica Today* for others.

Academia Tica de Español
Tel: 229 0013
Fax. 292-7136
E-mail: actica@sol.racsa.co.cr
Located on a coffee farm in Coronado. Offers beginners, elementary, intermediate and advanced levels. Technical Spanish and composition exercises available.

Centro Cultural Costarricense Norteamericano
P.O. Box 1489-1000,
San José, Costa Rica
Tel: 207 7500
Fax: 224 1480. Also at:
www.cccncr.com
Standard, intensive classes. Special courses and individual tutoring. Conversation club. The center sponsors plays and concerts. Homestays. Academic credit available.

Costa Rica Spanish Institute
Tel. 234- 1001
Fax: 253 2117
Toll free: 1 800 7715184
Also online at: www.cosi.co.cr
Intensive classes for groups and private tutition. Programmes from 1–16 weeks. Classes start every Monday.

Instituto Británico
Tel: 253 1894
Fax: 253-1894
E-mail: instbrit@sol.racsa.co.cr
Students are placed in the appropiate class through a written exam. General Spanish, technical Spanish and Express Spanish.

Instituto de Español Costa Rica
Tel/fax: 283 4733
E-mail: iespcr@sol.racsa.co.cr
Role playing, discussions, listening exercises and videos are part of the classes. Courses on all levels for individuals or in groups. Also cultural Programmes such as Costa Rican cooking or Latin-American dance workshops.

ILISA
Dept. 1420, Box 25216 Miami, FL 33102–5216, USA.
Tel: 225 2495
Fax: 225 4665
E-mail: spanish@ilisa.com
Courses with a maximum of four students. Also one-to-one programmes. Spanish for professionals available. ILISA uses a communicative approach rather than a method. Homestay and hotels. Free email and computer access.

Mesoamerica Language Institute
PO Box 1524
2050 San Pedro, Costa Rica
Tel: 224-8910.
A department of the Institute for Central America Studies which is dedicated to the causes of peace, justice and the well-being of the people and land of Central America. Offers a one-day survival Spanish class for tourists.

Further Reading

Books

Because reference books are often unavailable or expensive in Costa Rica, consider purchasing books before leaving home. The ones listed below give a good insight into Costa Rican life.

Above the Jungle Floor, by Donald Lire Perry. New York: Simon and Schuster, 1986.

Al Calor del Fogon, by Marjorie Ross de Cerdas. Promotora de Cultura y Arte Costarricense, SA, 1986. A culinary history of Costa Rica with recipes. Illustrated. A beautifully designed book. In Spanish.

The Children of Mariplata, by Miguel Benavides. Eleven fables from Costa Rica with local colour and deep on human feelings. Translated into English. Forest books, London.

Coastal Talamanca: A Cultural and Ecological Guide. History of the Talamanca region, both the indigenous and the African-Caribbean. Information on the area and hints on how to be a considerate visitor. Available in the office of the Talamanca Association for Ecotourism and Conservation (ATEC) in Puerto Viejo.

Cocos Island, by Christopher Weston. San José, Trejos Hermanos Sucesores S.A., 1992. Legendary treasures and the wonderful submarine world of the Pacific Costa Rican Island.

Costa Rica: National Parks, by Mario Boza. Incafo S.A., Madrid.

Costa Rica Nature Atlas, by Wilberth Herrera. Notes, maps and pictures of diverse sites, from mountains peaks and volcanoes, to rivers and valleys. Editorial Incafo S.A., Heredia.

Costa Rican Natural History, by Daniel H. Janzen. University of Chicago Press, 1983.

The Costa Ricans, by Richard, John and Mavis Biesanz. Englewood Cliffs, New Jersey, Prentice Hall, Inc., 1987. A readable sociological approach to Costa Ricans – a classic.

Costa Rica: A Traveler's Literary Companion, by Barbara Ras (editor). Whereabouts Press, 3145 Geary Boulevard #619, San Francisco, CA 94118. A collection of 26 short stories by Costa Rican writers, skillfully translated into English.

Guide to the Birds of Costa Rica, by Gary F. Stiles and A.F. Skutch. Cornell University Press, 1989.

Hostile Acts: US Policy in Costa Rica in the 1980s, by Martha Honey. Gainesville, Florida: University of Florida Press, 1994.

Naturalist on a Tropical Farm, by Alexander F. Skutch, Berkeley and Los Angeles. University of California Press, 1980. An engaging account of naturalist Alexander Skutch's early days at Los Cusingos, his tropical farm near San Isidro del General.

The New Key to Costa Rica, by Beatrice Blake, Anne Beecher. Berkeley, CA, Ulysses Press, 1997. A guide full of detailed, practical information on travel by bus, hotels, restaurants and bars, and all tourist destinations.

Pura Vida: The Waterfalls and Hot Springs of Costa Rica, by Sam Mitchell. Catarata Press, 1993. A self-published guide to 25 waterfalls, seven hot springs, and camping sites. Includes a variety of suggested excursions.

The Quetzal and the Macaw, by David Rains Wallace. San Francisco. Sierra Club Books. A history of Costa Rica's national parks.

What Happen, A Folk History of Costa Rica's Talamanca Coast, by Paula Palmer. San José,

Ecodesarrollos, 1977.

The Windward Road, by Archie Carr. Tallahasse, FL. University Presses of FL. 1955. The story of Tortuguero and the green sea turtle.

Newspapers

The *Tico Times* is the most important English language newspaper in Central America. Subscriptions are mailed worldwide. They publish a tourist guidebook annually. The classified section contains valuable information. They will often answer your questions about Costa Rica if you write to them. US Address: Department 717 PO Box 025216, Miami, FL 33102.

Online

For information on Costa Rica's Travel Net:
calypso@cosricon.com
Costa Rica Internet Directory:
www.cr
Info Costa Rica (has its own built-in search function):
www.info.co.cr
The *Tico Times*:
www.ticotimes.co.cr
Costa Rica Tourism and Services Directory:
www.yellowweb.co.cr
Costa Rican Tourist Board (ICT):
www.tourism-costarica.com
www.turismo-sostenible.co.cr
Chamber of Tourism
(CANATUR): www.tourism.co.cr
Costa Rica General Guide:
www.costarica.com/9
Hotels Information:
www.cr/hotelscr.html
Costa Rican Foreign Relations Ministry:
www.rree.go.cr
Costa Rican Enviromental Ministry: www.minae.go.cr
Embassy of Costa Rica in London: www.embcrlon.
demon.co.uk
La Nación Newspaper (has useful tourist information):
www.nacion.co.cr
Medical Directory:

www.edenia.com/medical
Grupo Taca (information about flights in Latin America):
www.grupotaca.com

Videos

Costa Rica: Land of the Pure (56 minutes). Video Visits, International Video Network Ltd., 107 Power Road, Chiswick, London W4 5PL, UK.

Costa Rica: Making the Most of Your Vacation (96 minutes). Marshall Productions, PO Box 534, Carlsbad, NM 88221.

Costa Rica Today (60 minutes), by Carlos Thomas, PO Box 5042, Department TT, New York, NY 10185.

Costa Rica Video Guide, by The Young and New Tone of Costa Rica. Apartado Postal 6709–1000, San José, Costa Rica.

National Parks (40 minutes). La Mestiza Productiones, Apartado Postal 1721–2100, San José, Costa Rica.

Other Insight Guides

Other *Insight Guides* which highlight destinations in this region include:

Insight Guide: Belize offers a full portrait of one of the world's leading eco-tourism destinations, including its rainforests and coral reefs.

Insight Pocket Guide: Yucatán Peninsula sifts through Mayan history and Spanish heritage to unveil the mysteries of southern Mexico.

ART & PHOTO CREDITS

Glyn Genin Front flap, Spine, Back cover, Back flap, 17, 25, 27L, 45, 82/3, 90, 96, 135T,138, 139, 139T,140, 140T, 147T, 149T,151, 151T, 155T, 156T, 159, 159T, 160, 161T, 166/167, 171T, 172, 174T, 183T, 184, 187T, 188, 189T, 193T, 196, 197T, 198, 199, 201, 209T, 216, 217, 218T, 221T, 223T, 229, 231T, 233T, 234, 235, 235T, 238T, 239T, 254T, 253T, 255T, 259T, 260, 261, 262T, 263
André Bårtschi 6/7, 12/13, 88, 148, 190, 208, 237, 239, 242/243, 254, 255, 259
Gary Braasch 85, 202, 228, 232, 233, 247
John Elleston 98
Michael & Patricia Fogden 1, 8/9, 78/79, 80/81, 86, 87, 147, 175, 206, 207, 209, 222, 223, 258
Henry C Genthe 10/11, 14, 20/21, 24, 28, 31R, 31L, 33R, 33L, 36, 37, 43, 44, 49, 56/57, 59, 60, 67, 68, 71, 74R, 104, 108, 110, 11, 112, 113, 114, 115, 117, 118/119, 122/123, 124, 134, 136,137, 142/143, 149, 152, 153, 154, 155, 158, 161, 169, 171, 173, 182, 191, 192, 200, 218, 220, 221, 226/227, 249, 250, 251, 252, 264

Genthe/Haber 23, 32, 35, 40, 41, 42
Lode Greven Free Lens 150
Harvey Haber 16, 22, 34R, 34L, 38, 39, 69, 73
Harvey Haber Collection 46/7, 48, 52/53, 61, 238
Chip and Jill Isenhart 18, 54, 74L, 84, 89, 120/121, 132, 180, 181, 214, 254, 257, 262
Carlos Jinesta 76, 141, 156, 157, 186, 231
Julio Lainez 62/63, 64/65, 72, 174
Miriam Lefkowitz 99
Neil P Lucas, BBC Natural History Unit 212/213
Luiz Claudio Marigo/Bruce Coleman Ltd 241
Buddy Mays/Travel Stock 26, 58, 77, 91, 97, 100, 109, 183, 187, 195, 203, 205
Carl Purcell 66, 70, 145
Jerry Ruhlow 102L
John Skiffington 27R, 29, 30, 50/51, 55, 75, 94/95, 101, 102R, 103, 105, 106/7, 116, 128/129, 133, 135, 162, 163, 168, 176/177, 185, 189, 193, 194, 197, 215, 219, 236, 240, 253
Marco T Saborio 19
Carlos M Uribe 204

Picture Spreads

Pages 92/93
Top row from left to right: Michael & Patricia Fogden, Michael & Patricia Fogden, Michael & Patricia Fogden, Buddy Mays
Centre row: both by Michael & Patricia Fogden
Bottom row: Buddy Mays, Buddy Mays, Buddy Mays, Glyn Genin.
Pages 164/165
Top row from left to right: Glyn Genin, Glyn Genin, Buddy Mays
Centre row: Glyn Genin, Glyn Genin, Marco T Saborio
Bottom row: all by Glyn Genin
Pages 210/211
Top row from left to right: Buddy Mays, Michael & Patricia Fogden, Michael & Patricia Fogden
Centre row: Michael & Patricia Fogden, Gerry Ellis/BBC Natural History Unit, Michael & Patricia Fogden
Bottom row: Michael & Patricia Fogden, Jeff Foott/BBC Natural History Unit
Pages 224/225
Top row from left to right: Marco T Saborio,Marco T Saborio, Marco T Saborio, Glyn Genin
Centre row: Glyn Genin, Buddy Mays
Bottom row: all by Glyn Genin

Map Production Colourmap Scanning Ltd
© 1999 Apa Publications GmbH & Co. Verlag KG (Singapore branch)

INSIGHT GUIDE
COSTA RICA

Cartographic Editor **Zoë Goodwin**
Production **Stuart A. Everitt**
Design Consultants
Klaus Geisler, Graham Mitchener
Picture Research **Hilary Genin**

Index

Numbers in italics refer to photographs

66 I was first drawn to the Insight Guides by the excellent "Nepal" volume. I can think of no book which so effectively captures the essence of a country. Out of these pages leaped the Nepal I know – the captivating charm of a people and their culture. I've since discovered and enjoyed the entire Insight Guide series. Each volume deals with a country in the same sensitive depth, which is nowhere more evident than in the superb photography. 99

Sir Edmund Hillary

INSIGHT GUIDES

The world's largest collection of visual travel guides

Insight Guides – the Classic Series that puts you in the picture

Alaska
Alsace
Amazon Wildlife
American Southwest
Amsterdam
Argentina
Asia, East
Asia, South
Asia, Southeast
Athens
Atlanta
Australia
Austria

Bahamas
Bali
Baltic States
Bangkok
Barbados
Barcelona
Bay of Naples
Beijing
Belgium
Belize
Berlin
Bermuda
Boston
Brazil
Brittany
Brussels
Budapest
Buenos Aires
Burgundy
Burma (Myanmar)

Cairo
Calcutta
California
California, Northern
California, Southern
Canada
Caribbean
Catalonia
Channel Islands
Chicago
Chile

China
Cologne
Continental Europe
Corsica
Costa Rica
Crete
Crossing America
Cuba
Cyprus
Czech & Slovak
    Republic
Denmark
Dominican Republic
Dresden
Dublin
Düsseldorf

East African Wildlife
Eastern Europe
Ecuador
Edinburgh
Egypt
England

Finland
Florence
Florida
France
Frankfurt
French Riviera

Gambia & Senegal
Germany
Glasgow
Gran Canaria
Great Barrier Reef
Great Britain
Greece
Greek Islands
Guatemala, Belize &
    Yucatán

Hamburg
Hawaii

Hong Kong
Hungary

Iceland
India
India's Western
    Himalayas
India, South
Indian Wildlife
Indonesia
Ireland
Israel
Istanbul
Italy
Italy, Northern

Jamaica
Japan
Java
Jerusalem
Jordan

Kathmandu
Kenya
Korea

Laos & Cambodia
Lisbon
Loire Valley
London
Los Angeles

Madeira
Madrid
Malaysia
Mallorca & Ibiza
Malta
Marine Life ot the
    South China Sea
Mauritius &
    Seychelles
Melbourne
Mexico City
Mexico
Miami
Montreal

Morocco
Moscow
Munich

Namibia
Native America
Nepal
Netherlands
New England
New Orleans
New York City
New York State
New Zealand
Nile
Normandy
Norway

Old South
Oman & The UAE
Oxford

Pacific Northwest
Pakistan
Paris
Peru
Philadelphia
Philippines
Poland
Portugal
Prague
Provence
Puerto Rico

Rajasthan
Rhine
Rio de Janeiro
Rockies
Rome
Russia

St. Petersburg
San Francisco
Sardinia
Scotland
Seattle
Sicily

Singapore
South Africa
South America
South Tyrol
Southeast Asia
    Wildlife
Spain
Spain, Northern
Spain, Southern
Sri Lanka
Sweden
Switzerland
Sydney
Syria & Lebanon

Taiwan
Tenerife
Texas
Thailand
Tokyo
Trinidad & Tobago
Tunisia
Turkey
Turkish Coast
Tuscany

Umbria
USA: Eastern States
USA: Western States
US National Parks:
    East
US National Parks:
    West

Vancouver
Venezuela
Venice
Vienna
Vietnam

Wales
Washington DC
Waterways of Europe
Wild West

Yemen

Complementing the above titles are 120 easy-to-carry Insight Compact Guides, 120 Insight Pocket Guides with full-size pull-out maps and more than 60 laminated easy-fold Insight Maps